THE AMERICAN NATION
A HISTORY

FROM ORIGINAL SOURCES BY ASSOCIATED SCHOLARS

EDITED BY

ALBERT BUSHNELL HART, LL.D.
PROFESSOR OF HISTORY IN HARVARD UNIVERSITY

ADVISED BY
VARIOUS HISTORICAL SOCIETIES

15251

THE AMERICAN NATION
A HISTORY

LIST OF AUTHORS AND TITLES

COMMITTEES ORIGINALLY APPOINTED TO ADVISE AND CONSULT WITH THE EDITOR

The Massachusetts Historical Society

Charles Francis Adams, LL.D., President
Samuel A. Green, M.D., Vice-President
James Ford Rhodes, LL.D., 2d Vice-President
Edward Channing, Ph.D., Prof. History Harvard University
Worthington C. Ford, Chief of Division of MSS., Library of Congress

The Wisconsin Historical Society

Reuben G. Thwaites, LL.D., Secretary and Superintendent
Frederick J. Turner, Ph.D., Prof. of American History, Wisconsin University
James D. Butler, LL.D., formerly Prof. Wisconsin University
William W. Wight, President
Henry E. Legler, Curator

The Virginia Historical Society

William Gordon McCabe, Litt D., President
Lyon G. Tyler, LL.D., Pres. of William and Mary College
Judge David C. Richardson
J. A. C. Chandler, Professor Richmond College
Edward Wilson James

The Texas Historical Society

Judge John Henninger Reagan, President
George P. Garrison, Ph.D., Prof. of History, University of Texas
Judge C. W. Raines
Judge Zachary T. Fullmore

JEFFERSON DAVIS

THE AMERICAN NATION: A HISTORY

VOLUME 19

CAUSES OF THE CIVIL WAR

1859–1861

BY

FRENCH ENSOR CHADWICK

REAR-ADMIRAL U.S.N.
RECENT PRESIDENT OF THE NAVAL WAR COLLEGE

WITH MAPS

NEW YORK AND LONDON
HARPER & BROTHERS PUBLISHERS

Jan. '38 Stechert 1.50 (Carnegie)

CONTENTS

CONTENTS

MAPS

EDITOR'S INTRODUCTION

THE most dramatic and most momentous episode in the history of the United States is undoubtedly the Civil War, into which the country slowly drifted for nearly ten years, but which burst out with amazing suddenness and unexpectedness. From one point of view all the volumes of the *American Nation*, after the Revolutionary period, deal with the friction between the North and the South. Hart, *Slavery and Abolition* (Volume XVI.), specifically discusses the controversy over slavery and anti-slavery. Smith, *Parties and Slavery* (*American Nation*, XVIII.), brings out the political divergences. In the first four chapters of this volume, Admiral Chadwick intentionally restates this discussion in the light of the intense sectional rivalry and mutual dislike revealed over the election of Abraham Lincoln to the presidency; and he shows the economic importance of slave-grown products and the significance of the political theory of state rights at the time of the outbreak. The narrative begins where Professor Smith's volume leaves off in 1859, with the John Brown raid (chapter v.). In the next chapter the political events of 1859 and

1860 are described. Chapters vii. and viii. are on the election of 1860. The process of secession and the attitude of Buchanan occupy chapters ix. and x. Chapter xi. deals with the first and utterly unsuccessful attempt at compromise. In chapters xii. to xv. there is a thorough discussion of the status of the Federal forts in the South, and of the attitude of Buchanan's administration, culminating in the episode of the *Star of the West*. Chapter xvi. is upon the second attempt at compromise, in February, 1861. With chapter xvii. begins Lincoln's administration and the development of its policy. Chapter xix. in detail expounds the final outbreak in the fall of Fort Sumter.

A West Virginian by birth, a graduate of the Naval Academy in 1864, and acquainted with many of the principal actors in this great drama, Admiral Chadwick brings an impartial spirit to his difficult task. The question of responsibility for the Civil War is one which cannot be settled off-hand, and no two writers, even occupying about the same stand-point, will agree as to the character of all individuals or the question of aggression; but the author has aimed in moderate phrase to state the results of a careful study of the men and the principles involved. The volume leads directly to the story of the events of the war in Hosmer's *Appeal to Arms* and *Outcome of the Civil War* (*American Nation*, XX. and XXI.).

AUTHOR'S PREFACE

IN preparing this volume I have had in mind throughout, both the limitations of space and the extent of the field described by its title. By "Causes of the Civil War," I understand those events, principles, and personalities, which were finally focussed in the exciting period from 1859 to 1861; but it is not possible to bring out the significance of all those influences in a narrative confined to those two years, however eventful. The subject is one of such long continued and deep nationalistic and psychologic influences, that I have devoted several preliminary chapters to the state of mind of those who took the responsibility for the final arbitrament of civil war. No such crisis can be explained in any other way than as a slow development; and though I have in those introductory chapters freely referred to earlier volumes of this series, and have so far as possible avoided going over the ground which they have traversed, I have aimed to make the volume self-explanatory, even at the risk of some slight repetition in the work as a whole.

The crisis of the secessionist movement was in the government's attitude in the questions of Forts

Sumter and Pickens; this part of the subject has thus been dealt with in especial detail.

Many friends have given information, or made suggestions on text and maps. I beg to express my obligations to them, and particularly to the officials of the War and Navy Department Libraries, of the Libraries of Congress, of the United Libraries of New York City, of Brown and Harvard Universities, of the Boston Public Library, and the Redwood Library, Newport, whose courtesy and helpfulness have lightened the task of preparation.

F. E. CHADWICK.

CAUSES OF THE CIVIL WAR

CAUSES OF THE CIVIL WAR

CHAPTER I

DRIFT TOWARDS SOUTHERN NATIONALIZATION
(1850–1860)

SEVENTY - TWO years after the adoption of the Constitution, called into being to form "a more perfect union," and eighty - five years after the declaration of independence (a space completely covered by the lives of men then still living), a new confederacy of seven southern states was formed, and the great political fabric, the exemplar and hope of every lover of freedom throughout the world, was apparently hopelessly rent. Of these seven states but two were of the original thirteen— Louisiana and Florida had been purchased by the government of the Union; a war had been fought in behalf of Texas; two states, Alabama and Mississippi, lay within original claims of Georgia, but had been ceded to the Union and organized as Federal territories.

April 11, 1861, found a fully organized separate

government established for these seven states, with a determination to form a separate nation, most forcibly expressed by the presence of an army at Charleston, South Carolina, which next day was to open fire upon a feebly manned fort, and thus to begin a terrible civil war. The eight other slave states were in a turmoil of anxiety, leaning towards their sisters of the farther South through the common sympathy which came of slavery, but drawn also to the Union through tradition and appreciation of benefits, and through a realization by a great number of persons that their interests in slavery were much less than those of the states which had already seceded.

The North, in the middle of April, was only emerging from a condition of stupefied amazement at a condition which scarcely any of its statesmen, and practically none of the men of every-day life, had thought possible. It was to this crisis that the country had been brought by the conflicting views of the two great and strongly divided sections of the Union respecting slavery, and by the national aspirations which, however little recognized, were working surely in each section, but upon divergent lines.

In the period of the Revolution the four most southerly states were the only ones deeply interested in slavery from an economic point of view. The general sentiment in other states, among statesmen, at least, was averse to slavery, though the objection was rather philosophic than practical. Even the Virginia House of Burgesses in 1772 petitioned against the traffic, but was resisted by the British crown.[1] In the Articles of Association drawn up by the first Continental Congress, October 20, 1774, it was agreed that the United Colonies would "neither import nor purchase any slave" and would "wholly discontinue the slave trade."[2]

The North Carolina and Virginia Conventions sending delegates to that congress pledged themselves not to import slaves and not to purchase them when imported by others.[3] And Congress itself, April 6, 1776, resolved, without opposition, that "no slaves be imported into any of the thirteen United Colonies."[4] Though this action was directed against British commerce, it was an indication of a general feeling of opposition to the traffic. No mention, however, was made of the subject in the Articles of Confederation submitted November 15, 1777; the farther South had begun to look to its supposed interests, and the results were the compromises of the Constitution, a necessity to the formation and immediate well-being of the Union, but fatal to its later peace.[5]

[1] *Journal of Va. House of Burgesses*, 131; *Tucker's Blackstone*, I., pt. ii., App. 5.
[2] *Journals of Congress* (ed. of 1904), I., 77.
[3] Wilson, *Slave Power*, I., 14.
[4] *Journals of Congress* (ed. of 1904), IV., 258.
[5] Cf. McLaughlin's *Confederation and the Constitution*, chaps. xiv., xvi.; Hart, *Slavery and Abolition*, chap. xi. (*Am. Nation*, X., XVI.).

The almost universal deprecation of slavery by
the public men of the eighteenth century need not
be repeated here. The author of the Declaration
of Independence, which declared all men created
free and equal; the Virginia orator whose impassioned declamations had done so much to forward
it; the great man and the great general whose lead
was so indispensable to its success; and yet another
Virginian who aided in making and expounding the
Constitution, all declared their abhorrence of the
system, but continued to hold their slaves. On
the other hand, many northerners and Englishmen
stood by the system. Even Jonathan Edwards left,
as part of his property, two negroes, a man and a
woman.[1] Whitefield regarded slavery as arranged
by Providence for the instruction and salvation
of the blacks; he had no doubt of the "lawful-
ness of keeping slaves,"[2] and died owning seventy-
five, who, classed among his goods and chattels,
were bequeathed to Lady Huntingdon.[3] Lord Thurlow, in 1799, could denounce the proposal to abolish
the slave-trade as "altogether miserable and ridiculous."[4]

In the face of these facts it is not surprising that
probably the great majority of lesser men, North as

[1] See Lunt, *Origin of the Late War*, 8.
[2] Whitefield, *Works*, II., 404; Tyerman, *Whitefield*, II.,
272.
[3] Tyerman, *John Wesley*, III., 183.
[4] Summary of debate July 5, 1799, *Parliamentary History of
England*, XXXIV., 1138–1139.

well as South, regarded slavery as no sin. It was
not until a great psychological wave of religious and
altruistic enthusiasm swept over the North shortly after the Missouri contest that deprecation of
slavery took a concrete form which made its destruction but a question of time. And this would
have spread southward but for the simultaneous
development of an immense and overpowering interest through the demand for cotton, the invention of the cotton-gin, and the consequent expansion
on a gigantic scale of cotton production. This gave
the slave a money value which it was hardly in
human nature to ignore; and it gave an exultant
feeling of superiority over the North in possessing
a commercial monopoly. As put by a southern
writer: "The cotton culture, then, and negro civilization, have grown up rapidly and equally together
and their interests are now inseperable; whatever
injures the one injures the other, and it is impossible to destroy the one without destroying the
other. This alliance between the negroes and cotton, we venture to say, is now the *strongest power* in
the world; and the peace and welfare of Christen-
dom absolutely depend upon the strength and security of it. The whole world is under the heaviest
bonds to promote and strengthen this connection." [1]
The supply of slaves could not keep pace with the
demand; the more cotton, the more negroes needed.

[1] Wright, " Cotton and Negroes," in *De Bow's Review*, XXIX.,
139 (August, 1860).

Every additional three and a half bales meant an additional field-hand, so that in round numbers 1,400,000 more were employed in the cotton-fields in 1860 to produce 5,400,000 bales than to produce the 450,000 bales of 1820. [1]

In these forty years cotton had become not only the support of the South and the main-stay of our foreign commerce, but an equal necessity to England, the home of the cotton manufacture. There was then a basis for the belief, held without reserve, that without slavery there could be no cotton. The results of freedom in Haiti and Jamaica afforded good grounds for such a view, and in any case the South had full belief that the result of a general emancipation would be totally to destroy the cotton industry by the refusal of the blacks to labor; thus reducing the region to the depressed condition of these islands. [2] This feeling was a powerful element in the political situation. None foresaw that in less than forty years from 1860 the crop of cotton would be more than doubled under free negro labor. Could they have done so, politics would have taken a different aspect. The change of conditions effected by the rapidly increasing demand for cotton was by 1830 a great economic revolution.

[1] Cf. Morse, " Southern Slavery and the Cotton Trade," in *De Bow's Review*, XXIII., 475 et seq. (November, 1857).

[2] *De Bow's Review*, XXVIII., 87, 201 (January and February, 1860).

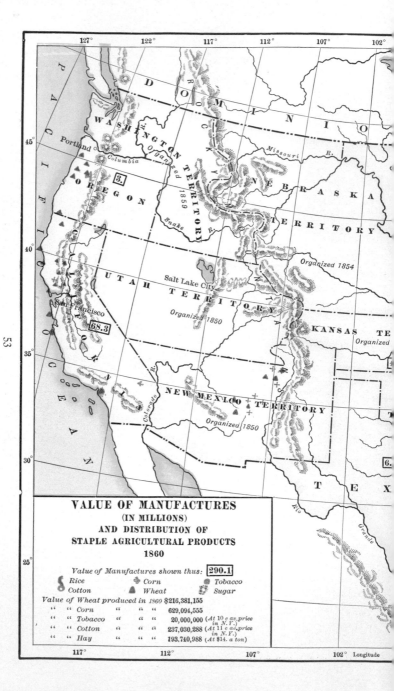

VALUE OF MANUFACTURES
(IN MILLIONS)
AND DISTRIBUTION OF
STAPLE AGRICULTURAL PRODUCTS
1860

Value of Manufactures shown thus: 290.1

Rice   Corn   Tobacco
Cotton   Wheat   Sugar

Value of Wheat produced in 1860				$216,381,155	
" " Corn	"	" "		629,094,555	
" " Tobacco	"	" "		20,000,000	(At 10 c av. price in N.Y.)
" " Cotton	"	" "		237,030,288	(At 11 c av. price in N.Y.)
" " Hay	"	" "		193,740,988	(At $14. a ton)

117°   112°   107°   102° Longitude

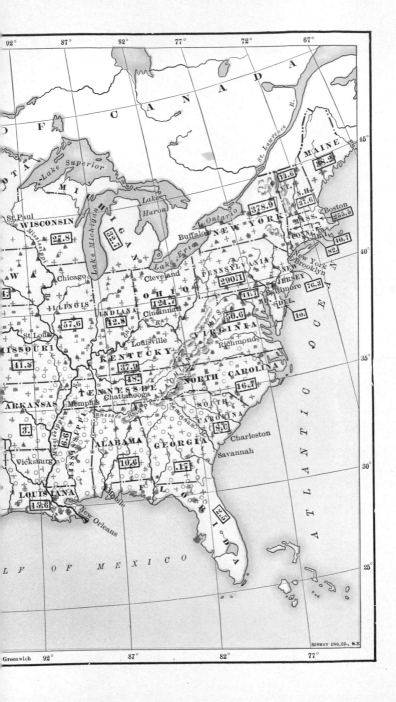

Cotton cultivation rolled like a car of Juggernaut over every lesser industry, and marched into new territory as an invading army. Public lands to the amount of 20,242,017 acres were sold from 1833 to 1840 in the Gulf states, Arkansas, and Tennessee. The cotton crop rose from 1,070,438 bales in 1833 to 1,801,497 bales in 1838. Almost the whole of the increase was in the new slave states, whose slave population increased in the decade 1830–1840 by nearly four hundred thousand, proving how great had been the shifting of blacks from farther North, Virginia showing an actual decrease of nearly twenty - three thousand, and Maryland of over thirteen thousand.[1] The natural effect of cheap land, the necessity of continually seeking fresh soil for unchanging crops, could have but one effect: there could be no careful cultivation, "no adequate system of fertilization, southern husbandry was, for the most part, a reckless pillage of the bounty of nature."[2]

Southern slavery wore a more humane aspect than the slave societies which preceded it. By the partial closure of the African slave-trade the supply was limited, and the economic well - being of the planter required such treatment of the slaves as would insure not only a good labor efficiency, but, still more important, would tend to a rapid increase in numbers. Says the excellent southern

[1] *Democratic Review*, XXIII., 102 (August, 1848).
[2] Reed, *Brothers' War*. 432

authority just quoted: "The southern slaves, regarded as property, were the most desirable investment open to the generality of people that has ever
been known. . . . Their labor was richly remunera-
tive; their market value was constantly rising; they
were everywhere more easily convertible into money
than the best securities; and their natural increase
was so rapid that a part of it could be squandered
by a shiftless owner every year to make both ends
meet, and he still be left enough of accumulation to
enrich him steadily. And so the plantation, or,
rather, the slave system, swallowed up everything
else." [1]

To preserve this system meant to extend and
give it at least political equality, if not actual pre-
ponderance in the Union; this became the aim and
demand of the South; to restrict it became the
equally fixed resolve of the North. Failing pre-
ponderance in the Union, the only course of the
South was to nationalize itself in correspondence
with its peculiar social and economic organization,
and face the world as a nation whose corner-stone
was negro slavery. [2]

The outward manifestations in the history of the
separation of the North and the South stand out in
strong relief: the Missouri question; the protective
tariff and South Carolina nullification; the abolition
attacks which wrought the South into a frenzy sui-
cidal in character through its impossible demands

[1] Reed, *Brothers' War*, 433.   [2] *Ibid.*, chap. iv.

upon the North for protection; the action of the southern statesmen in the question of petitions; the passage of a fugitive-slave law which drove the North itself to nullification; the Kansas-Nebraska act and its outcome of civil war in the former territory; the recognition, in the dicta of the supreme court in the Dred Scott case, of the South's contention of its constitutional right to carry slavery into the territories, and the stand taken by the North against any further slavery extension. To these visible conflicts were added the unconscious workings of the disruptive forces of a totally distinct social organization. The outward strifes were but the symptoms of a malady in the body politic of the Union which could have but one end, unless the deep, abiding cause, slavery, should be removed.[1]

The president and vice-president of the Southern Confederacy, in their elaborate defences written after the war, have endeavored to rest the cause of the struggle wholly on constitutional questions. Stephens, whose book, not even excepting Calhoun's utterances, is the ablest exposition of the southern reading of the Constitution, says: "The struggle or conflict . . . from its rise to its culmination, was between those who, in whatever state they lived, were for maintaining our Federal system as it was established, and those who were for a consolidation of power in the central head."[2]   Jef-

---

[1] Cf. *Am. Nation*, XIV., XVI.–XVIII., passim.
[2] Stephens, *War between the States*, II., 32.

ferson Davis is even more explicit. "The truth remains," he says, "intact and incontrovertible that the existence of African servitude was in no wise the cause of the conflict, but only an incident. In the later controversies . . . its effect in operating as a lever upon the passions, prejudices, or sympathies of mankind, was so potent that it has been spread like a thick cloud over the whole horizon of historic truth."[1]

This is but begging the question. The constitutional view had its weight for the South in 1860 as it had for New England in the Jefferson-Madison period. Jefferson's iron domination of the national government during his presidency, a policy hateful to New England, combined with the fear of being overweighted in sectional influence by the western extension through the Louisiana purchase, led to pronounced threats of secession by men of New England, ardently desirous of escaping from what Pickering, one of its most prominent men, termed the Virginian supremacy.[2] Exactly the same arguments were used, *mutatis mutandis*, later by the South.

As we all know, the movement, which never had any real popular support and which had its last spasm of life in the Hartford Convention at the close of the War of 1812, came to naught. Freed by the fall of Napoleon and the peace with England from the

---

[1] Davis, *Confederate Government*, I., 80.
[2] Adams, *New England Federalism*, 144-146.

pressure of the upper and nether mill-stones which had so ground to pieces our commerce, a prosperity set in which drowned the sporadic discontent of the previous twenty years. The fears of the eastern states no longer loomed so high and were as imaginary in fact, and had as slight a basis, as were, in the beginning of the era of discord, those of the South. Could slavery have been otherwise preserved, the extreme decentralizing ideas of the South would have disappeared with equal ease, and Stephens's *causa causans*—"the different and directly opposite views as to the nature of the Government of the United States, and where, under our system, ultimate sovereign power or paramount authority properly resides," would have had no more intensity of meaning in 1860 than to-day.

Divergence of constitutional views, like most questions of government, follow the lines of self-interest; Jefferson's qualms gave way before the great prize of Louisiana; one part of the South was ready in 1832 to go to war on account of a protective tariff; another, Louisiana, was at the same time demanding protection for her special industry. The South thus simply shared in our general human nature, and fought, not for a pure abstraction, as Davis and Stephens, led by Calhoun, would have it, but for the supposed self-interest which its view of the Constitution protected. Its section, its society, could not continue to develop in the Union under the northern reading of the document, and the irrepressible and certain nationalization, so different from its own tendencies, to which the North as a whole was steadily moving.

Slavery drove the South into opposition to the broad, liberal movement of the age. The French Revolution; the destruction of feudalism by Napoleon; the later popular movements throughout Europe and South America; the liberalizing of Great Britain; the nationalistic ideas of which we have the results in the German empire and the kingdom of Italy, and the strong nationalistic feeling developing in the northern part of the Union itself had but little reflex action in the South because of slavery and the South's consequent segregation and tendency to a feudalistic nationalization.

As pointed out by one, himself a distinguished son of the South, "In 1789 the states were the creators of the Federal Government; in 1861 the Federal Government was the creator of a large majority of the states. In 1789 the Federal Government had derived all the powers delegated to it by the Constitution from the states; in 1861 a majority of the states derived all their powers and attributes as states from Congress under the Constitution. In 1789 the people of the United States were citizens of states originally sovereign and independent; in 1861 a vast majority of the people of the United States were citizens of states that were originally mere dependencies of the Federal Government, which was the author and giver of their political being." [1]

These words of a southern orator convey a serious truth. The conditions of settlement were instigators of national feeling, as well as the tendencies of the century and the general conditions of American life. The immigrant, the traveller abroad, the commercial world, the great merchant fleet of the country, the army and navy, knew no state. But the South, except for its representatives in the military and naval services, was outside the pale of these influences; it had no merchant marine; its only travellers were from among the very few who owned slaves; it clung necessarily, through slavery, to agriculture, and lived the secluded and separate life of the husbandman; and when attacked by abolitionism it bent all its energies to the preservation of the only life it knew. It was not touched, except in a remote way, by the wonderful industrial change which came over the world with steam; its spirit not being commercial, it did not strive to link itself with the great West, as did New York, Boston, Philadelphia, and Baltimore. Its harbors were few and mostly shallow, and though of depth sufficient for the ships of the period, its distance from Europe was so much greater when the steamship began to be the carrier and took a direct route, independent of trade-winds and Gulf Stream, that this distance became an im-

[1] Lamar, quoted by Curry, *Southern States*, 187.

portant element in the change from busy to deserted ports.

The impulses working in the North and West, liberal, industrial, and national, were thus unfelt in the South, which planted and gathered in 1860 much as it did in 1820. Its illiteracy was very great, its reading public small. There was less movement between North and South than between the southern East and West, and the sections grew in painful ignorance of each other; an ignorance which increased as intercourse diminished through the sensitiveness of slavery. There was left but one kinship—that of blood. All other bonds disappeared in the gulf of economic interest, the outcome of its special form of labor, the preservation of which became an obsession. Under the circumstances there was but one step finally for the South to take—to set up a nationality of its own. It was impossible for it to remain under a polity almost as divergent from its sympathies as the Russian autocracy of that period was from the United States of to-day.

CHAPTER II

THE SLAVE-HOLDING SOUTH

(1850–1860)

SLAVERY followed the natural law of every vice or disease — of moving towards health or towards dissolution. To denounce it now seems, in the words of a distinguished historian, "like trampling on a grave"[1]; the system is in the limbo of the inquisition and of witchcraft; a generation has sufficed to still much of the passion and hush the arguments which fifty years ago possessed the minds of the great majority of the South and many of the North. They can now only serve to illustrate the extraordinary psychologic aberrations to which the best of men are prone and teach the charity which all of us are so unapt to extend to the opinions of our fellow-man. Its study leads to the feeling that in this instance the mantle of charity cannot be too broad; it needs to be stretched over both North and South. For all slave-owners were not vicious; all anti-slavery men were not enemies or wishers of evil to the South. Nor were all slaves under the incessant application of

[1] Goldwin Smith, *United States*, 221.

the lash; families were not always torn apart, though there were enough such instances to point a moral.

Almost all Americans now agree with Clay's dictum that slavery was "a curse to the master and a wrong to the slave," but the wrongs of the latter had many alleviations, and in the main the great body of negroes in slavery enjoyed the happiness of an ignorant and unprogressive race to which to-day is much more than the morrow. It was a race which in its native land, though in contact with the highest civilizations through thousands of years, had not risen beyond the savagery which enslaved, destroyed, and sacrificed its kind; perhaps the most ancient of mankind, and which has come down to us unchanged through the ages in company with the gigantic and wonderful fauna of its mysterious continent.

Few of the southern blacks of the period of 1860 were far removed from their ancestral state by an interval of more than a hundred and fifty years, a short time in which to change the nature of any race of men; and the traditions also of the old life were kept alive by the steady influx of new African blood, seventy thousand being considered a "very moderate and even low" estimate of these importations into the United States so late as the decade 1850 to 1860.[1] To the credit side of slavery must be placed this transplantation into conditions where the characteristic imitativeness of the race

[1] Collins, *Domestic Slave Trade*, 2c

had an opportunity. It was the African's one real stepping-stone to better things.

Slowly there grew up among all classes of the North the feeling which had always existed among the few, that slavery was an immense wrong. The twenty years from 1835 to 1855, which may be taken as the special period of this growth, saw also, as natural outcome of an attack, the development of a fierce defence, through which the mind of the southern states became almost completely unified in a belief that slavery was a positive good. This feeling, even of God - fearing, upright, and conscientious people in the South, of whom there was as large a proportion as in the North, is expressed in the reminiscences of a southern lady: "We never raised the question for one moment as to whether slavery was right. We had inherited the institution from devout Christian parents. Slaves were held by pious relatives and friends and clergymen to whom we were accustomed to look up. The system of slave holding was incorporated in our laws, and was regulated and protected by them. We read our Bible and accepted its teachings as the true guide in faith and morals. We understood literally our Lord's instructions to His chosen people and applied them to our circumstances and surroundings."[1] The Old and New Testaments were regarded as impregnable buttresses of their faith and practice, and diligently and triumphantly

[1] Clayton, *White and Black under the Old Régime*, 51.

quoted as full authority for the social regimen of the South.[1] This reliance on Biblical authority permeated the South and is epitomized by Alexander H. Stephens in a speech on the Mexican War. "Until Christianity be overthrown, and some other system of ethics be substituted, the relation of master and slave can never be regarded as an offence against the Divine laws."[2]

While the slaves enjoyed, on the face of it, none of the essentials of manhood named in the Declaration of Independence, they probably thought very little on the subject, and then vaguely; while the certainty of freedom from want, from care for the future, from many of the demands of the law which touch society in general, went far to make up for the loss of liberty and brought them at least content. That the mass of negroes in the South were not dissatisfied with their condition would appear almost self-evident from the fact that during the four years of civil war none sought to change their condition by insurrection. This was due partly to their affection for their masters, partly to their childlike simplicity of mind and their ignorance and fear of the unknown; all of which last was a portion of the psychical make-up which had in the first instance doomed them to slavery, which continued to hold them in its all-powerful grasp, and is still far from having let go its hold.

[1] See Hart, *Slavery and Abolition* (*Am. Nation*, XVI.), chap. x.
[2] *Cong. Globe*, 29 Cong., 2 Sess., App., 354.

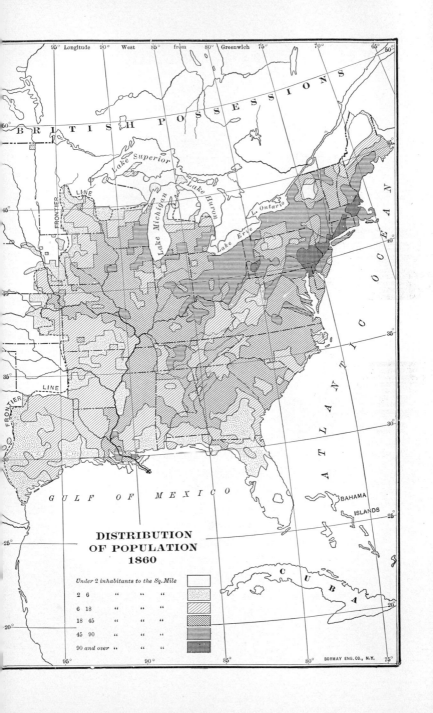

DISTRIBUTION
OF POPULATION
1860

Under 2 inhabitants to the Sq. Mile
2 — 6 " " " "
6 — 18 " " " "
18 — 45 " " " "
45 — 90 " " " "
90 and over " " " "

BORMAY ENG. CO., N.Y.

The fifteen slave-holding states, including Delaware, with 1798 slaves and 19,829 free colored, and Maryland, with 87,189 slaves and 83,942 free colored, had, in 1860, a total population of 12,240,000, of whom 8,039,000 were whites, 251,000 free colored, and 3,950,000 slaves. This was a gain of the whole southern population in ten years of 2,627,000, or 27.33 per cent. The slaves advanced in numbers 749,931, or 23.44 per cent., the lowest rate for many decades. The nineteen free states (including Kansas) and seven territories, together with the Federal district, contained 19,201,546 persons (including 27,749 Indians), of whom 18,936,579 were white and 237,218 free colored, a smaller number of the latter, it should be observed, than in the South. The northern increase in the decade was 5,598,603, or 41.16 per cent.[1] The population of the South was thus but little more than two-fifths that of the North. Calhoun foresaw, as did others, that if a struggle was to come it should come early if the South was to have a hope of victory.

The area of the fifteen slave states was 882,245 square miles; of the free, 824,622. But it was clear by 1860 that all the territories would be added to the list of the free states, making a free area of 1,903,204 square miles, or much more than twice the extent of the slave, and in this lay the crux of southern discontent.

Virginia, in 1790 the most populous of the states,

[1] U S. Eighth Census (1860), *Preliminary Report*, 5.

with 748,308 people, of whom 293,427 were slaves, had dropped to the fifth place, with 1,596,318 inhabitants, of whom 490,865 were slaves. New York, with but 340,120 in 1790, had in 1860 the first place, with 3,880,735, of whom all but 49,005 were whites. The one state had more than doubled; the other had increased more than ten times. Of the whites, the increase in Virginia had been 137 per cent.; South Carolina, 108; North Carolina, 119; Maryland, 147. Georgia, however, had increased in this period from 52,886 whites to 591,588, a ratio of 11.18, the only one of the original thirteen states of the South to make a showing in any degree comparable with that of the more important states of the North. In all the border slave states the white population was gaining steadily upon the black. The census of 1810 was the last which showed an increase of the slaves in Maryland; they reached their maximum, 111,502, in 1810, and slowly decreased to 87,189 in 1860; the white population had nearly doubled. The whites in Virginia increased more than twice as fast as the slaves. The ratio of whites to slaves in Kentucky had risen steadily from three-fourths in 1830 to four-fifths in 1860.

The rapid proportionate increase of whites in Missouri should have convinced thoughtful minds that the fierce struggle for the extension of slavery in the territories then included under the name of Nebraska was lost effort, even had it been successful in the first instance. The note of alarm was sounded loudly by De Bow, who nevertheless makes the error of ascribing the decline to the troubles in Kansas instead of to the immigration of foreigners. Between 1851 and 1856 the increase of slaves in Missouri was 12,492, and of whites 205,-703; in ten counties adjoining Iowa they had gained 238 against an increase of whites of 31,691; in twenty-five counties the slaves had actually decreased 4412. In 1860 Missouri was nine-tenths white. It is not surprising to have De Bow, who had become eager for disunion, write: "Surrounded on three sides by non-slaveholding communities, can any one in his right mind expect to see slavery maintain itself in Missouri? Under the present Union the border states must all in a short time be lost to us. Were the Union at an end, the South would become at once a *unit*, and continue such for perhaps a century. The terms of a new confederation would secure this. The Union may be and doubtless is on a thousand accounts, very valuable; but let it be understood that this is one of the items of the price that is paid for it."[1]

The system was a serfdom to both races; to the black chiefly physically only; but a severe mental servitude to the six millions of whites who had no connection with slave-holding and who formed more than three-fourths of the white population of the South. To the vast majority of these people slavery was a complete closure to the higher reaches

[1] *De Bow's Review*, XXIII., 521 (November, 1857).

of social and financial well-being; for white labor would not compete with slave labor, but was relegated to the cultivation of petty farms, from which a bare subsistence was extracted and a peasantry brought into being wretchedly housed, isolated, and living a life which through generations was almost wholly without civilizing influences. In the lowlands this class, by its mere proximity to slave labor, sank to lowest depths of ignorance and unthrift, despised by the negro himself, too isolated to be able to hold his own against the deadening influences of his surroundings, and with no chance of entering into the knowledge of the world, since he was reached by neither book nor schoolhouse.

Scattered over the plains and foot-hills from North Carolina south were not less than two and a half millions of such people, for whom under slavery there was no hope; who had no place in southern polity or society; who aimed at nothing because there was nothing to aim at, and who are only now emerging into the light under the influence of the new industrial world which has risen in their midst. These people, however, were fiercely southern in feeling through the ever-present need of asserting the superiority of their white blood, which was all they had to differentiate them in social consideration from the lowliest black; and it was these men, never owning a slave, or hoping to own one, who, led by the slave-owner, made the military power of the

South and fought the fierce and manly fight of the
Civil War.

The condition of this great mass was the direct
outcome of its segregation from the social organization of the slave-owning class of the South by its
isolation through want of roads, through want of
schools, through want of interest on the part of the
planter in any laboring class but the slave, with
whom in the large slave-owning districts the poor
whites would not work, and with whom it was not
desired to have them work. Where slaves were
smaller in number this last difficulty disappeared
through a reversal of conditions. On numbers of
farms in Virginia, Maryland, and West Virginia, in
districts where slaves were few, whites and blacks
frequently worked together in good-fellowship and
harmony; the owner of hundreds of acres, but of
very few—perhaps three or four—slaves, himself a
gentleman and perhaps a member of the legislature
or justice of the peace, lending a hand in the fields
if occasion needed.

In a district larger than the German empire,
stretching in the Appalachian region from the
northern part of West Virginia into Georgia and
Alabama, a great bay of mountain and valley
reaching into the heart of the South, a region in
which there are thirty-seven peaks higher than
Mount Washington, there dwell to-day over two
millions of people whose earlier conditions of isolation was physical and not social, as was that of their

lowland brothers of like degree.   They are the after-
math of the great "crossing," stranded through
stopping "to make a crop" to support the family
through a coming winter.   Their vast region was
without roads, without navigable rivers, but with
an enchanting scenery of wild and heavily wooded
mountains, beautiful brooks, and valleys elevated
into one of the most delightful summer climates of
the world.

The mountaineer, though his life was necessarily
one of a rude half-savagery through its lonely isolation, retained the independence and hardihood of
his ancestry.   Slavery was almost unknown among
these men, and when the war came they took
largely the opposite side from that taken by the
poor whites of the lowlands, with whom they had
nothing in common but poverty.   Abraham Lincoln, himself a product of the mountain race and of
the lowliest of them, is a startling example of their
possibilities under changed opportunities.   In his
case it was transplantation which gave him growth;
but education, enlightenment, and contact with the
rest of the world, all of which were for generations
denied them, will yet work similar miracles in this
great mass.   The blood of the people of the Appalachian region is of the best; it is the blood of
Boone, of Harrod, of Clark, of the pioneers who
gained for us the empire of the West, who under
Jackson—himself one of them—won the victory of
New Orleans, and under Clark, through the Kas-

kaskia campaign, enabled our negotiators to make
the Mississippi our boundary in 1783; above all, it
is the blood of the mighty and heroic man who
saved the Union.

Neither would nor could the laborers of Europe,
entering our doors by the hundred thousand, bring
themselves to a competition with great numbers of
slaves, more than the poorer whites bred in the
South. Of a foreign-born population of 4,136,175
in 1860, but 118,585 were south of the border slave
states. South Carolina had but 9986; Georgia,
11,671; Alabama, 12,352; Mississippi, 8588; Louisiana, 81,029, and Texas, 43,422. Missouri had
nearly as many (160,541) as all the cotton states
together, a fact which itself should have shown the
South the impossibility of preserving it a slave state.

Everywhere throughout the South the small
farmer was very markedly in the ascendant. In
Louisiana there were 10,794 farms under 100 acres
to 6487 larger, of which but 1532 were plantations
of over 500 acres, and but 371 really great plantations of over 1000 acres. In Georgia 31,482 out of
53,897 farms were less than 100 acres, and there
were but 902 places of over 1000 acres, though
1000 acres of fair land could be readily bought for
$5000, and frequently for much less.

While the South was so strictly agricultural, the
low value of slave labor became apparent in results.
It produced in 1860, in comparison with the North,
but one-eightieth the cheese, one-fourth the wheat,

one-fifth the oats, one-tenth the hay. On the other hand, it produced somewhat more than half the Indian - corn, two-thirds the swine, five-sixths the tobacco, all the cane sugar (40,000,000 pounds of maple - sugar were produced in the North), and all the cotton. But the hay alone brought more money to the northern farmer than did cotton, sugar, and tobacco combined to his fellow-farmer of the South.

There was a like great difference in the manufactures of the two sections. Taking the more important industries in the two sections about to be formed—the Southern Confederacy of eleven states and the remaining twenty-three states of the Union in 1861 — the relative values of production, North and South, were (in millions): agricultural implements, 16, against $1\frac{1}{2}$; iron (pig and other), 39, against $2\frac{1}{2}$; steam machinery, 43, against 4; iron-founding, 26, against $2\frac{1}{2}$; coal, 19, against $\frac{1}{2}$; lumber, 78, against 18; flour and meal, 193, against 30; cotton goods, 108, against 7; woollen goods, $68\frac{1}{2}$, against $2\frac{1}{2}$; leather, 59, against 4; boots and shoes, 86, against $2\frac{3}{4}$. The North, in these industries, the most important in sustaining the demands of a great war, was thus producing at its outbreak to the value of $735\frac{1}{2}$ millions, against $75\frac{1}{4}$ of the South. In the great aggregate of manufactures, the value of productions of the two sections stood $1,730,-330,000 in the North, against $155,531,000 in the eleven southern states of the coming Confederacy.

The enormous disproportion of two and a half times the fighting men, and a manufacturing productivity eleven times as great, showed, had it taken time to think, a hopeless outlook for the South should its contention end in war. A close blockade, such as was to come, could only mean death to Confederate aspirations. The facilities for interior transportation were also greatly disproportionate; the Southern Confederacy contained 8947 miles of the total 31,196 of the railways of the whole Union; nearly all of this, both North and South, was east of the Mississippi; the North had about three times as much mileage per square mile as the South.[1]

The great importance of cotton rested not so much in its money value as in the fact that it was the principal export of the United States and the main basis of supply both to Europe and America. Of the cotton consumed by the mills of Great Britain, continental Europe, and the United States in the five years ending August 31, 1860, the growth of the South supplied an average of 84½ per cent.[2] Two-thirds of the values exported from the United States were thus from the South. The North had not as yet become a very great exporter of food stuffs or manufactures, but sent quantities of both to the South, to be paid for chiefly by the income from cotton. In 1855, excluding specie, the total

---

[1] U. S. Eighth Census (1860), passim.
[2] Shepperson, *Cotton Facts* (ed. of 1904), p. xi.

exports amounted to $192,751,000, of which $67,-626,000 were from the North and $125,124,000 from the South, $88,143,000 being in cotton alone. If the cotton in manufactures exported by the North be added (400,000 bales valued at $2,000,000), the value of cotton exported would have exceeded the total values exported by the North by $13,-000,000. There was thus much ground for the belief of the South that cotton was king. It was difficult for any one to understand how it would be possible for the spinning world to get on without its American supply, how the United States could manage its foreign exchanges without the eighty to a hundred millions balance supplied by cotton, or how the northern farmer or manufacturer could withstand the loss of his southern market; for the North not only clothed the South, supplied its furniture and agricultural implements, but in a very considerable degree supplied the food, the large planters finding it cheaper to buy supplies for the slaves in the northern markets than to raise it at home.

The impression of some writers of southern birth that there was in the southern county towns a decided anti-slavery sentiment and sense of rivalry to the planters has little or no basis. The anti-slavery sentiment, instead of increasing, had diminished. A strong pro-slavery sentiment existed among men who had no personal interest whatever in slavery by reason of ownership of slaves; nor does there ap-

pear, from the census records at least, that there had
been such considerable growth of "handsome and
fairly enterprising and prosperous county towns."[1]
The census of 1860 could find only fifteen in Alabama worth mentioning, and of these nine had less
than a thousand inhabitants, dwindling to as few
as 117. But two towns in Arkansas rose in degree
above the merest villages, one having only eighty
people. Of the thirty-six "cities and towns" in
Georgia, seventeen were of the same insignificant
character; Louisiana had but three towns of over
two thousand population, besides New Orleans (including Algiers) and its capital, Baton Rouge. All
but five of the towns enumerated in Mississippi were
small villages. It was the same in North and
South Carolina, the latter state having but three
towns, besides Charleston, of over one thousand
population, and neither of these three having as
many as seventeen hundred. Virginia, as is well
known, was a state of petty villages, the *locale* of
the court-house having often so slight a population
that it had no other popular designation, and the
census notes places in this state with as few as
thirty-nine people.

It is of great importance that there should not
be a false impression of the economic and social
conditions of the South of that period. The usual
descriptions of southern life presented a glamour of
general well-being and luxury, an impression of con-

[1] Burgess, *Civil War and Constitution*, I., 29.

stant house-to-house visiting, a life of feudal dignity
and impressiveness, all this pictured by pens guided
by minds much too imaginative and far from the
rather prosaic facts. Some of the southern estates
had handsome houses, a considerable degree of comfort, and, in comparatively rare cases, luxury. The
life of the largest establishments was, in the main,
of a somewhat rude plenty, with abundant service,
and the horses and carriages, without which the life
would have been imprisonment. Along with this
there was the hospitality to their kind which such a
life naturally demands. But it was not a life of
ease even to the master and still less to the mis-
tress. The latter supervised the clothing, the doc-
toring, the nursing of a great family, sometimes of
hundreds, of a people who never grew out of childish
ways and simplicity. The master had an overseer,
and his province was mainly the fields, but the
master's wife was a woman of many and varied
burdens, whose life was as far as possible from
frivolity and ease; and the greater the estate the
greater the burdens. There was a spirit of self-
sacrifice and acceptance of the hard duties of the
situation, a serious recognition of obligation to the
childlike race committed to their care, for which the
women of the South should have the highest meed
of praise. It was the cultivation of a noble life,
and made the brightest side of slavery.

How few were the well-to-do is shown by the fact
that only 10,781 families held as many as fifty or

more slaves in 1860, and these may, without great error, be taken as representing the number of the larger productive estates of the South. The great plantations in rice, cotton, or sugar were held by the 1733 owners of as many as 100 slaves. Of the 52,-128 slave-holders in Virginia, one-third held but one or two slaves; half held one to four; there were but 114 persons in the whole state who owned as many as 100 each, and this out of a population of over a million whites.[1] On the supposition that each slave-holder in the Union represented a family of five persons, there were in the whole South in 1860 less than two million persons, old and young, directly interested in slavery through ownership, as against over six million whites who had no slave property or interests, and whose own interest it would be supposed would be felt to be directly antagonistic to the system through competition in all branches of labor and through the social inferiority, that most galling of feelings to the American man, and more especially to the American woman, which non-ownership of slaves involved. Even a South Carolina journal, itself of secessionist views, could quote the following with approval from another paper of the same state: "The white mechanic is forced to eke out half a living beside the sturdy negro who fattens upon a price for his labor at which a white man cannot work with anything like

[1] See estimates in Hart, *Slavery and Abolition* (*Am. Nation*, XVI.), chap. v.

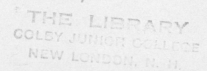

an effort to maintain the distinction to which he should aspire. He is not only forced to labor for the same remuneration as the slave mechanic, but oftentimes finds difficulty in securing work enough to keep him employed on account of the plenitude of negro mechanics and the accommodating terms upon which they may be obtained." [1]

That this body of three-fourths the white men of the whole South should have fought stubbornly for four years to fasten more completely bonds which restricted them to every inferiority of life is one of the extraordinary facts of history. It was a disfranchised population almost as fully as the negro, in so far as any part in the higher and directive life of the country was concerned. No one of them ever appeared in any office of importance unless returned from the sections where slavery had slight hold. But this was no small part of the South; in the counties of Virginia now forming West Virginia, with a population of 376,886 (about one-third that of the entire state), there were but 18,497 slaves, of whom 11,235 were in the nine counties bordering on what is now Virginia. The northwestern part of the state, with a white population of 175,006, had but 1797 slaves, or one to every 100 whites. The eastern parts of Tennessee and Kentucky, the western region of North Carolina and northern Georgia, while not so marked, were

[1] *Edgefield Advertiser*, January 18, 1860, quoting *Camden* (S. C.) *Journal*.

akin to this in conditions. In fact, West Virginia and parts of the states just mentioned had, as had Delaware, the attributes practically of free states.

The decayed and decaying agriculture of Virginia and of North and South Carolina caused, particularly from the last two, a great drift of owners and negroes to the cotton belt. It is a common error, however, to suppose that white Virginians went farther south in great numbers. Nearly four hundred thousand persons born in Virginia were, in 1860, living in other states, and only 68,341 had come in to offset this loss; only about fifty thousand had gone south. The chief migration from Virginia was to Ohio, Tennessee, Kentucky, Missouri, and Indiana; there were 75,874 in Ohio alone. South Carolina, with her meagre 276,868 people, had living in other states 193,389 of her sons and daughters, 50,112 in Georgia, 45,185 in Alabama, and 26,577 in Mississippi. South Carolina was, in fact, a decaying, or at least a stationary, state; the 237,440 whites of 1820 had only become 291,388 in 1860, and the emigrants to states farther south carried their slaves with them.

The trade in negroes was great and continuous from all the more northern slave states. Kentucky and Tennessee furnished largely, sometimes many, sometimes fewer; the drift from Maryland and Virginia was continuous and on a large scale. Niles, always conservative and trustworthy, says: "The march of the slaves is south, south. Already they may be said to have crossed the Potomac—for in Maryland they are not generally esteemed as a permanent possession, and the sale of them for the supply of the southern 'market' checks their increase in this state. Free white laborers are taking their place in our most flourishing counties; and as some will not *sell* them, 'runaways' are not so ardently sought for. There is a larger export from Virginia. 'Old Virginia' has a lessened use for them, *new* Virginia will not receive them, and Middle Virginia is already pretty well filled with industrious freemen." [1]

[1] *Niles' Register*, XLV., 180.

CHAPTER III

DOMINANCE OF CALHOUN'S POLITICAL CONCEPTIONS

(1850 – 1860)

CALHOUN'S ascendency over the southern mind is a basal historic element of our national life. Its study includes the political history of the South from 1830 to 1850 and the springs of southern action thenceforward until the sword put an end to debate. He was the amanuensis of his state when it desired to declare a policy, and in the Senate he was the prophet whose pronouncements were as a gospel to the South, which moulded itself to his views. From 1833 onward he urged an interpretation of the Constitution which legitimatized, in the southern mind, the extremity of action in 1861. The history of the movement towards secession is part of the story of his life and influence. Never has man exercised a more complete intellectual dominancy over his section, but sadly to its undoing.

Calhoun was a constitutionalist, but he obeyed a greater power than the Constitution—the necessity of preserving the society of which he was a part.

His strength lay in believing in the wisdom and righteousness of the southern social organization. Crittenden was right when he said that Calhoun, while seeing clearly the tendency of events, was unable to restrain himself from focussing the mind of the country upon the unhappy subject, and unable to see that his own action upon the subject of petitions had given the greatest impetus to the feeling he wished to allay.[1] His habit of thrusting forward the dogmas of which he was so fond, and which apparently had lain dormant in his mind until hope of the presidency had passed, after which he felt free to be true to himself, could have no result but impassioned and limitless debate, the necessary result of which was to spread throughout the South, by official publication, a literature similar in character to that for the repression of which he was willing to alter the character of the government. Resolutions such as those he finally pressed to a vote were simply abstractions; their passage could effect nothing, could bind no other persons, organization, or state. Their futility was perfectly expressed by Adams in a resolution offered December 13, 1838—"That the powers of Congress, being conferred by the Constitution of the United States, no resolution of this House can add to or deduct from them."[2]

Every step of the kind Calhoun took, every for-

[1] *Cong. Globe*, 25 Cong., 2 Sess., App., 55.
[2] *Ibid.*, 3 Sess., 33.

mal expression of his peculiar views of the situation, only gave new ground for the abolitionists to stand upon, and took from the northern friends of the South their arguments for quietude. His peculiar characteristics made him a disrupter of our national fabric in spite of himself. He recognized every explosive charge laid by the Constitution and by the circumstances of the South, and, where not already laid, he placed others of his own invention, and could not resist lighting every fuse.

Calhoun's ability "to look to the farthest consequences of every question" has been dwelt upon by many writers, notably by Von Holst, but his forecasts were no more remarkable than those of Jefferson, John Quincy Adams, and others. It was perfectly clear to every thoughtful man that the slavery question was an imminent danger to the Union. To Calhoun the danger appeared only in permitting the abolitionists and even the anti-slavery men to meet, discuss, print, and petition upon slavery. He called on them to drop the subject, and all would be happy; but he himself was the great, insistent discusser, and, through the instrumentality of the government, the printer and distributer of the discussions. He insisted upon slavery taking precedence in importance of any other question; for this he would muzzle the press, search the mails, make the laws of the individual states overbear the Federal statutes, and reduce the Federal government to a nullity which could only end in disintegration.

His theories, taken together, led straight to anarchy.

If Calhoun had the "prophetic vision" and the logical mind with which so many endowed him, should he not have been able to see this result as clearly as others saw it then and all see it now? There could be only one excuse for Calhoun's policy—the hope of extending slavery throughout the Union. If such possibility existed, he was justified, logically, in all he said and did. Otherwise we can only suppose him blind to the great moral change in mankind, to the greater feeling of brotherhood which had come over the world, and which among civilized powers was rapidly making slavery impossible.

The steamship, the railway, the press, the post-office, though yet in infancy, were even then great instrumentalities of this change. It is difficult for us now to conceive of the almost absolute separation of individuals and communities which ruled even much less than a hundred years ago. Interchange of thought was confined to the very few, and ignorance, dense as that of the Middle Ages, reigned among much of the mass the world over. Calhoun, born before this change, and, but for his time at Yale College, reared amid surroundings which had not felt the touch of the new life, dwelt, physically and mentally, in this mediæval atmosphere, thought slavery a blessing, believed that a superior race had a right to enslave an inferior one, and was ready to suppress all dissent in such a question, whether founded upon moral and religious grounds or on any other. To suppose that a string of resolutions, passed by thirty or forty men sitting in the Senate chamber, could stop millions from thinking and from acting within their plainest rights was not the belief of a sane mind.

Calhoun's spirit is revealed in an account of a two hours' conversation recorded by Horace Binney in 1834: "He obviously considered society as consisting only of two classes, the poor who were uneducated, and doomed to serve, and the men of property and education, to whom the service was to be rendered. Regarding these two classes as discriminating the people of Pennsylvania as much as South Carolina, he said, emphatically, 'The poor and uneducated are increasing; there is no power in a republican government to repress them; their number and disorderly tempers will make them in the end efficient enemies of the men of property. They have the right to vote, they will finally control your elections, and by bad laws or by violence they will invade your houses and turn you out. Education will do nothing for them; they will not give it to their children; it will do them no good if they do. They are hopelessly doomed as a mass to poverty, from generation to generation; and from the political franchise they will increase in influence and desperation until they overturn you. The institution of slavery cuts off this evil by the root. The whole body of our servants, whether in the family or in the field, are removed from all influence upon the white class by the denial of all political rights. They have no more tendency to disturb the order of society than an overstock of horses or oxen. They have neither power nor ambition to disturb it. They can be kept in order by methods which a republican government, as well as a monarchical or a military one, can apply. They have no jealousy of the other class, nor the other of them. They never stand on the same platform with the white class. They only require supervision and domestic discipline to keep them in good order; and such means are easily applied and become normal in the state. The white class is therefore left to pursue without apprehension the means they think best to elevate their own condition. Slavery is indispensable to a republican government. There cannot be a durable republican government without slavery.' " [1]

Of Calhoun's love of the Union there can be no question, but the Union had to be one which sheltered slavery. He moved gradually to this attitude. As a member of Monroe's cabinet he had, in the Missouri question, along with Crawford and Wirt, accepted the principle of freedom applied to territories in the Ordinance of 1787; he had had leanings to protection in the earlier part of his congressional career; but he had thrown over such views, and the

[1] Binney, *Binney*, 313.

"Exposition" of the South Carolina legislature, which he wrote in 1828,[1] and his letter of August 28, 1832, to Governor Hamilton, written for the guidance of the convention to meet in the following November,[2] was the torch which lighted the way to the establishment of the Southern Confederacy.

Calhoun's pre-eminence as the champion of the South began with this defence of nullification from 1828 to 1833, though South Carolina went much further in her resolves, in her threats, and in her military preparations than Calhoun had expected. Jackson's determined attitude, his reinforcement of the Charleston forts, the occupancy of Charleston harbor by ships of war, the indisposition of other states to follow her lead, and the passage of the force bill were events which would have had much deeper significance but for Clay's compromise on the tariff, which left a moral victory with South Carolina. Seldom, judged by the logic of events, has there been greater fatuity than in the action of Clay and his weak supporters, which made war in the not distant future a certainty.

But the force bill gave Calhoun opportunity for perhaps his ablest effort in his speech of February 13, 1833, on his resolutions of January 22, which in power and ability was the equal of that of his great opponent, Webster, whose answer, January 30, with his earlier speech in reply to Hayne, made him the idol of the Unionists, North and South. It was

---

[1] Calhoun, *Works*, VI., 1–59　　　[2] *Ibid.*, 144–193.

upon the principles of Calhoun's resolutions that the South took its stand; it was upon the principles of Webster's answer that the North fought the Civil War. They need to be quoted here, though, in fact, they never came to a vote.

Calhoun's resolutions were as follows:

"That the people of the several states . . . are united as parties to a constitutional compact to which the people of each state acceded as a separate sovereign community, each binding itself by its own particular ratification; and that the Union . . . is a union between the states ratifying the same.

"That the people of the several states . . . delegated to that government . . . certain definite powers, reserving at the same time, each state to itself, the residuary mass of powers, to be exercised by its own separate government; and that whenever the general government assumes . . . powers not delegated by the compact, its acts are . . . of no effect; and that the same government is not made the final judge of the powers delegated to it, since that would make its discretion,

The propositions maintained by Webster were:

"1. That the Constitution of the United States is not a league, confederacy, or compact between the people of the several states in their sovereign capacities; but a government proper, founded on the adoption of the people, and creating direct relations between itself and individuals.

"2. That no state has authority to dissolve these relations; that nothing can dissolve them but revolution; and that consequently there can be no such thing as secession without revolution.

"3. That there is a supreme law, consisting of the Constitution of the United States, and acts of Congress passed in pursuance of it, and treaties; and that, in cases not assuming the character of a suit in law of equity, Congress must judge of and finally interpret this

and not the Constitution, the measure of its powers; but that, as in all other cases of compact among sovereign parties, without any common judge, each has an equal right to judge for itself, as well of the infraction as of the mode and measure of redress.

"That the assertions that the people of these United States, taken collectively as individuals, are now or ever have been united on the principle of the social compact, and as such are now formed into one nation or people, or that they have ever been so united . . . ; that the people of the several states . . . have not . . . retained their sovereignty; that the allegiance of their citizens has been transferred to the general government; that they have parted with the right of punishing treason through their respective state governments; and that they have not the right of judging in the last resort as to the extent of the powers reserved, and, of consequence, of those delegated; are not only without founda-

supreme law so often as it has occasion to pass acts of legislation; and in cases capable of assuming the character . . . of a suit, the Supreme Court of the United States is the final interpreter.

"4. That an attempt by a state to abrogate, annul, or nullify any act of Congress, or to arrest its operation within her limits, on the ground that, in her opinion, such law is unconstitutional, is a direct usurpation on the just powers of the general government, and on the equal rights of the states, a plain violation of the Constitution, and a proceeding essentially revolutionary in its character and tendency.''

---

[1] Curtis, *Webster*, 1., 450.

tion in truth, but are con-
trary to the most certain
and plain historical facts
and the clearest deductions
of reason; and all exercise of
power . . . claiming au-
thority from so erroneous
assumptions must of necessity be unconstitutional,
must tend directly to sub-
vert the sovereignty of the
states, to destroy the federal
character of the Union, and
to rear on its ruins a consolidated government, without constitutional check or
limitation, and which must
necessarily terminate in the
loss of liberty itself." [1]

From this period on, Calhoun took the rôle in American politics of a Cassandra; every speech was a prediction of impending woe and every stand taken was increasingly impossible for the North to accept. His treatment of the question of incendiary documents; his denial of the right of the petitioner to the acceptance by Congress of his petition; his extraordinary committal, in his correspondence as secretary of state, of the government of the United States to the view that the freedom of the negro would not be tolerated in Texas, and that the United States was forced to annex the country rather than such freedom should exist; his leader-

[1] *Debates of Congress*, IX., 191.

ship in the action of southern legislatures in 1847
against the Wilmot proviso, of which his resolutions
of February 17 of that year (which were never
brought to a vote) were the cue—all these acts mark
him as under the obsession of an evil genius which
forced him to stir the fires of sectionalism.[1] For
twenty years his gloomy mind and great powers
were absorbed in the work; and when his life
ended, the South was already prepared for the
fatal leap from the precipice to which he had
led it.

But to fully understand the lengths to which he
had allowed his views to stray we must look to a
letter of the stormy period of 1847 written by Calhoun to a member of the Alabama legislature. In
this he declared it necessary to force the issue upon
the North, as the South was now stronger relatively
than it would be later. "Delay to us," he said,
"will be dangerous indeed." He welcomed the
Wilmot proviso as an occasion of successfully asserting the South's equality. "Something of the
kind was indispensable to rouse and unite the
South; . . . I would regard any compromise or adjustment of the proviso, or even its defeat, without
meeting the danger in its whole length and breadth
as very unfortunate for us. It would lull us to
sleep again without removing the danger." His
remedy—a most extraordinary one for a constitu-

---

[1] See Hart, *Slavery and Abolition*, chap. xviii.; Garrison, *Westward Extension*, chap. xvi. (*Am. Nation*, XVI., XVII.)

tionalist—was to refuse the right of northern ships and commerce to enter southern ports, leaving open the trade of the Mississippi Valley, so as to detach the Northwest from the northeastern states, and for this to be effective a convention of all the southern states would be indispensable. "The non - slave-holding states would be compelled to observe the stipulations of the constitution in our favor, or abandon their trade with us, or to take measures to coerce us, which would throw upon them the responsibility of dissolving the Union." [1]

March 4, 1850, the country heard Calhoun's last formal utterance on the subject which filled his mind and dominated his soul. It was a comparison of northern and southern expansion, showing how the South had lost in political power through the Ordinance of 1787 and the establishment of the Missouri Compromise line. Had neither existed, he argued, the South would have divided the immigration with the North, would thus have equalled it in population, and would have maintained an equality in number of states; the result had been to give the North an absolute control over the government, so that wherever there was a diversity of interests those of the South would be sacrificed. The next day, in an interlocution with Foote, of Mississippi, he embodied his thought in a single sentence— . . . "I will say—and I say it boldly—that as things now stand the southern states cannot remain in the

[1] See Benton. *Thirty Years' View*, II., 698–700.

Union." [1] Four weeks later he was dead. His work was completed; he had attained his aim—the practical subjection of the southern mind to the view that the South could not remain in the Union unless on its own terms.

Two other great figures in Congress in this generation shared with Calhoun the nation's interest: Clay, representing slavery in its mildest form; Webster, the reasonable antagonism of the North. All three showed in their attitude on the question the overpowering influence of environment. Clay, however, was the insistent compromiser; he was never able to see that a deep sentiment could not be set aside by a trade in principles; that the best of compromises—and such he regarded the great compromise of 1850—could produce but a condition of unstable equilibrium. His anxiety for the Union overpowered, in this, his judgment, which was true and sound as to slavery extension. In answer to Jefferson Davis's proposed ultimatum (January, 1850), of the extension of the Missouri line to the Pacific, he could say, "coming from a slave state as I do, I owe it to myself, I owe it to truth, I owe it to the subject, to say that no earthly power could induce me to vote for a specific measure for the introduction of slavery where it had not before existed, either south or north of that [Missouri] line." [2]

Whatever criticism may be made of Clay's and

[1] Calhoun, *Works*, IV., 575.
[2] *Cong. Globe*, 31 Cong., 1 Sess., 249.

Webster's attitudes in this stirring and hazardous year, there can be no question of their lofty patriotism and overpowering anxiety for the preservation of the Union.   The country owed much to Webster besides that due to his classic speeches in the nullification period.   He was a great instrument for the nationalization of the Union through one of his chief victories in law: the case Gibbons *vs*. Ogden (1824), which involved the question of monopoly of steam navigation in the waters of a state, granted by New York to Fulton and Livingston.   The decision of the supreme court in this case fixed the meaning of what thus became a momentous phrase of the Constitution, "The Congress shall have power to regulate commerce among the several states." It was a decision which became a mighty element in cementing the Union.[1]   A consistent opponent of slavery and its extension; opposed to the annexation of Texas and to the Mexican war, to Webster's anxiety for the Union was due the conservatism of his Seventh of March speech (1850) which called upon his head the deepest wrath of the abolitionists and the unjust censure of many who were not of the fanatical party of the anti-slavery public.   He saw as clearly as Calhoun whither the Union was tending under the excitement of the South, and could say at this moment "your eyes and mine are never destined to see that miracle [of peaceable secession]. . . . I see that . . . [disruption] must produce . . .

[1] Cf. Reed, *Brothers' War*, 140.

such a war as I will not describe in its twofold
character." [1] It was this feeling which caused the
utterances in this speech, which with Webster's acceptance of the unfortunate and exasperating fugitive-slave law of the compromise (the latter a profound error both of judgment and heart) brought
a condemnation throughout the North which destroyed his influence, embittered the short remainder of his life, and hastened his death.

No more common-sense statement could have
been made than that by Webster, that California
and New Mexico were "destined to be free . . . by
the arrangement of things ordained by the Power
above us. . . . I would put in no Wilmot Proviso,
for the mere purpose of a taunt or a reproach. I
would put into it no evidence of the votes of superior
power, . . . to wound the pride, whether a just and
a rational pride, or an irrational pride, of the citizens of the southern states. . . . Whether they expect to realize any benefit from it or not, they
would think it at least a plain theoretic wrong."
In these words was an epitome of the situation.
Webster was right when he said "there is not at
this moment within the United States, or any territory of the United States, a single foot of land,
the character of which, in regard to its being free
territory or slave territory, is not fixed by some
law, and some irrepealable law, beyond the power
of the action of the government." [2]

[1] Webster, *Works*, V., 361.   [2] *Ibid.*, 340, 351.

Had the statesmen North and South accepted the dispassionate and wise views of this speech there might have been many years of calm, and perhaps as an end, could the fugitive-slave law have been modified to a more kindly form, a general disposition such as that expressed by Webster, "to incur almost any degree of expense" for a scheme of colonization upon a large scale. One southerner at least accepted his convictions as to conditions. Jefferson Davis himself said "the climate of Kansas and Nebraska was altogether unsuited to the negro and the soil was not adapted to those productions for which negro labor could be profitably employed. . . . As white laborers adapted to the climate and its products flowed into the country, negro labor would have inevitably become a tax to those who held it, and their emancipation would have followed that condition as it has in all the Northern states old and new—Wisconsin furnishing the last example." [1]

That slavery should have been prohibited by mandatory act, had invasion of these territories by it been imminent, all now must agree, but it is questionable if it was wise statesmanship to pass a law of supererogation, and one which could only have been a profound irritant to a great section. Neither the Wilmot proviso nor the South's contention could have any practical result beyond placing the two sections finally in an attitude of

[1] Davis, *Confederate Government*, I., 30.

strong antagonism, though of an intensity in the
South far from dreamed of at the North, where
feeling, except among the few, was very mild in
comparison.

The strength of those antagonistic to slavery extension lay in waiting; the greater basis of northern
representation in Congress, now rapidly increasing,
with the certainty that the adverse sentiment of
the North to slavery must in the very nature of
things increase and not diminish, made it certain
that, whatever the attempts by the South, no
further annexations of territory would be made to
the southward. That a fear of such annexations
existed is unquestionably true, but it was baseless
by reason of the impossibility of such a concession
on the part of the North, even at this period.
Cuba even now, without slavery, is not a part of
the Union. The nation had been sufficiently sati-
ated with conquest for many years, but those who
so pressed the Wilmot proviso and kindred legislation were impelled by a like psychical force with
that which drove the South towards its impossible
demands.

CHAPTER IV

EXPECTATIONS OF THE SOUTH
(1850–1860)

THAT every ebullition of feeling in this stormy epoch had its following period of quiescence and acceptance of the situation, showed the strong desire of the people North and South to live in accord. However strong the passions involved in the Missouri controversy, the compromise of 1820 met with so general an acceptance that the principle involved did not reappear until brought forward by new issues. That this discussion had not changed the moderate views of slavery held in the border states at the time was shown by the strong invectives against slavery in the Virginia legislature in 1832.[1]

The nullification action of South Carolina, in a way, strengthened the feeling for the Union; for it brought out the powerful defence of Webster, which, whether it fully met the arguments of Calhoun or no, was accepted as conclusive by the country at large; and it was significant that Jackson himself based his nullification proclamation upon

[1] Hart, *Slavery and Abolition* (*Am. Nation*, XVI.), chap. xii.

Webster's answer to Hayne. The president's action gave the country a new view of the federal power to act; and argument and action combined to foster a feeling of security which dominated the North, and strongly affected the South, to the very eve of actual secession.

The success of abolitionism of the Garrison type was in the too-ready acceptance of the South to take up the gauntlet. The South was demoralized by a movement which, if it could have been quietly ignored, would have lost itself in the more reasonable anti-slavery sentiment, the growth of which the conditions of the age made certain. The abolitionists scorned the idea of compensation to slave-holders, though that remedy, found in the speeches of Seward as well as of Webster, was growing in favor, and, had the South shown the slightest willingness to accept the freedom of the negro under any conditions, might have become a working basis for such action.[1] The results of manumission in the West Indies, however, which brought financial ruin to the great majority of planters, and the fear of the political equality of the negro, aided in supporting the view of Calhoun that emancipation was an impossible supposition.

"Whatever," said McDowell, of Virginia, in 1850, "the opinions I have expressed or entertain upon the institution of slavery in the abstract, I have

[1] Cf. Hart, *Slavery and Abolition* (*Am. Nation*, XVI.), chap. xxi.

never doubted for a moment, that as the white and black races now live together in the southern states, it is an indispensable institution for them both." [1] This, coming from one who had made an eloquent plea for emancipation in the Virginia Legislature in 1832, and who "had acquired a national reputation by his ardent patriotism, his broad and statesman-like views in pleading for the best interests of his own commonwealth," [2] marks a change in southern sentiment regarding manumission. If a wise conservative could utter such an opinion, the notion of freedom through purchase was hopeless.

The abolition societies had their apogee before 1840. The explosive elements which they included brought dissensions among themselves which became fatal to their influence as organizations. Amos A. Phelps, "one of the earliest and ablest of the writers, orators and organizers of the anti-slavery movement," in resigning his membership, in 1839, of its board of managers, said, "The society is no longer an anti-slavery society simply, but in its principles and modes of action has become a women's - rights, non-government, anti-slavery society." [3] "At this time," says Wilson (than whom there can be no authority more favorable to the abolitionists), "there were probably two thousand societies in the country, containing, it was esti-

---

[1] *Cong. Globe*, 31 Cong., 1 Sess., App., 1678.
[2] Wilson, *Slave Power*, II., 288.
[3] *Ibid.*, I., 415.

mated, some two hundred thousand members. They had, however, already attained their maximum of numbers and influence, and had accomplished the largest share of their peculiar work. Afterward their numbers and distinctive labors were diminished rather than increased." [1]

More effective than anything else in rousing anti-southern feeling in the North (using this phrase as distinct from anti-slavery sentiment) was the struggle in Congress in 1835 over the acceptance of anti-slavery literature in the mails, and the continuance, for several years thereafter, of bitter debate on the question of anti-slavery petitions: the existence of an institution which could not even permit discussion in the press, once realized by the northern public, doomed that institution. The unwise vituperation of so many of the southern papers; their asking the impossible; their inability to see that the attempt to stifle discussion was revolution, and that the denial of the right of petition or the suppression of petitions was touching a right dear to all free people, gave the impetus to a new sentiment which slowly came over the North, and which in its beginnings was against southern ideals and action, against the arrogant and dictatorial tone of southern public men and the insult and abuse in the southern journals, rather than against slavery as a thing not to be tolerated.

The general acquiescence in the compromise of

[1] Wilson, *Slave Power*, I., 422.

1850, despite sporadic disunion movements in the South, shows how strong was the Unionist feeling. Had not the South committed the folly of forcing the passage of a new fugitive-slave law unnecessarily severe and unfair, and had not the Kansas-Nebraska bill been brought forward in 1854, it is not unreasonable to suppose that the status of good feeling would have indefinitely extended itself, and much would have been settled by natural causes. There was a lull of political strife in the South which brought to silence the agitators of the Quitman and Yancey type; the country was prosperous and content in general, except for sporadic cases of violent opposition to the execution of the fugitive-slave law, but even these were apparently diminishing. Seemingly, the disunionism of 1850 was buried in the overwhelming victory which brought Pierce to the presidency, the Democratic party to a dominancy more complete than ever before, and the Whigs to annihilation.

Much as Douglas has been blamed, both for act and motive, in rousing the country from its calm by bringing forward squatter sovereignty in the Kansas-Nebraska act, and in being the instrument for abolishing the Missouri Compromise, despite his earlier views of the sacred character of the compromise of 1820, he was but yielding to an unconscious pressure which he could not resist. He "rode the whirlwind" but did not "direct the storm." Though he averred that the bill was all his own, he

was acting under a sub-conscious southern pressure
felt by his quick soul to be as actual, as mandatory,
and as necessary to Democratic success as if specifically formulated by the party caucus. He little
foresaw that the gloss he put upon this was to be
the disruption of the Democratic party and his own
ruin. The Kansas-Nebraska bill, supplemented by
the emotions which overran the country under the
influence of *Uncle Tom's Cabin*, a book which drew
with irresistible power a picture of slavery which
outside the South was accepted the world over as
true of the whole, gave new force to the resistance
to the fugitive-slave law and swept the North into
an opposition which culminated in the formation of
the Republican party, developed from abstract antagonism into concrete civil war in Kansas, and, in
the election of 1856, reared a spectre, the mere apprehension of which, to the South, was to end in
secession. The dictum of the supreme court in the
Dred-Scott case, the decision in which was given
out but two days after Buchanan's inauguration,
gave the final blow to northern patience in the
slavery question.

There still, in 1859, remained over eight hundred
thousand square miles in territories, enough, measured by mere area, to make eighteen states of the
size of New York or Pennsylvania; but which, as
pointed out elsewhere, even Davis, to whom the
mantle of Calhoun had fallen, acknowledged was
unfitted for slavery.

The contention of the South was thus a violation of every principle of logic and in the face of the great fact that European emigration must naturally overwhelm slave labor in regions in which land was sold so cheap. Nearly three and a half millions of immigrants arrived in the years 1848–1858,[1] a number within half a million of the total number of slaves in the Union; and it was impossible that any southern migration could compete with this, particularly as it was not the well-to-do owner of slaves who would attempt to establish himself in a new and, to the southerner, inhospitable region, in which, even on his own theory, slavery might be abolished when the territory became a state.

The bloody story of Kansas; the formation of emigration societies North and South, but in much greater numbers in the North; the arming of the emigrants; the development of a minor civil war, is told elsewhere in these volumes.[2] It was but a phase of the extension and development of two civilizations antagonistic in every fibre of their nature; a struggle between the men who desired an opportunity to work with their own hands and those who thought it right to own and use an inferior race to do the labor which they directed.

Nothing in the history of the subject presents a more curious psychological problem than the action at this period of the statesmen of the South in their

---

[1] 3,416,923. U. S. Eighth Census (1860), *Preliminary Report*, 13.
[2] Smith, *Parties and Slavery* (*Am. Nation*, XVIII.).

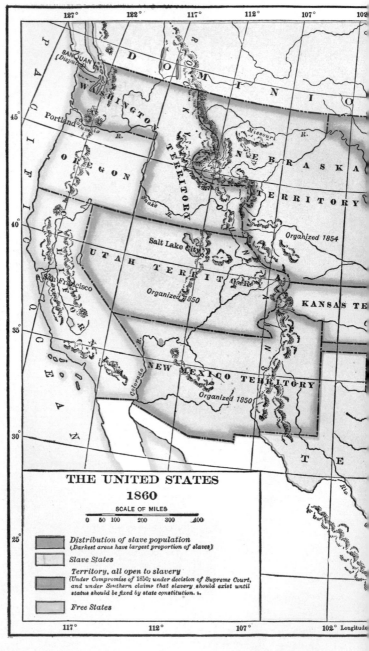

THE UNITED STATES
1860

SCALE OF MILES
0 50 100 200 300 400

Distribution of slave population
(Darkest areas have largest proportion of slaves)

Slave States

Territory, all open to slavery
(Under Compromise of 1850; under decision of Supreme Court,
and under Southern claims that slavery should exist until
status should be fixed by state constitution. ı.

Free States

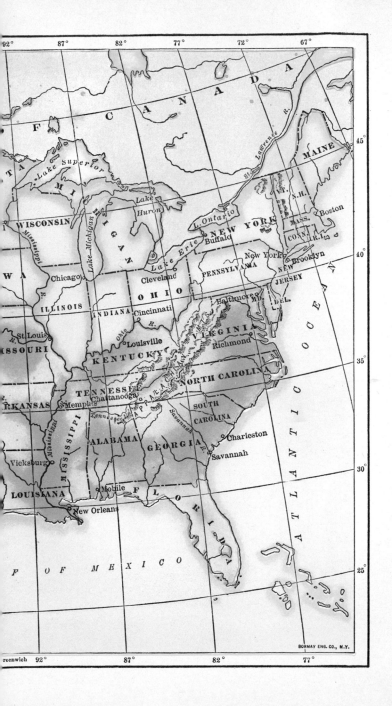

insistence that the North should yield to a demand absolutely empty unless they looked to new extensions of territory to the south in which slavery could actually be applied. The suspicion of a project of expansion southward was confirmed by President Buchanan's attempt to purchase Cuba and to occupy a part of Mexico, termed by the message "a wreck upon the ocean, drifting about as she is impelled by different factions." [1] The South had also good reason to hope that the filibuster William Walker would succeed in Nicaragua, and that Central America would be added as a field for slavery extension.[2] Without such hopes as to Mexico and the regions farther south, it is impossible to understand the bitterness of southern contention as to territorial rights after 1857, except as the barest and emptiest sentiment.

More logical and equally destructive of good feeling between the sections was the wide-spread movement for the reopening of the African slave-trade, based on the claim that the South had too few slaves, and that the supply must be reinforced by importation; a claim which reversed the logic of diffusion of slavery applied to the territories. The price of a good field-hand had risen in the cotton states to as much as $2000, and was still rising. The consumption of cotton was increasing at the

---

[1] Richardson, *Messages and Papers*, V., 568.
[2] See Walker, "Central American Affairs," in *De Bow's Review*, XXVIII., 154 (February, 1860).

rate of over six per cent. per annum. If that rate was to be kept up and met, besides the natural increase, an additional 70,000 field-hands, or, with their families, 215,000 slaves, would be needed in the cotton-growing states in the five years from 1855 to 1860, which would mean an additional yearly investment in such labor of $44,000,000.[1] With reason it was asked, "Where are they to come from?" No wonder that, with their now passionate belief in slavery, many in the South favored the reopening of the African slave-trade. But why, in the face of such needs, and of such values as those to which the slave had risen, should there be a wish to still further deplete the labor of the cotton states and raise prices to a prohibitive point by transporting to the territories such labor already employed in its most profitable field—cotton? That territorial slavery should have been to the interest of the border states, whose only real interest was in the sale of the negroes, can be understood; but it was essentially otherwise where the slave was the only laborer and was not an exotic, as he was in Virginia and Kentucky.

De Bow was able to say in the beginning of this year, "Certainly no cause has ever grown with greater rapidity than has that of the advocates of the slave trade, if we may judge from the attitude it is assuming in most of our southern legislatures."[2]

---

[1] *De Bow's Review*, XXI., 599 (December, 1856).
[2] *Ibid.*, XXVI., 51 (January, 1859).

The Southern Convention, a body formed for advancing the commercial interests of the South, in its meeting, May, 1858, at Montgomery, Alabama, gave its time almost entirely to the question. Yancey, prominent in all its proceedings, clearly stated their position. "If it is not wrong to hold slaves and buy and sell them, it is right in morals and under the Constitution which guarantees the institution, that we should buy them in whatever place we may choose to select. He did not wish to be compelled to go to Virginia and buy slaves for $1500 each, when he could get them in Cuba for $600, and upon the coast of Guinea for one sixth of that sum."

The report of the committee favoring reopening of the African slave-trade was laid upon the table, but taken up at the next meeting of the convention, at Vicksburg, Mississippi, May, 1859, and adopted by over two to one.[1] It was not entirely cheapness which determined the views of those favoring the trade, "for," said the committee, with extraordinary blindness to the physical and other conditions of the problem, "we believe that an importation of one or two hundred thousand slaves will enable us to take every territory offered to the West."[2]

The advocacy of the reopening of the slave-trade by so many South-Carolinians in the last decade of

---

[1] *De Bow's Review*, XXVII., 96–99 (January, 1860).
[2] *Ibid.*, XXIV., 490 (June, 1858).

slavery would seem anomalous in face of the fact that South Carolina was herself a slave-selling, or, at least, a slave-deporting, state. The fact that slaves were not profitable in the economy of South Carolina is shown by the dark picture of the condition of the state in 1859, drawn by Spratt, of Charleston, the chairman of the committee of the Southern Convention of 1859, reporting in favor of reopening the slave-trade. The depressed condition of the state was, in his opinion, wholly due to the want of African labor. He said: "Upon the suppression of . . . [the slave] trade the splendors [of the town and parishes of the Charleston district] waned; their glories departed; progress left them for the North; cultivation ceased; the swamps returned; mansions became tenantless and roofless; values fell, lands that sold for fifty dollars per acre, now sell for less than five dollars; trade was no longer prosecuted; . . . and Charleston, which was once upon the line of travel from Europe to the North, now stands aside, and while once the metropolis of America is now the unconsidered sea port of a tributary province." [1]

His statement of conditions was true; his reasoning erroneous. The state was already black in the proportion of four negroes to three whites, and further flooding with Africans would not have made it a cotton state in the sense that Alabama and Mississippi were such. The conditions were intrinsic.

[1] *De Bow's Review*, XXVII., 211.

The state was not in the true cotton belt; the yield per acre was but three-fifths that in Alabama and less than half that in Mississippi.[1] Its advance in cotton production in the decade 1850–1860 was but eighteen per cent; in Mississippi it was one hundred and forty-six per cent. It is true that the sea-island cotton of South Carolina and Georgia had a special value, but of this the South Carolina production rarely exceeded seven thousand bales.

It is not unfair to suppose that some of the strength of the secession movement in South Carolina was due to a vain hope of recovering something of her former prosperity by being free to import African slaves. But causes deeper than those mentioned lay at the root of South Carolina's decadence. In 1775, when her exports of rice and indigo were valued at over one million pounds, she was one of a fringe of colonies on the Atlantic seaboard, and she was one of the few which raised specialties for export. There was no "back country" except that given over to the Indian and the buffalo. But when population crossed the mountains, and great states grew northwest and west of her, she could have little share in that trade on account of the barrier of mountains and because the others had their own natural commercial ports of Mobile and New Orleans. The Mississippi was the highway of the West until railroads found their

[1] U. S. Seventh Census (1850), *Compendium*, 178.

way west over the easier routes of the North, and New York, Philadelphia, and Baltimore took the trade because ships could load both ways. Charleston ceased to import, as she once did, for the northern trade, and found herself with deserted wharves. No additions of slaves, no efforts of masters, could have prevented such a change. Charleston was left aside, with nothing to carry outward except South Carolina's own comparatively limited production. The deep discontent with conditions which no efforts on their part could, to any great extent, have overcome ripened into sullen dissatisfaction with the Union, at whose door was laid the cause, instead of at that of nature.

CHAPTER V

THE JOHN BROWN RAID
(1858–1859)

THE civil war in Kansas was ending, and the territory was certain to be one of the free states which, by the admission of Minnesota and Oregon, now numbered eighteen as against fifteen slave states—Delaware and Maryland were not dependent on slavery, and four others, Virginia, Kentucky, Tennessee, and Missouri, had large areas where the slaves were so few that there was no positive and insistent pro-slavery feeling. There was still a wide-spread and powerful Union sentiment throughout all parts of the South, except in South Carolina, though even there it was far from unknown.

The Whig party, which had been the stronghold of Unionist feeling, had now as a party disappeared, its following in the South finding refuge in the ephemeral organization known as "Americans" or "Know-Nothings," and many of the northern Whigs drifting to the new Republican party, a name which to the South, unfortunately and incorrectly, was the synonym of abolitionist. New England was now solidly Republican; New York elected a Republican governor in 1858, and Pennsylvania in 1859 for the first time left the Democratic ranks. Ohio, Indiana, Michigan, Wisconsin, Iowa, and Minnesota were Republican. Maryland elected a "Know-Nothing" governor, Hicks, in 1858. Houston left the Senate to become governor of Texas. Quitman, who for seven years had been a firebrand, had died in July, 1858. Alexander H. Stephens was no longer in Congress. Leaving Washington, March 5, 1859, he stood at the stern of the boat gazing at the Capitol. A friend remarked, "I suppose you are thinking of coming back to these halls as a senator." Stephens replied: "No, I never expect to see Washington again, unless I am brought here as a prisoner of war," a prophecy which was to be fulfilled.[1]

October 17, 1859, the country was startled by the news of the seizure, the previous night, of the United States arsenal at Harper's Ferry, and the domination of the village by a small body of men led by John Brown, whose name was already known throughout the Union by a series of bloody exploits in Kansas, ending in the summer of 1858 with a raid into Missouri to free some slaves.[2]

Born at Torrington, Connecticut, in 1800, reared in the Western Reserve in northern Ohio, in his father's occupation as a tanner; married at twenty years

---

[1] Johnston and Browne, *Stephens*, 348.
[2] Smith, *Parties and Slavery* (*Am. Nation*, XVIII.), chap. xi.

and again at thirty-three; the father of twenty children, thirteen of them by his second wife; by turns tanner, farmer, land surveyor, wool dealer, cattle drover, sheep raiser, a migrant for years between Ohio and Massachusetts, and always unsuccessful in his affairs, he finally, after a ruinous visit to Europe in 1849 to sell wool, settled his family, but not himself, on a small farm in the Adirondacks, at North Elba, Essex County, New York. It was in this region that Gerrit Smith, a large-hearted philanthropist, had given farms to a considerable number of colored people, though a region where Indian-corn would not ripen and stock had to be fed six months in the year was wholly unfitted by climate and production to the negro race. It was among these that Brown established himself somewhat as an adviser and helper, and no doubt also because he obtained a home for his family under favorable conditions.

Brown himself states that he becarr an abolitionist during the War of 1812, through witnessing the maltreatment of a colored boy, a slave.[1] It is not surprising, with his intensity of character, that as early as 1839 he had decided upon some such course as was taken in 1859. He seems to have kept this steadily in view and to have looked upon his whole family as instruments in the cause.[2] Coming of Puritan stock, he inherited the intense

[1] Sanborn, *John Brown*, 12–17.
[2] Sanborn, in *Atlantic Monthly*, XXXV., 21 (January, 1875).

religiosity associated with the Puritan character and a firm faith in the Bible, of which he was a constant reader and quoter; he was a religious man and a kindly one, as religion and kindliness presented themselves to such a soul, which, when fired with an idea, recked little of the law and morality which lay across his way.

Six of Brown's seven living sons and a son-in-law migrated to Kansas in 1855. The wretched conflict, which was the forerunner of the greater war later, caused Brown to find the true *métier* for which nature had fitted him—that of the partisan leader.

Whatever other dark and savage deeds were done in the dark period, none, it must be said in the truth of history, was more savage and more ruthless than the murder (for it can be called nothing else) at Pottawatomie during the night of May 24, 1856, when five men were taken at midnight from their beds and their heads split open by a heavy, old-style navy cutlass, but one shot being fired. Even Sanborn, the intimate associate of Stearns and Higginson on the Boston Kansas committee, and Brown's biographer and ardent admirer, can find no better excuse for this outrage than that Brown "knew—what few could believe—that slavery must perish in blood; and though a peaceful man, he had no scruples about shedding blood in so good a cause . . . we who praise Grant for those military movements which caused the bloody

death of thousands, are so inconsistent as to denounce Brown for the death of these five men in
Kansas."[1]

The savagery of Kansas conditions roused the
fighting instincts of the man, and he reverted to
views expressed to Frederick Douglass as early as
1847 regarding a scheme of an Appalachian stronghold: "To take at first about twenty-five picked
men and begin on a small scale; supply them with
arms and ammunition, and post them in squads
of five on a line of twenty-five miles, the most per-
suasive and judicious of whom shall go down to
the fields from time to time, as opportunity offers,
and induce the slaves to join them, seeking and
selecting the most reckless and daring."[2]

Brown's three guerilla years in Kansas may be regarded as a preliminary study for his work of 1859.
His organization of a corps of "Kansas Regulars"
in 1856 and the rules for their government are
much in keeping with his later action.[3] In January, 1857, Brown first came in contact with the
Massachusetts Kansas committee, of which Mr. G.
L. Stearns was chairman, and he received the
custody of certain arms in western Iowa belonging
to the committee and was furnished with a considerable sum of money to transport them.[4] Later

[1] Sanborn, *John Brown*, 268.
[2] Douglass, *Life and Times* (ed. of 1881), 280.
[3] Sanborn, *John Brown*, 287–290.
[4] Sanborn, in *Atlantic Monthly*, XXXV., 232.

in the same month he was urging in New York, before the national Kansas committee, the organization of a company of a hundred mounted rangers.

The chaotic conditions of public feeling is shown by the effort to induce the Massachusetts legislature to vote ten thousand dollars for use in Kansas; and Brown, in February, 1857, appeared before the committee appointed to consider such petitions, and gave a powerful description of Kansas outrages,[1] omitting, however, a description of his own. In the fall of 1857 Brown was in Iowa, associated with an English adventurer, Forbes, who had been Italian silk merchant, Garibaldian, and New York fencing-master, and who was engaged by Brown as an instructor in military matters. In November, 1857, Brown was again in Kansas. He was soon back in Iowa, where his views were revealed to a small following of nine persons besides Forbes; a revelation which caused a good deal of wrangling.[2] The property of the Massachusetts committee, consisting of about two hundred Sharps rifles, a like number of revolvers, blankets, clothing, and ammunition, were shipped to Ashtabula County, Ohio, whence they finally found their way to the Kennedy farm in Maryland.

Brown's plan was fully revealed Monday, February 22, 1858, at the house of Gerrit Smith, at Peterboro, New York, where Brown had asked to meet

[1] Redpath, *John Brown*, 176–184.
[2] Cook's confession, in *Ibid.*, 198.

him, Theodore Parker, George L. Stearns, T. W. Higginson, and F. B. Sanborn, all of Boston, and his intimate supporters. Sanborn alone came, but was empowered to represent the others. "After dinner," says Sanborn, "I went with Mr. Smith, John Brown, and my classmate Morton [Smith's secretary] to the room of Mr. Morton in the third story. Here in the long winter evening which followed, the whole outline of Brown's campaign in Virginia was laid before our little council . . . the middle of May was named as the time of the attack. To begin this hazardous enterprise he asked for but eight hundred dollars, and would think himself rich with a thousand." [1]

The colloquy lasted late into the night and was resumed next day, with the result that Smith and Sanborn agreed that funds must be raised and Brown supported. Sanborn continues: "I returned to Boston on the 25th of February and . . . communicated the enterprise to Theodore Parker and Wentworth Higginson. At the suggestion of Parker, Brown, who had gone to Brooklyn, N. Y., was invited to visit Boston secretly, and did so on the 4th of March, taking a room at the American House, in which he remained for the most part during a four days' stay." Brown could write to his son John, March 6: "My call here has met with a most hearty response, so that I feel assured of at least tolerable success. . . . All has been effected by quiet

[1] Sanborn, *John Brown*, 438.

meeting of a few choice friends." [1]   Brown's letters at this time to his family show how fully he was possessed with the spirit of his project, and also illustrate the wildness of his views, which included a possible return after the accomplishment of "the great work of my life" and "'rest at evening.'" [2]

Sanborn makes it clear that at least Higginson, Stearns, Parker, and Howe were informed at this period of Brown's plans of attack and defence in Virginia, though he does not know that any besides himself knew of his purpose to surprise the arsenal and town of Harper's Ferry. [3]

May 8, 1858, found Brown (known for some time for safety as Shubel Morgan) at Chatham, Canada, with eleven young white associates and one colored man whom he had attached to himself and who had been with him in Kansas and elsewhere. At Chatham, by these men and thirty-four colored persons, was adopted an extraordinary "Provisional Constitution and Ordinance for the people of the United States," which was written in January, 1858, at the house of Frederick Douglass, in Rochester, a paper in itself a witness of the abnormality of the mind of the author. [4]   Brown was elected commander-in-chief, Richard Realf, secretary of state; J. H. Kagi, secretary of war; George B. Gill, secretary of the treasury. Two colored men were

[1] Sanborn, *John Brown*, 440.   [2] *Ibid.*, 441.   [3] *Ibid.*, 450.
[4] For this constitution in full, see Hinton, *John Brown and His Men*, 619–634.

elected members of the congress, and seem to have
formed the entire body; commissions were issued
signed by W. C. Munroe, a colored man, as president of the convention.

Suspicions of Brown's intentions reached Senator Henry Wilson from Forbes, the English adventurer mentioned. A letter to Dr. Howe from
Wilson caused the committee, of which Stearns was
chairman, to write Brown, May 14, 1858, not to use
the arms furnished him for any other purpose than
the defence of Kansas. This was evidently a blind
to cover responsibility, as May 31 found Brown
back in Boston in consultation with Smith, Stearns,
Howe, Parker, Higginson, and Sanborn. Here, notwithstanding the danger of publicity, Higginson protested against delay, regarding "any postponement
as simply abandoning the project." [1] But all the
others of the committee were against him, Sanborn
writing him, May 18: "Wilson, as well as Hale and
Seward, and God knows how many more, have heard
about the plot from Forbes. To go on in the face of
this is mere madness." [2]

The duplicity of the committee is shown by a
letter of May 12, 1858, to Senator Wilson, sent by
Howe, saying: "I understand perfectly your meaning. No countenance has been given to Brown for
any operations outside of Kansas *by the Kansas
Committee*," [3] and three days later, "Prompt meas-

---

[1] Sanborn, *John Brown*, 459.   [2] *Ibid.*, 460.
[3] The emphasis is in the letter.

ures have been taken and will be resolutely followed up to prevent any such monstrous perversion of a trust as would be the application of means raised for the defence of Kansas to a purpose which the subscribers of the fund would disapprove and vehemently condemn." [1]

The meaning of this gross prevarication was that the arms having been furnished by Stearns, he now made claim to them, withdrew them from the Kansas committee, and, meeting Brown in New York about May 20, arranged that they should be in Brown's hands as the agent, not of the committee, but of Stearns alone. [2] It is not a pleasant story. It was a curious salve to the consciences of the conspirators, who thus far had been in the fullest degree accessories. These arms and a thousand pikes contracted for by Brown in Collinsville, Connecticut, were to be the arms of an army of liberation.

Brown, consulting Higginson, proposed to blind Forbes by going to Kansas, and that the committee in future should not know his plans. June 3 he left Boston with five hundred dollars in gold, and reached Lawrence, Kansas, June 25, 1858.

A massacre of Free State men at Marais des Cygnes by a party of "Border Ruffians" in May, 1858, a deed which raised the North to a dangerous heat, was a good reason for Brown's return; but seven months later, at the end of December, 1858, he was in Kansas, and the leader of a party of fa-

[1] Sanborn, *John Brown*, 462.   [2] *Ibid.*, 463.

miliars which crossed the Missouri border and carried away eleven slaves and some horses and wagons, killing one of the owners who had attempted to defend his possessions. The slaves were safely landed in Canada and the horses were sold at Cleveland, Ohio, by Brown, who had the grace, however, to warn the purchasers of a possible defect in the title.[1]

Brown wandered in many places until July 1859, when he appeared in the rough, semi-mountainous country of the upper Potomac, immediately on the highway, and six miles north from Harper's Ferry, where he rented for a year a small place known as the Kennedy farm, on which were two houses. Thither he transported by degrees all his arms and gathered together his twenty-one followers (five of whom were colored), for whom his daughter Anne and his sixteen-year-old daughter-in-law, wife of Oliver Brown, "kept house." Nor were most of the men much older. Except John Brown and his son Owen, they ranged in age from eighteen to twenty - eight. Only five of the whites were over twenty-four years of age; one was not yet nineteen; three were Brown's sons.

Brown's pretence of looking for a better climate and for a location for raising sheep, imposed upon the unsophisticated neighbors, and no suspicions seem to have been roused by the presence and the going to and fro in this secluded district of a number of strangers, who wandered freely over the

[1] Sanborn, *John Brown*, 494.

mountains of the vicinity. The time in-doors was spent in what they called drill and in looking after the arms. The heads of the pikes had come separately from the shafts, which latter passed for fork-handles; they were fitted together at the farm.

An anonymous letter dated at Cincinnati, August 20, 1859, to the secretary of war, gave full information of the intended movement, but received no attention. It indicated so clearly Brown's movements that it was evident later that it had been written by one thoroughly informed. Not until 1897 was the name of the writer made public, and it was then shown to have been written in Iowa by a young man urged on by the solicitude of some in the Quaker settlement, which he was visiting, for the safety of the young Iowans accompanying Brown.[1]

Sunday, October 16, the party was assembled in an all-day council at the Kennedy farm, the "constitution" was read for the benefit of four new-comers, commissions for newly made officers made out, and orders given detailing the movement, which Brown had decided should be that evening. "Captains" Owen Brown, Merriam, and Barclay Coppoc were to remain and guard arms and effects until morning, when, joined by some men from Harper's Ferry, they were to remove the arms with teams to an old school-house in Virginia three-quarters of a mile from Harper's Ferry. Two were to go ahead of the wagon in which Brown was to

[1] B. F. Gue. in *Am. Hist. Mag.*, I., 162 et seq. (March, 1906).

go and cut the telegraph wires; two were to capture the watchman at the railroad bridge, and two
were detailed for each of the following posts: the
covered Potomac bridge, the engine-house, the
armory, and the rifle factory. "Captain" Stevens,
after the engine-house should be seized, was to go
into the country with five companions and take
certain persons prisoners, among them Colonel
Lewis Washington, owner of the Washington sword
which tradition has falsely ascribed as a present
from Frederick the Great, which Brown coveted,
and which, when received, he theatrically wore.

The invading procession left the Kennedy farm
at eight o'clock. Brown, with his wagon and party,
having captured the bridge watchman, went on to
the armory, forced the door, and seized the watchman. The several stations assigned were occupied
by eleven o'clock. A shot fired at a relief bridge
watchman gave the alarm. The stoppage of an
eastward-bound train at midnight at first suggested
to the passengers a strike among the arsenal workmen; at daylight it was allowed to proceed with a
knowledge of the true situation, Brown himself seeing the conductor across the bridge, as he "had no
intention of interfering with the comfort of passengers or hindering the United States mails." [1]

With daylight, October 17, came a four-horse
wagon-load of Colonel Washington's slaves. Washington himself, when aroused and captured, had

[1] Hinton, *John Brown and His Men*, 288.

been ordered to give in charge to Anderson (a colored man) the historic sword, and a pair of pistols from Lafayette. He was brought in his own carriage to the armory, where he was kept as a prisoner, as were several other neighboring slave-owners. The Washington wagon and fourteen slaves were sent to the Kennedy farm to assist in removing the arms to the Virginia school-house.[1]

Two deaths had by this time occurred; the first that of a colored porter at the hotel who would not stop when ordered; the other that of the village mayor, Beckham, who was passing unarmed in range from the engine-house, and whose body was left exposed for some hours. An inquisitive bartender had been seized, but was exchanged for breakfast from the hotel for forty persons.

The countryside being now aroused, men with arms of all sorts poured into the village. Militia began to arrive from all the neighboring and some of the more distant towns, and desultory fighting began with a number of casualties on either side. At nightfall Brown held the engine-house with four men and ten prisoners, his son Oliver dead and another son, Watson, dying. Six others were dead, three wounded, and one a prisoner. At eleven in the evening a company of United States marines arrived from Washington, accompanied by Colonel Robert E. Lee, of General Scott's staff, who took over the command. At seven the next morn-

---

[1] Hinton, *John Brown and His Men*, 294.

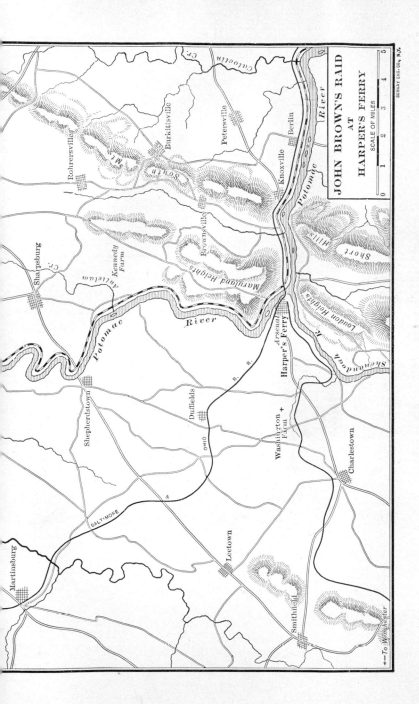

JOHN BROWN'S RAID
AT
HARPER'S FERRY

SCALE OF MILES

0 1 2 3 4 5

BORMAY LITHO. CO., N.Y.

ing (Tuesday, October 18) Lieutenant J. E. B.
Stuart was sent by Lee, under a flag of truce, to
demand an unconditional surrender. Brown refused all offers unless he should be allowed to leave
with his prisoners, to go, unpursued, as far as the
second toll-gate, where he would free his prisoners,
and the soldiers thereafter be permitted to pursue.
A renewal of the demand and of advice to trust to
the clemency of the government was refused by
Brown, with the remark, "I prefer to die just here."
The failure to obtain a surrender was followed by
an assault by the marines, in which the door was
battered in, with the loss of one man. Brown received a bayonet wound and several severe sword-
cuts in the mêlée. Owen Brown and six others
escaped.[1]

After Brown was brought out he revived and
talked earnestly in response to various questions.
His conversation bore the impression of the conviction that whatever he had done to free slaves
was right, and that in the warfare in which he was
engaged he was entitled to be treated as a prisoner
of war.[2]

Brown's prisoners all testified to their lenient
treatment, and Colonel Washington spoke of him
as a man of extraordinary coolness and nerve.
Brown and the other prisoners, to whom were added
two captured later, were transferred to the county

[1] Hart, *Am. Hist. told by Contemporaries*, IV., §§ 47, 48.
[2] *Harper's Weekly*, III., 695.

jail at Charlestown. On examination at the Kennedy farm a large quantity of blankets, clothing, and the arms previously mentioned were found, as also a carpet-bag containing a copy of Brown's "constitution" and a number of papers connected with his movement.[1]

Brown's trial began October 25, two Virginia lawyers, Lawson Botts and C. J. Faulkner, being assigned to his defence. These gentlemen were replaced later by S. Chilton, of Washington; H. Griswold, of Cleveland, Ohio, and a young Boston lawyer, G. E. Hoyt. The indictment was, first, for conspiring with negroes to produce insurrection; second, for treason to the commonwealth of Virginia; and, third, for murder. October 31 he was found guilty, and was hanged December 2. All of the other prisoners in turn suffered the same punishment.

Brown's conduct throughout his imprisonment and trial was of great dignity and reserve, and commanded respect and sympathy. He appeared in court wounded and ill and in a cot. His speech previous to being sentenced was the only blot upon his action at this time, in so far as he disclaimed "murder or treason, or the destruction of property, or to make insurrection." He claimed an intention simply to carry slaves to Canada. But one cannot do all he did and then disclaim the intention of using force.

[1] Hinton, *John Brown and His Men*, 319.

Governor Wise himself gave high praise to Brown.[1] Thousands of letters poured in upon him urging Brown's pardon. Many threatened; others deemed the execution ill-advised. Wise's message to the legislature, written after Brown's death, gave good reasons for not taking such advice.[2]

The emotional feelings among the abolitionists caused throughout the North expressions of an extraordinary character which enthroned Brown among the saints, and scarcely left anything for future use in characterizing our most exalted philosophic or religious ideals. It is painful testimony to a national habit of emotional exaltation. A Virginia transcendentalist could say, "John Brown was executed on December 2, 1859, and two days later my sermon exalted him to the right hand of God."[3] Forty-four years later the same man could say, "Reading his career by the light of subsequent history, I am convinced that few men ever wrought so much evil."[4]

The oratorical governor of Virginia saw in the event principally a means of arming his state to meet events which he too clearly foreboded. The whole available militia of the state was assembled, and Harper's Ferry became a camp of some eighteen hundred men. "I brought the force into the field," said Wise, "in the first place to rouse the military spirit of the state; and in my humble estimation

[1] Wise, *Wise*, 246.
[2] *Ibid.*, 250–254.
[3] Conway, *Autobiography*, I., 302.
[4] *Ibid.*, 303.

that was worth all the money spent.   In the next place . . . to assure the people of the border of their safety and defense." [1]   In his message of December 5 he called upon the legislature to "organize and arm."

The South, under the circumstances, was much calmer than might have been expected.   This was due in part, no doubt, to a reassurance because the blacks failed to rise, and showed evident loyalty to their masters.   Their attitude justified much of what the South had so long upheld as to the contentment of the slaves; and this, with a removal of much of the fear which had hung over the section since Nat Turner's insurrection in 1831, nurtured a satisfaction which did much to offset the indignation which was poured out abundantly upon Brown's northern abettors and upon the many who proclaimed him a martyr.   Motions in both houses of the Massachusetts legislature to adjourn on the day of Brown's execution, though lost, very properly rankled in the southern mind, as did also meetings in many parts of the North prompted by ill-advised fanaticism.   The strength and extent of this spirit was illustrated by Theodore Parker's belief that "No American has died in this century whose chance of earthly immortality is worth half so much as John Brown's." [2]   Parker was also one who could say, "I should like of all things to see

[1] *Richmond Enquirer* (semi-weekly ed.), January 31, 1860.
[2] Frothingham, *Parker*, 463.

an insurrection of slaves. It must be tried many times before it succeeds, *as at last it must*," [1] an expression which was the outcome of his own full knowledge as to what was brewing. Of this the others of the Boston secret committee, Parker, Stearns, Higginson, Howe and Sanborn as already shown on the authority of the last, also had full information, as had Gerrit Smith, with the exception, perhaps, of the exact place at which Brown was to strike. Brown's funds were supplied by these men, who were accessories before the fact in the fullest meaning of the phrase.

It is impossible to justify such action. That they had full appreciation of the results should Brown succeed is shown in Howe's feeling, when, early in 1859, returning from Cuba and "accepting the hospitality of Wade Hampton and other rich planters . . . it shocked him to think he might be instrumental in giving up to fire and pillage their noble mansions." [2] If Brown and his coadjutors were justified, then Orsini's attempt, to which Lincoln himself compared Brown's, was justifiable; the death of Lincoln himself was a result of the same want of principle. For the men just mentioned were conspirators in the same sense as those who aided Orsini and Booth, both of whom were acting upon the extreme view of "the higher law" which makes man a law unto himself. Stearns and his fellows were not martyrs; they did not risk their

---

[1] Frothingham, *Parker*, 475.   [2] Sanborn, *John Brown*, 491.

lives; they were not in open warfare; they were
simply in secret conspiracy to carry by bolder instruments throughout the South the horrors of
Hayti, still vivid in the recollection of many then
yet living.

One can respect the fanatical spirit which so
often goes with martyrdom.   Brown was undoubtedly willing to lay down his life in order to instigate
the blacks to move for freedom.   But his willingness was no more a justification than Orsini's or
Booth's.   No result of the kind intended could possibly have justified the overriding of every law of
the country from the formation of the Constitution.   That the negroes had themselves a right to
rise, and, if necessary to their freedom, to slaughter
and burn, cannot be denied.   Every man has the
right, at all hazards, to resist enslavement; it is a
right of nature.   But the men who bought the arms
and supplied the money for the pikes carried to
the Kennedy farm, with full knowledge of the uses
which they were to be put to, and the whites who
were to use them, were fighting, not against the
South, but against all organized society.   We could
palliate such action on the part of the quarter of
a million of free negroes in the North, working in
behalf of their race, and respect the southern free
negro who was willing to fight for such a cause.
But of such willingness there was too faint a sign
to suppose such action, unaided by higher leadership, possible.

While Brown had a blood-thirst which made him a willing leader in some of the worst incidents of the bloody epoch in Kansas, he had the high qualities of undaunted courage and an unflinching willingness to give his life for the cause he had at heart. Such willingness is, however, by no means so infrequent that it need elevate such a case as Brown's to a foremost rank of martyrdom. For, however willing to be a martyr, he did not expect that glory; he was, in his own mind, to be the head of a great and successful movement, and herein his conduct showed too much insanity or folly to deserve sympathy. In all the important phases of his plot he showed extreme ignorance and want of good sense. His original scheme was as wild and impossible as could be imagined. It was stamped with ignorance and incapacity. His intent to occupy the rough region of the Alleghanies with a large body of blacks, led by a score of whites, most of whom were mere boys, wanting in any supplies of clothing or food, in an unsettled region, one of the roughest of the continent, was one showing absolute want of the judgment necessary in a leader. Starvation would have met him at the threshold of his eyrie. The choice both of his theatre of action and of the time showed a want of balance of mind. The theatre was a region where the whites were in an overpowering majority; the time the beginning of the season when the support of life is most difficult and in which the negro would be most unlikely to yield the warm comfort of his cabin for the wintry heights of the West Virginia mountains. The whole scheme, so far as it expected slave support by insurrection, was one of complete folly.

That Brown, despite his speech when condemned, did expect a rising, must be taken as unquestionable. If proof beyond his own statement were needed, we have it in that of his "Adjutant-General" Kagi (killed at Harper's Ferry), as follows: "It was not anticipated that the first movement would have any other appearance to the masters than a slave stampede or local insurrection at most. The planters would pursue their chattels and be defeated. The militia would then be called out, and would also be defeated. . . . They anticipated after the first blow had been struck that by the aid of the free and Canadian negroes who would join them, they could inspire confidence in the slaves, and induce them to rally; . . . the design was to make the fight in the mountains of Virginia, extending it to North Carolina and Tennessee and also to the swamps of South Carolina if possible."[1] "The mountains and swamps of the South were intended by the Almighty," said Brown, "for a refuge for the slave and a defence against the oppressor,"[2] a remark not in disaccord with Brown's claim to being directed by the Lord in visions.[3]

When Brown found himself face to face with the

[1] Hinton, *John Brown and His Men*, 673.
[2] Redpath, *John Brown*, 204.   [3] *Ibid.*, 113.

actuality of conflict it seemed to take from him all
power of initiative or movement, and led him to
sacrifice himself and his party in a defence which
could only have one end. Whatever may be said
as to his bravery, and he was certainly brave, or as
to his loftiness of spirit, which is undeniable, he
was, if it be granted that he was attempting that
which every act, every writing, every explanation
by himself, leads us to believe he attempted, a man
wanting in knowledge of the race he was urging to
rise, and so lacking in common-sense that he was
plainly unfitted for such a leadership.

Nor could the South fail to be gratified with the
rebound in northern sentiment. The sporadic cases
of public approval of Brown could not outweigh
the general indignation throughout the North. It
needed the events of the next and later years, with
which his acts had but remote connection, to can-
onize John Brown, whose name became the con-
venient watchword of antagonism to disruption of
the Union, and gained a fame, whether good or ill,
which will last as long as the memories of the great
Civil War.

CHAPTER VI

RISING SPIRIT OF ANTAGONISM IN CONGRESS
(1859–1860)

WHEN Congress met, December 5, 1859, the new House was a conglomerate of 109 Republicans, 88 administration Democrats, 13 anti-Lecompton Democrats, 26 Americans, and 1 Whig. All the Americans were from the South with four exceptions, and they included half the delegations from Maryland, Kentucky, and North Carolina, and six of the ten representatives of Tennessee. Charles Francis Adams, Morrill, Burlingame, Conkling, Grow, Corwin, Sherman, Colfax, Windom were among the Republicans; Miles, Pryor, Curry, Lamar, Reuben Davis, Vallandigham, S. S. Cox, Sickles were among the Democrats. Henry Winter Davis, Gilmer, and Maynard were of the Americans. In the Senate from the northern states were Seward, Sumner, Wilson, Wade, Douglas, Chandler, of Michigan, and Grimes; Davis, Toombs, Slidell, Benjamin, Mallory, and Crittenden (the last an American) from the South.

It was not strange that, with the general feeling strongly accentuated by the Harper's Ferry raid,

the slavery question should at once arise, and in the
House render impossible for many weeks the election of a speaker. Sixty - four Republican representatives had signed a circular in which it was proposed to issue at a very cheap price a compendium
of the *Impending Crisis*, a book written by Hinton
R. Helper, a North-Carolinian of the poorer middle
class, appealing to the poor whites of the South
to emancipate themselves. It was not in human
nature to refuse the challenge offered by the circulation of a document which, however true in its
statistics, showing the immense disparity of even
the agricultural progress between the sections, was
deeply abusive of the slave-holder and revolutionary
in its advice. The purpose stated in the circular
was to diffuse the book particularly in Pennsylvania, New Jersey, Indiana, and Illinois, the states
which were to decide the next presidential contest.
Clark, of Missouri, introduced a resolution that no
member of the House who had "indorsed the book
and recommended it or the compend from it, is fit
to be a Speaker of this House," and termed the
action an incipient movement of treason.[1]

Sherman, the Republican candidate, stated that
while he had lent his name, he had not seen a copy
of either the book or compendium,[2] an action which
he fitly characterized in a private letter "a thought-
less, foolish, and unfortunate act." [3]   He reinforced

[1] *Cong. Globe*, 36 Cong., 1 Sess., 3.
[2] *Ibid.*, 547.   [3] *Sherman Letters*, 78.

his public statement by declaring that his opponents would scan his record "in vain for anything to excite insurrection, to disturb the peace, to invade the rights of the states, to alienate the North and South from each other, or to loosen the ties of fraternal fellowship by which our people have been and should be bound together. I am for the Union and the Constitution, with all the compromises under which it was formed and all the obligations which it imposes." [1] But this did not avail. He was supported until January 30 by the Republicans, when he withdrew his name, and Pennington, of New Jersey, a new member, was elected February 1, on the forty-fourth ballot, by 117 votes, the bare number necessary.

Though the southern leaders retaliated on the friends of Helper's book, they made the same blunder as twenty years before in regard to other incendiary documents. The book which they desired to suppress received an advertisement which spread it over the South, to its deep resentment, and gave it an enormous circulation in the North, where, convincing as were its arguments as to the effects of slavery, it made still more sure Republican success in the doubtful northern states.

Personal encounters on the floor of the House were imminent, arms were carried by many in both Houses, and the animosities in Congress were more than equalled by those of the southern press and by

[1] *Cong. Globe*, 36 Cong., 1 Sess., 548.

much of the northern. Every expression of members of prominence in both Houses showed how firmly had become fixed in the southern mind the idea of secession should a Republican president be elected. The speech, December 15, 1859, of Martin J. Crawford, of Georgia, against the election of Sherman as speaker, may be taken as the type of many which gave expression to the now dominant feeling of the South. "To talk," said Crawford, "of the settlement of this slavery question is folly; to talk of a compromise upon this subject of slavery is worse than folly; . . . this question has resolved itself at last into a question of slavery and disunion, or no slavery and union, . . . I have this to say, and I speak the sentiment of every Democrat on this floor from the state of Georgia: we will never submit to the inauguration of a Black Republican president." (Applause from the Democratic benches and hisses from the Republicans.) [1]

This language had its fitting counterpart in the speech of Hickman, of Pennsylvania, an anti-Lecompton Democrat, who said: "The North will never tolerate a division of the territory. . . . I am neither a prophet nor the son of a prophet; but I express my belief that there is as much true courage in the North, though it may not be known by the name of chivalry, as there is in the South. . . . I believe . . . that with all the appliances of art to assist, eighteen millions of men reared to industry,

[1] *Cong. Globe*, 36 Cong., 1 Sess., 163, 164.

with habits of the right kind, will always be able to cope successfully, if need be, with eight millions of men without these auxiliaries." [1]

A private letter from Senator Hammond shows a situation impossible of continuance: "I assure you and you may philosophize upon it, that unless the slavery question can be wholly eliminated from politics, this government is not worth two years', perhaps not two months', purchase. So far as I *know*, and as I believe, every man in both houses is armed with a revolver—some with two—and a bowie knife. . . . Seeing the oldest and most conservative *senators* on our side . . . get revolvers, I most reluctantly got one myself. . . . I can't carry it. . . . But I keep a pistol now in my drawer . . . as a matter of *duty* to my section. . . . While regarding this Union as cramping the South, I will nevertheless sustain it as long as I can. Yet I will stand by my side—as you would—to the end. I firmly believe that the slaveholding South is now the controlling *power* of the world—that no other power would face us in hostility. This will be demonstrated if we come to the ultimate; . . . cotton, rice, tobacco, and naval stores command the world; and we have sense enough to know it. . . . The North without us would be a motherless calf, bleating about, and die of mange and starvation." [2]

---

[1] *Cong. Globe*, 36 Cong., 1 Sess., 120.
[2] Letter to Francis Lieber, April 19, 1860, Perry, *Francis Lieber*, 310.

With such existing and growing antagonism
marked by such action as an act by the Virginia
legislature for "a full and complete arming of the
state," separation was a mere question of time and
opportunity. Every utterance of the kind in Congress had its echo in the press, North and South, but
much more powerfully in the latter, since the North
was far from being awakened to the imminence of
the situation. The close analogy between the irrec-
oncilables of both sections failed when applied to
the effects of their utterances; the abolitionists
were taken seriously by the South; the secessionists
were never so taken by the North until actual secession came. The Republicans adopted the habit of
simply disbelieving these predictions. Seward said:
"I remain now in the opinion I have uniformly expressed here and elsewhere that these hasty threats
of disunion are so unnatural that they will find no
hand to execute them." [1] Senator Wilson could
speak, January, 1860, of the "disunion predictions,
arguments, and threats" with which "every breeze
from the South is burdened," as "THIS BROAD
FARCE." [2]

In the Senate, where there were 37 Democrats,
24 Republicans, and 2 Americans, with one vacancy
each from Oregon, Minnesota, and Texas, the spirit
was no better. The resolution of Mason, of Virginia,
December 6, 1859, to appoint a committee to inquire

[1] *Cong. Globe*, 36 Cong., 1 Sess., 914.
[2] *Ibid.*, 572.   The emphasis is his own.

into the facts of the Harper's Ferry invasion brought out a sectional discussion, through an amendment offered by Trumbull, of Illinois, to extend the inquiry to the seizure, December, 1855, from the United States arsenal at Liberty, of a quantity of arms (including three field-pieces) by a large body of Missourians for use in Kansas. Nor did the discussion end with the unanimous adoption of the resolution, unamended, December 14; it extended throughout the session, with the added acrimony and personality which the approaching political conventions naturally induced. Toombs, in a very able speech, apostrophizing his state, exclaimed: "Never permit this Federal government to pass into the traitorous hands of the Black Republican party. It has already declared war against you and your institutions. It every day commits acts of war against you; it has already compelled you to arm for your defense. Listen to 'no vain babblings,' to no treacherous jargon about 'overt acts'; they have already been committed. Defend yourselves, the enemy is at your door; wait not to meet him at the hearth stone—meet him at the doorsill and drive him from the temple of liberty or pull down its pillars and involve him in a common ruin." [1]

Stephen A. Douglas, January 16, offered a bill of demagogic propitiation to the South, for the protection of states from invasion by another state, based upon Wise's communication, as governor, to

[1] *Cong. Globe*, 36 Cong., 1 Sess., App., 93.

the president, regarding reported conspiracies, and
calling upon the latter to take steps to preserve the
peace between the states; to which Buchanan had
replied that he was at a loss to discover any provision in the Constitution or laws which would authorize him to take steps for such a purpose. In
his speech supporting the bill, Douglas had "no
hesitation" in expressing his "firm and deliberate
conviction that the Harper's Ferry crime was the
natural, logical, inevitable result of the doctrines
and teachings of the Republican party. . . . The
great principle that underlies the organization . . .
is violent, irreconcilable, eternal warfare upon the
institution of American slavery, with the view of
its ultimate extinction throughout the land." Its
"vitality consists in appeals to northern passion,
northern prejudice, northern ambition against
southern states, southern institutions, and southern
people." [1] The speech was one which could have
well been made by a senator from South Carolina
instead of from Illinois. Throughout it was typical
of Douglas's want of serious conviction of any kind,
and of the spirit which we have come to call that of
the politician, which will bid for votes at any price;
and his action had no other effect than to give opportunity for a long debate on slavery, ending in
a strong disunion sentiment by Senator Hunter,
of Virginia, a cruel analysis by the keen mind of
Davis, and a discussion which showed the general

[1] *Cong. Globe*, 36 Cong., 1 Sess., 553.

crudeness of the mental make-up of Douglas, who will stand in history, almost with Calhoun, as a marplot against the peace of the Union.

Davis offered a bill to issue to any state or territory, on application, arms made at the United States armories on payment of an amount sufficient to replace by manufacture the arms issued, which had in the light of coming events a sufficiently ugly look to cause a united Republican vote in the negative.[1]

William H. Seward was with one consent regarded by the South as the coming nominee of the Republican party; his nomination was looked forward to with double bitterness throughout the section, because of the boldness of his expressions on slavery in and out of Congress, and Governor Letcher, of Virginia, gave form to the almost universal sentiment of the South in his message of 1860 to the legislature of Virginia: "The idea of permitting such a man to have the control and direction of the army and navy of the United States, and the appointment of high judicial and executive officers, postmasters included, cannot be entertained by the South for a moment."

The southern leaders recognized that the presidential contest of 1860 would under any circumstances be close, and dangerously so in the divided state of the Democratic party. For while Douglas was looked upon by the Democracy of the North as certain to be its next candidate, he had been dis-

[1] *Cong. Globe*, 36 Cong., 1 Sess., 1352.

carded by the South through the very action by
which he had hoped to ingratiate himself with the
southerners. His abrogation of the Missouri Compromise at the time of the passage of the Kansas-
Nebraska bill was in line with southern views; but
when squatter sovereignty failed to make Kansas a
slave territory, Douglas and his doctrine became to
the South anathema.

To bring out this internal division of the party,
Jefferson Davis, February 2 and March 1, 1860, submitted a series of resolutions, the first and second
of which were substantially the state - sovereignty
doctrine of Calhoun; the third affirmed it to be the
duty of the Senate, "which represents the states in
their sovereign capacity," to resist all attempts to
discriminate as to persons or property in the territories; the fourth attacked Douglas's Freeport Doctrine by declaring that "neither Congress nor a
territorial legislature, by direct or indirect legislation, has the power to annul or impair the constitutional right of any citizen, to take his slave
property into the common territories and there
hold and enjoy the same while the territorial condition remained"; the fifth made it the duty of
Congress to supply remedies, if adequate protection should not otherwise be afforded; the sixth
provided that the inhabitants of a territory, when
admitted as a state, might decide whether to have
slavery or not; the seventh demanded that the
constitutional provision as to fugitive slaves and

the laws made to secure its execution should be honestly and faithfully observed and maintained by all; and that all acts of individuals or state legislatures to defeat or nullify these were "hostile in character, subversive of the constitution and revolutionary in effect." [1]

These resolutions abandoned all theories of "non-interference" and of popular sovereignty in favor of the startling proposition that slavery was the normal and constitutional status in every territory, and that Congress must protect that status. The views were not new to Davis's mind; he had stated them broadly July 12, 1848, in a speech upon the Oregon bill, when he "denied that there was any power in Congress or in the people of the territory to interrupt the slave system," and "asserted it to be the duty of the United States to protect the property of a slave-owner during the transit from one state to another," [2] views at the time the more remarkable inasmuch as, when secretary of war in 1854, he cordially assented to Douglas's squatter-sovereignty views and aided in advancing them. Davis's resolutions were, however, now offered in effect as the platform of the southern wing of the Democratic party, and Douglas was given to understand that he must stand on this ground or lose the support of the South, which had come to view his doctrine as a bar against the admission or

[1] *Cong. Globe*, 36 Cong., 1 Sess., 658, 935.
[2] *Ibid.*, 30 Cong., 1 Sess., 927.

establishment of slavery in any territory as effectual
as the Wilmot proviso.[1]

While the two foremost representatives of the
Democratic party, Douglas and Davis, were thus at
sword's point, two Republicans of unequal prominence made nearly at the same moment speeches
which attracted the attention of the country. The
one expected, with almost the certainty of receiving it, the Republican candidacy for president; the
other but a year since had been disappointed in the
only hope of high political station which he seems
to have really held out to himself—the seat in the
Senate so long held by Douglas. The possibility of
being president but slowly dawned in Lincoln's
mind. But he had stepped into greatness, and
was carried far on the road to fame, by his debate
with Douglas in 1858.

These speeches were speedily published and had
a wide circulation. Their truth, fairness, and logic
made Lincoln a marked man in the thoughtful
minds of the East as well as among the populace of
the West, many thousands of whom he had faced
from the platform. He was called upon during
1859 for speeches and addresses in several of the
western states—in Kansas, in Wisconsin, in Ohio;
and it is not strange that he should have received
an invitation from the Young Men's Central Republican Union of New York City to come east. His

[1] Speech of Iverson, of Georgia, January 9, 1860, *Cong. Globe*,
36 Cong., 1 Sess., 380.

speech in response, at the Cooper Institute, February 27, 1860, before a brilliant and intellectual audience, was a marked and, if we could trace all the threads of politics, perhaps a momentous event. His text was the understanding of those who framed the Constitution as to the power of the Federal government to control slavery in the territories. No better or more powerful presentation of the subject, it may be said none so good or powerful, has been made; and it deserved the praise of Greeley as being "the very best political address to which I ever listened—and I have heard some of Webster's grandest."[1] Lincoln in his final sentence epitomized the principles which were later to give him strength in a period of stress such as seldom falls to man: "Let us have faith that right makes might, and in that faith let us to the end dare to do our duty as we understand it."[2]

A marked feature of Lincoln's speeches throughout is the frequency with which he speaks of the United States as a "nation." It illustrates the fact that the West, the child itself of the Federal government,[3] had become permeated with the idea of nationality, distinct from that of an easily broken association which had become so dear to the mind of the South.

Seward spoke in the Senate but two days later, February 29. His political prominence, the philos-

---

[1] *Century Magazine*, XX., 373 (July, 1891).
[2] Lincoln, *Works* (ed. of 1898), I., 599–612.   [3] See above, p. 3.

ophy, restraint, and general nobility of his speech, made it an event in the history of the time. He used as a text the memorial from the legislature of Kansas for admission to the Union, and made a powerful analysis of slavery. "What is just," he said, "to one class of men can never be injurious to any other; and what is unjust to any condition of persons in a state is necessarily injurious in some degree to the whole community." The slave state "affects to extinguish the personality of the laborer, not only as a member of the political body, but also as a parent, husband, child, neighbor, or friend. He thus becomes, in a political view, merely property without moral capacity, and without domestic, moral, and social relations, duties, rights, and remedies. . . . The state protects not the slave as a man, but the capital of another man which he represents. On the other hand, the state which rejects slavery encourages and animates and invigorates the laborer by maintaining and developing his natural personality in all the rights and faculties of manhood, and generally with the privileges of citizenship. In the one case capital invested in slaves becomes a great political force, while in the other labor thus elevated and enfranchised becomes the dominating political power." [1]

This speech, reasonable and temperate, was, however, not of the kind to suit the fanatical spirit of those abolitionists whose leaders exalted John

[1] *Cong. Globe*, 36 Cong., 1 Sess., 910.

Brown to sainthood, but it pleased the reasonable
man, to whom Seward was appealing, and met the
views of the sober part of the North which, having no fellowship or sympathy with the murder-
ous and disunionist spirit of the Garrison school,
was practically the whole North, including not only
sympathizers with slavery, but the great body of
middle-state and western abolitionists.

May 24, Davis's resolutions came to a vote, and
were passed unchanged. On the first resolution
there was a strict party vote, 38 to 19. The amendment offered by Harlan, of Iowa, to the second resolution, that "free discussion of the morality and
expediency of slavery should never be interfered
with," and that "freedom of speech and of the
press . . . should be maintained inviolate," received
but twenty votes. Most of the Republicans re-
frained from voting on the later resolutions, which
were all tranquilly passed.

Congress lingered on into summer, the victim of
factional strife. Keitt, in the House, epitomized
the beliefs which were at the bottom of southern
tactics a year later. "Touch a Southern state," he
said, "with armed hand and the whole South would
rush to its defense, and would emerge from the
struggle with an organized slaveholding confederacy. And how vast would be the power of the
South! She is now more imperial than Rome ever
was. . . . The South has the monopoly of tropical
productions and upon them hang the destinies of

peace, civilization and empire." [1]   Mad as this now
seems, it was then to the southerner an axiom.
Cotton was king, and civilization would halt and
disappear with the ruin which would come to
southern labor with freedom.

Lovejoy, brother of the man murdered at Alton,[2]
brought, by a violent anti-slavery speech, a scene
of disorder in the House, with threats of violence
which barely escaped leading to a bloody general
fight; and this was followed by a challenge to a
duel from Pryor, of Virginia, to Potter, of Wisconsin,
who named bowie-knives as the weapons, a quarrel
which attracted the attention and intensified the
feeling of the whole Union.   Legislation which involved any question of slavery was at a stand-still.
A bill to admit Kansas under the Wyandotte constitution passed the House April 11 by 134 to 73,
but was laid aside by the Senate June 5, and the
Pacific Railroad bill was postponed by relegation to
a select committee.

The authorization of a committee under the
chairmanship of Covode to inquire into the conduct of the president was another evidence of
the violent partisan feeling in the House.   The report added to the unpopularity of the president
throughout the country by the dissemination of
"a crude mass of malicious matter," [3] though with

---

[1] *Cong. Globe*, 36 Cong., 1 Sess., App., 97.
[2] See Hart, *Slavery and Abolition* (*Am. Nation*, XVI.), chap.
xvii.   [3] Schouler, *United States*, V., 451.

much of truth deeply injurious to the administration.

Mexican anarchy of the period was a question worthy of the thought and space given it in the president's message. Juarez's government, acknowledged by the United States as the constitutional authority, held Vera Cruz, but was powerless in the interior, which was given over to lawlessness. Under the so-called Miramon government the republic was deeply in debt to foreign powers, and there was already hanging over her an invasion by Spain, England, and France, from which the two first were soon wisely to withdraw. The president, though only hinting at such possibility, proposed to forestall the movement by like action of our own, and "employ a sufficient military force to enter Mexico for the purpose of obtaining indemnity for the past and security for the future." His expressed intention was to aid the constitutional forces of Mexico, the country being "entirely destitute of the power to maintain peace upon her borders or to prevent the incursions of banditti into our territory." [1] A treaty "of transit and commerce" and a convention "to enforce treaty stipulations and to maintain order and security in the territory of the republics of Mexico and the United States" was signed by our minister, McLean, December 14, 1859. For the payment of four millions the United States was to have control and a cer-

[1] Richardson, *Messages and Papers*, V., 568.

tain lien upon Mexican customs dues. While it
gave the United States great advantages of isthmus
trade and commerce, it gave Juarez a capital
which might have enabled him to forestall the empire of Maximilian, but it would, almost beyond
doubt, have fixed the grasp of the United States
upon Mexico and have made a great extension
of the slave power possible. Attempts (and they
could only be the attempts of folly in the political
situation) to secure Cuba or to extend our influence
in Central America or Mexico disappeared in the
caldron of sectional feeling. The underlying design was too evident; it was impossible to pass such
a treaty in face of such a declaration as that of Senator Brown, of Mississippi: "I want Cuba; I want
Tamaulipas, Potosi, and one or two other Mexican
states; and I want them all for the same reason,
for the planting and spreading of slavery. . . . I
would spread the blessings of slavery, like the religion of our divine Master, to the uttermost ends
of the earth." Brown could also say: "I would
make a refusal to acquire territory because it was
to be slave territory, a cause of disunion, just as I
would make the refusal to admit a new state, because it was to be a slave state, a cause for disunion." [1]

The very favorable convention with Spain concluded at Madrid in March, 1860, establishing a
joint commission for the adjudication and pay-

[1] Quoted by Wilson, *Cong. Globe*, 36 Cong., 1 Sess., 571, 573.

ment of all claims, was to meet a like fate. The final blow to the hopes of southern extremists was, however, not to come until the very eve of the time when all effort was to be turned against the North, for September 30, 1860, William Walker was captured on the Honduras coast, and twelve days later was shot.

CHAPTER VII

PRELIMINARIES OF THE PRESIDENTIAL ELECTION

(1860)

THE Democratic convention was thus brought together at Charleston, April 23, 1860, under circumstances which foreboded trouble. Caleb Cushing, of Massachusetts, was chosen chairman. Davis's resolutions in the Senate, supported as they were throughout the South, were evidently to be the *motif* of action for the more extreme southern members; and the committee on resolutions, one from each state, came together with irreconcilable views. The western members, besides a strong personal enthusiasm for Douglas, were well aware of the danger to their party in the North if an extremist platform were adopted, and insisted firmly on a platform which Douglas, as the only Democratic candidate who could carry the North, could accept. But southern members "thought Douglas as bad as Seward and popular sovereignty as hateful as Sewardism." [1] It had been determined long before that under no circumstances should Douglas be ac-

[1] Rhodes, *United States*, II., 443.

cepted on his own platform. The result, after four
days' discussion in the committee, was the presentation, April 27, of a majority report, representing
seventeen states (including California and Oregon),
with 127 electors, and a minority report representing 172 electoral votes. The majority reaffirmed
the Cincinnati platform of 1856 of "non-interference by Congress with slavery in state or territory,
or in the District of Columbia"; but added the
fateful principle that during the existence of the
government of a territory all citizens of the United
States have an equal right to settle with their
property in the territory, without their rights,
either of person or property, being destroyed or im-
paired by congressional or territorial legislation;
and that it was the duty of the Federal government, in all its departments, to protect, when
necessary, such rights.

The minority report also readopted the Cincinnati platform, but, to cover the "differences of
opinion . . . as to the nature and extent of the
powers of a territorial legislature, and as to the
powers and duties of Congress under the Constitution of the United States over the institution of
slavery within the territories," added a resolution
"That the Democratic party will abide by the de-
cisions of the Supreme Court . . . on the questions
of constitutional law." [1] Benjamin F. Butler, of

---

[1] Stanwood, *Hist. of the Presidency*, 282, 284; McKee, *National
Conventions and Platforms*, 108.

Massachusetts, later general, made a separate report of his own, proposing simply to reaffirm the Cincinnati platform as it stood.

Henry B. Payne, of Ohio, in offering the minority report, said: "It is not a personal victory which we seek to achieve, God knows, but every gentleman on that committee has felt in his conscience and in his heart that upon the result of our deliberations and the action of this Convention, in all human probability, is dependent the fate of this party and the destiny of this Union." He dwelt upon the earnest and patriotic desire to adjust the party differences, but claimed that the trouble came from the South. "I can prove," he said, "here, by the recorded testimony of almost every distinguished Senator or Representative from the Southern States, that from 1850 to 1856 there was not a dissenting opinion [to the principle of the Cincinnati platform] expressed on the records of Congressional discussion—not one. . . . I say to you, in the solemnity of my heart, that if the resolutions presented here by the majority of the committee be adopted, . . . you cannot expect any assistance from the Democracy of the Northern States in electoral votes or in members of Congress. . . . I do not believe we can elect a single member of Congress in the whole Northwest, unless it be in Lower Egypt."[1]

Yancey, of Alabama, whose oratory, to a southern audience, was irresistible, and who, though in early

[1] *National Intelligencer*, May 1, 1860.

life an ardent Unionist, had long stirred the fires of separation until he now had them ablaze, held up a lurid picture of the superlative evils which the adoption of the minority report must bring. "Ours," he said, "is the property invaded; ours are the institutions which are at stake; ours is the peace that is to be destroyed; ours is the property that is to be destroyed; ours is the honor at stake—the honor of our children, the honor of families, the lives perhaps of all—all of which rests upon what your course may ultimately make a great heaving volcano of passion and crime, if you are enabled to consummate your designs." [1]

Yancey scored the Democrats of the North because they "acknowledged that slavery was wrong. . . . You acknowledged that it could not exist anywhere by the law of Nature or by the law of God; that it could exist nowhere except by virtue of statutory enactment. In that you yielded the whole question. . . . If you had taken the position that has been taken by one gallant son of the North, who proclaimed, under the hisses of thousands, that slavery was right, that anti-slavery demon, if not dead, would long since have been in chains at your feet." [2] The southern leaders had come to that point of dementia where no difference of opinion upon slavery was to be tolerated.

When, on the sixth day of the convention, the

[1] *National Intelligencer*, May 8, 1860.   [2] *Ibid.*

minority report was adopted by 165 to 138, the effect of Yancey's influence was shown. The delegates from Alabama at once presented a written protest in obedience to the behest of their state convention, by which they were "positively instructed to withdraw" unless propositions, such as were affirmed in the majority report, should be accepted at the Charleston meeting. A majority of the delegates of South Carolina, Georgia, Florida, Louisiana, and Arkansas followed, the chairman of each making a speech of justification.

The main convention, now reduced to 253 votes, proceeded to ballot under the two-thirds rule.[1] After fifty-seven ballots, in which Douglas's highest vote was 151½, and the next highest was that of 66 for Guthrie, of Kentucky, it was clear that a choice was impossible so long as Douglas's supporters remained firm; and the convention adjourned, May 3, to meet in Baltimore, June 18. Meantime the seceding members had met, elected James A. Bayard, of Delaware, chairman, adopted the majority platform of the committee, and adjourned to meet at Richmond, June 10.[2]

The act of the Alabama delegation was the first step in the great drama of secession about to open, and it was with sober minds that many men returned North, convinced that the Democratic party

[1] For reasons for the adoption of this rule, see Buchanan's speech, Washington, July 9, 1860, in Curtis, *Buchanan*, II., 290.
[2] Hart, *Am. Hist. told by Contemporaries*, IV., § 49.

was hopelessly divided.   Even in the South this extreme doctrine found opposition. Gaulden, of Georgia, said: "I believe that this doctrine of protection to slavery in the territories is a mere theory, a mere abstraction.   Practically it can be of no consequence to the South for the reason that the infant has been strangled before it was born. . . . We have no slaves to carry into the territories. We can never make another slave state with our present supply of slaves."   To do this "you will be obliged to give up another state—either Maryland, Delaware or Virginia—to free soil upon the North." If the territories were to be occupied, he held that it was necessary to reopen the African slave-trade, which he strongly urged and which he said was less immoral and unchristian than the slave-trade of Virginia.[1]

May 9, a week before the meeting of the Republican convention, the delegates of the party calling itself the "Constitutional Union" met in Baltimore and nominated Bell, of Tennessee, and Everett, of Massachusetts, as president and vice-president. The members were chiefly of the disintegrated Whig and "American" parties, and represented the conservative element of the country, both in the North and in the South.   A platform was adopted recognizing "No political principles other than THE CONSTITUTION OF THE COUNTRY, THE UNION OF THE STATES, AND THE ENFORCEMENT OF THE

[1] Greeley, *Am. Conflict*, I., 316.

LAWS." [1] While it was clearly impossible to elect the candidates, it was hoped that the action would throw the election into the House, and it had unquestionable effect in staying, throughout the canvass, much disunion sentiment which otherwise would have had free course.

When the Democratic regular convention reconvened in Baltimore, June 18, a wrangle over the admission of delegates elected to replace some of those who had withdrawn, and who now wished admission again, ended in a second secession of delegates, including those from Virginia, North Carolina, Tennessee, and Kentucky. Caleb Cushing followed their example, as did the Massachusetts delegation led by Benjamin F. Butler, who announced that he would not sit in a convention "where the African slave trade, which is a piracy by the laws of my country, is approvingly advocated." Soulé, of Louisiana, still clung to Douglas, and was terribly severe upon the seceders as "an army of unprincipled and unscrupulous politicians." [2] Douglas was nominated upon the second ballot, his highest competitor, Guthrie, receiving but ten votes. Fitzpatrick, of Alabama, a southerner of the most advanced type, was chosen for vice-president; he declined, and Herschel V. Johnson, of Georgia, equally advanced, was substituted.

The Charleston seceders met at Richmond, June

---

[1] McKee, *National Conventions and Platforms*, 117.
[2] Wilson, *Slave Power*, II., 687.

11, but adjourned to Baltimore, where they met
June 28, twenty-one states being fully or partially
represented. Cushing was again president; the platform rejected there was now unanimously adopted,
and John C. Breckinridge, of Kentucky, and General Joseph Lane, of Oregon, were unanimously
nominated for president and vice-president.

The Republican convention met in Chicago, May
16. Besides all the free states, Delaware, Maryland, Virginia, Kentucky, Missouri, the District
of Columbia, and the territories of Kansas and
Nebraska had representatives. Four names were
prominently before the convention — Seward, Lincoln, Chase, and Bates; but there were few throughout the country who doubted the success of the
first. Chase's chances were greatly damaged by
the fact that Judge McLean and Senator Wade,
both of whom were candidates, were from the same
state. Schurz had frankly given his opinion to
Chase: "Governor, if the Republicans at Chicago
have the courage to nominate an advanced anti-
slavery man they will nominate Seward; if not,
they will not nominate you." [1]   Bates, a Missourian,
had weight with those who saw in him an opportunity for a compromise, as he was a conservative
southern man with anti-slavery principles strong
enough to cause him to free his slaves. His most
prominent supporter was Horace Greeley, who, for
private reasons as well as public, had brought all

[1] Bancroft, *Seward*, I., 526.

the great weight of the *Tribune* against Seward,[1] and to whose efforts both Seward himself and Weed, his bosom friend, mainly, though incorrectly, attributed Seward's defeat.

The platform quoted the clause of the Declaration of Independence beginning, "All men are created equal"; denounced threats of disunion; declared as essential to our system "the right of each state to order and control its own domestic institutions according to its own judgment"; denounced the invasion by an armed force of any state or territory; condemned the subservience of the administration "to the exactions of a sectional interest," and stigmatized as "a dangerous political heresy" "the new dogma—that the Constitution of its own force carries slavery into any or all of the territories."

The eighth resolution took a position never before adopted by a political party—"That the normal condition of all the territory of the United States is that of freedom; that as our republican fathers, when they had abolished slavery in all our national territory ordained that 'no person should be deprived of life, liberty or property without due process of law,' it becomes our duty by legislation, whenever such legislation is necessary, to maintain this provision of the constitution against all attempts to violate it; and we deny the authority of Congress, of a territorial legislature, or of individ

[1] Barnes, *Weed*, chap. xxi.

uals to give legal existence to slavery in any territory of the United States."

This advanced ground ignored the fact that Congress had both allowed and prohibited slavery in a territory. Under the compromise of 1820 it was tacitly allowed to continue south of 36° 30′; and by the compromise of 1850 New Mexico, which Clay believed to be free, was opened to slavery. The resolution was "a reading of the constitution diametrically opposed to the Southern reading. The political men who framed this 'platform' doubtless considered that the time had come for a direct antagonism between the North and South on this subject so that it might be decided by the votes of the people. . . . That such antagonism was the consequence and purpose of this declaration of a new principle of action on this subject will be denied by no one." [1]

In the remaining eight resolutions Congress was called upon to suppress finally the African slave-trade reopened under cover of our flag; the admission of Kansas was called for; a protective policy recommended; the passage of the homestead bill demanded; full protection to all citizens, native and naturalized, supported; river and harbor improvements of a national character favored; and immediate and efficient aid from Congress to a Pacific railroad demanded. [2]

[1] Curtis, *Buchanan*, II., 285.
[2] Stanwood, *Hist. of the Presidency*, 291, 294; McKee, *National Conventions and Platforms*, 113–116; Lincoln, *Works* (ed. of 1894), I., 635–637.

When it came to ballot for the candidates, 233 votes were necessary to a choice. The first ballot stood: Seward, 173½; Lincoln, 102; Cameron, 50½; Chase, 49; Bates, 48; scattering, 42. On the second ballot Seward had 184½; Lincoln, 181. On the third there were 180 for Seward, 231 for Lincoln. To make the necessary majority, four Ohio votes were changed from Chase to Lincoln, and others followed until he had 354 out of the whole 446, when Evarts, of New York, performed the melancholy courtesy of moving that the vote be declared unanimous.[1]

Hannibal Hamlin, of Maine, was nominated for vice-president.

The result was a shock of surprise to the country at large, and particularly in the East, as Seward's nomination had been looked upon as secure. The failure filled his followers with gloom and bitterness. Thurlow Weed shed tears.[2] The East knew Lincoln by report as abnormally uncouth, as the natural outcome of a rough early life spent in splitting rails and in flat-boating upon the Ohio and Mississippi. The South in addition, ignoring the conservative attitude involved in the full expression of his most sane and reasonable views,[3] regarded him as one of the monsters of depravity who had

[1] Rhodes, *United States*, II., 456–473; Greeley, *Am. Conflict*, I., 319–321; Stanwood, *Hist. of the Presidency*, 290–295; Hart, *Am. Hist. told by Contemporaries*, IV., § 50.

[2] Barnes, *Weed*, 271.

[3] See speech of October 16, 1854, Lincoln, *Works* (ed. of 1894), I., 187.

declared that war must be made upon slavery, selecting a single sentence, his declaration that "a house divided against itself cannot stand. I believe this government cannot endure permanently half slave and half free "[1] as typifying his stand and probable course of action. He was nominated largely because of this conservatism so unwisely disregarded by the South, and as a more available candidate for this reason than Seward. It is a striking fact that the Garrison school of abolitionists themselves were opposed to the result.[2]

Seward himself had been certain of success, despite the knowledge of an opposition, the grounds of which were frankly stated to him by an eminent member of his own party. When about leaving Washington he complained to Senator Wilson of the latter's antagonism. Wilson replied, substantially: "If I could elect a President, I should nominate you or Mr. Chase. . . . But . . . like Mr. Chase, you have by your ability and long devotion to the antislavery cause, excited prejudices and awakened conservative fears in the great states of Pennsylvania, Indiana, Illinois, New Jersey, and Connecticut which are to be the battle ground of the contest, and whose votes must be secured to give success. . . . I do not think your name will command the necessary strength." Nevertheless, Seward left the Senate chamber with Sumner, reiterat-

[1] Speech at Springfield, June 16, 1858, Lincoln, *Works* (ed. of 1894), I., 240.   [2] Garrisons. *Garrison*, III., 502.

ing his confidence, assured of both the nomination and election.[1]

Seward had failed to recognize the weight and influence gained by his western antagonist just preceding the election. Even a few in the South had begun to comprehend that Lincoln was more than the uncouth boor, the possibility of whose nomination had been derided. Benjamin, of Louisiana, was one of the southerners who had come to recognize the lofty qualities of his nature and mind. In his speech in the Senate against Douglas, of May 22, he said, referring to the category of questions put by Douglas to Lincoln in the debate of 1858,[2] the answers to which are among the finest in character of Lincoln's statements, "It is impossible, Mr. President, however we may differ in opinion with the man not to admire the perfect candor and frankness with which these answers are given; no equivocation—no evasion."[3]

The victory for Lincoln was in fact a simple question of availability. He had not been seriously thought of for the presidency until his acclaim at the Republican state convention at Decatur, Illinois, May 10, 1860. There can be little doubt that a large majority of those assembled at Chicago went expecting to vote for Seward. "Certainly two thirds of the delegates . . . preferred him

[1] Wilson, *Slave Power*, II., 694.
[2] Lincoln, *Works* (ed. of 1894), I., 306.
[3] *Cong. Globe*, 36 Cong., 1 Sess., 2237.

for president." [1] But Pennsylvania and Indiana were to hold elections for governor in October. Those who had nominated Curtin in Pennsylvania had not even yet taken the name "Republican." It was a party of fusionists in which the "American" element was strong, and this element was bitterly opposed to Seward through his favoring a division of school funds. "Without its aid the success of Curtin was simply impossible. A like condition of things existed in Indiana. . . . While the anti-slavery sentiment asserted itself by the election of a majority of Republicans to Congress in 1858, the entire Democratic State ticket was successful by majorities varying from 1534 to 2896. . . . The one thing that Curtin, Lane [the Republican nominee for governor in Indiana] and their respective lieutenants agreed upon, was that the nomination of Seward meant hopeless defeat in their respective States." [2]

Seward thus, in fact, though it was not apparent, was defeated before the convention met. The struggle really lay between Lincoln and Bates, and Lincoln had immensely the advantage in the *locale* of the convention. It was the first which had been held at Chicago, and it was in his own state. The environment was one which knew the man and his worth. The fact, too, that Douglas was certain to be the nominee of the regular Democratic conven-

[1] McClure, *Lincoln and Men of War Times*, 28.
[2] *Ibid.*, 31–33.

tion was greatly in Lincoln's favor. The publication of the speeches of the great contest of 1858 had shown the superior logic and ability of Lincoln, and if able to assert his superiority then, there could be little doubt of his ability to meet him on more than a favorable footing in the great contest about to come. If the hand of Providence is ever to be recognized in human affairs, it was in this debate and in this nomination.

CHAPTER VIII

THE TIDE OF SEPARATION
(September–November, 1860)

THE final days of the session of Congress, ending June 25, 1860, showed the nebulous state of mind of the prominent men of the North, and how slight a grasp they had upon the realities of the situation. At the instance of Sherman, of Ohio, the estimate for repairs and equipment of the navy was cut down a million; his influence had caused even a greater reduction the preceding year. Senator Pugh, of the same state, could say, "I think we have spent enough money on the navy, certainly for the service it has rendered; and for one I shall vote against building a single ship under any pretense at all." [1] The blatant Lovejoy, in the face of the rising storm, said, "I am tired of appropriating money for the army and navy when absolutely they are of no use whatever. . . . I want to strike a blow at this whole navy expenditure and let the navy go out of existence. . . . Let us blow the whole thing up! let these vessels rot; and when

[1] *Cong. Globe*, 36 Cong., 1 Sess., 3109.

we want vessels to fight, we can get mercantile vessels and arm them with our citizens." [1]

An absurd exhibition of want of naval power had
just been made in a demonstration against Para-
guay. The whole existing steam navy consisted of
but twenty-three vessels which could be called efficient and thirteen which were worthless, and while
there was a willingness and effort on the part of the
northern senators and representatives to add to the
force, it was put wholly upon the ground of the suppression of the slave-trade. Morse, of Maine, chairman of the naval committee in the House, urged
that this increase should take the form of a purchase of small steamers of six to nine feet draught
for African service. There appears no glimmering in
the mind of any one of the speakers of the coming
of a great war, then but nine months distant, and
in which the North could not have been successful
had it not been for the throttling by the blockade
and the occupancy of the Mississippi.

The last month of the session gave time for a four
hours' speech by Sumner on slavery,[2] "harsh, vin-
dictive," [3] brutal, and unwise, and however true in
its elaboration of statistics and statement of facts,
wholly unnecessary in such a place and at such a
time. It exhibited the full-fledged hatred which

[1] *Cong. Globe*, 36 Cong., 1 Sess., 2848, 2849.
[2] *Ibid.*, 2590–2603.
[3] Grimes, of Iowa, in a letter to his wife, June 4, 1860, Salter,
Grimes, 127.

had been in incubation during the four years of Sumner's absence caused by the brutality of Brooks, and, however true, could not redound to the author's good sense or good taste, nor to the benefit of his party, already overwhelmed with the charge of sectionalism. It is an excellent repository of comparative statistics, and would better have appeared as an abolition pamphlet.

The strain of the political situation was somewhat offset by the arrival of the first Japanese embassy to a foreign power, which reached Washington the middle of May and left for home the last of June, in the frigate *Niagara*. The Prince of Wales, later visiting Canada, added, on the invitation of the president, a tour in the United States. His stay of three weeks, from the end of September to October 20, during which he was everywhere received with enthusiastic welcome, may have had some influence to fix the kindly spirit of the queen, of which, in the stormy years following, we were to have such weighty evidences.

The defeat of the Democrats in Pennsylvania and Indiana in October, 1860, made the election of Lincoln almost a certainty. The result in the former state, which had been suffering from the depression of the iron trade, the outcome of the panic of 1857, had been greatly aided by the Republican advocacy of protection. The danger of secession, which might follow, was naturally cried down by Republican speakers, for a real fear of such an event would undoubtedly have lessened Republican energy and have reduced the vote. The North was in no humor to bring the question to such an issue, however strong the general anti-slavery sentiment. For this sentiment was not so determined against slavery itself as against its extension, and the North by this time was beginning to feel that it could control the territories in any case. Seward was but expressing the irrepressible American optimism which would not consider such threats as dangerous until the actuality was upon the country, when, November 2, he said at New York: "For ten—aye, twenty years, these threats have been renewed in the same language and in the same form, about the first day of November every four years, when it happened to come before the day of the presidential election. I do not doubt but that these southern statesmen and politicians think they are going to dissolve the Union, but I think they are going to do no such thing." [1]

Lowell spoke "of the hollowness of those fears for the Union in case of Mr. Lincoln's election," and called to mind that false alarms had been sounded before. "The old Mumbo Jumbo," he asserted, "is occasionally paraded at the North, but, however many old women may be frightened, the pulse of the stock market remains provokingly calm."[2]

Douglas, who from association knew the southern

---

[1] Seward, *Works* (ed. of 1884), IV., 420.
[2] Lowell, *Political Essays*, 26, 41.

mind more intimately, and who had had in the last
few years but too good reason to know its bitterness,
so much of which was directed against himself, saw
much more clearly. He declared at Chicago, "I
believe this country is in more danger now than at
any other moment since I have known anything of
public life."[1] There was no doubt of the danger
in the mind of any patriotic southerner. Bell and
Breckinridge, through the intermediation of Davis,
both offered to withdraw if an arrangement could
be made by which those opposed to the Republicans
could be united upon some one more generally acceptable than either of the three in nomination.
When this was stated to Douglas he said the scheme
was impracticable, as his friends, mainly northern
Democrats, would, if he were withdrawn, join in
support of Lincoln, rather than of any one who
should supplant him.[2] Douglas had little or no expectation of success; early in the canvass, in New
England, he expressed to Burlingame and Wilson
his conviction that Lincoln would be elected. Later
he mentioned to a friend in Washington that he had
renounced all hopes of election, but expressed the
conviction that "the Union would be safe under
Mr. Lincoln, if it could be held together long enough
for the development of his policy," though he con-
fessed his fears that that could not be done.[3] Moved

[1] *National Intelligencer*, October 5, 1860.
[2] Davis, *Confederate Government*, I., 52.
[3] Wilson, *Slave Power*, II., 699.

by his real Unionism, Douglas rose to a higher plane
than at any earlier period of his life.   His demagogy
disappeared as the danger, so persistently minimized
by the Republican leaders, loomed more porten-
tously in his perception.   "Receiving a despatch
October 8th, from his devoted friend John W.
Forney, announcing the result in Pennsylvania and
another announcing that of Indiana, he said to his
private secretary: 'Mr. Lincoln is the next president! We must try to save the Union. I will go
South.'" [1] He cancelled all western engagements,
and spoke in Kentucky, Missouri, Tennessee, Georgia, and Alabama, everywhere averring his patriotism and the necessity of standing by the Union.
At Norfolk, Virginia, to the question whether, if
Lincoln be elected, the southern states would be
justified in seceding, he said, "I emphatically answer 'no'" (great applause). To a second question,
"If they . . . secede from the Union upon the inauguration of Abraham Lincoln before he commits
an overt act against their constitutional rights, will
you advise or vindicate resistance by force to their
secession?" he said: "I answer emphatically that
it is the duty of the President of the United States
and all others in authority under him to enforce the
laws of the United States as passed by Congress,
and as the courts expound them. (Cheers.) And
I, as in duty bound by my oath of fidelity to the
Constitution, would do all in my power to aid . . .

[1] Wilson, *Slave Power*, II., 700.

in maintaining the supremacy of the laws against all resistance to them, come from what quarter it might. In other words, I think the President . . . whosoever he may be should treat all attempts to break up the Union by resistance to its laws, as Old Hickory treated the nullifiers in 1832 (applause)." [1] At Petersburg he said there was no evil in the country for which the Constitution and "laws do not furnish a remedy, no grievance that can justify disunion." At Raleigh he said he was ready "to put the hemp round the neck and hang the man who would raise the arm of resistance to the constituted authorities of the country." [2] Douglas's attitude then and thereafter atoned for much of his shortcomings of previous years.

In the campaign every one was active but Lincoln, who remained quietly at home, an observer only. Seward, who felt himself "a leader deposed . . . in the hour of organization for decisive battle," [3] showed a magnanimity in act and expression which was, in the words of Lowell, "a greater ornament to him and a greater honor to his party than his election to the presidency would have been." [4] "No truer or firmer defenders of the Republican faith," wrote Seward for an Auburn paper, "could have been found in the Union than the distinguished

[1] Du Bose, *Yancey*, 523.
[2] Wilson, *Slave Power*, II., 700.
[3] Letter to his wife, in Seward, *Seward*, II., 454.
[4] *Atlantic Monthly*, VI., 499 (October, 1860).

and esteemed citizens on whom the honors of the
nomination have fallen." [1] He proved this declaration by his works.

Seward had not always felt thus: it is a mark of
his generous character that he rose above a hasty
determination expressed before the election. Medill
expressed very strongly in the Chicago *Tribune*,
February, 1860, the view that Lincoln could be
elected that year and that Seward could not.
Meeting Medill in Washington, Seward spoke in
strong terms of his disappointment in the latter's
preference for that "prairie statesman," as Seward
called Lincoln. "He then proceeded to declare,
with much heat and temper of expression, that if
he was not nominated as the Republican candidate
for president at the ensuing convention, he would
shake the dust off his shoes and retire from the
service of an ungrateful party for the remainder of
his days." [2] How ephemeral was this feeling of
pique has just been shown, and added evidence of
the height to which he rose is in the series of great
speeches made throughout the North. He did not
shirk the question of an irrepressible conflict. He
said, October 31, "Upon what issue is the American
people divided in this political crisis, except a conflict between freedom and slavery?" [3] Nor did he
give any evidence of want of loyalty to the party

[1] Seward, *Seward*, II., 452.
[2] Letter of Medill to Frederic Bancroft, in Bancroft, *Seward*,
I., 531.   [3] Seward, *Works* (ed. of 1884), IV., 399.

nominee. November 2, four days before the election, he could say, "If you elect that eminent, and able, and honest and reliable man, Abraham Lincoln . . . and if, as I am sure you will during the course of the next four years, you constitute the United States Senate with a majority like him, and at the present election establish the House of Representatives on the same basis, you have then done exactly this: you have elected men who will leave slavery in the United States just exactly where it is now, and who will do more than that—who will leave freedom in the United States and every foot and every acre of the public domain . . . just exactly as it is now."[1] His references to the South were kindly; his course throughout wise, conservative, and conciliatory. It was the apogee of his greatness. But, as mentioned, his optimism played him false in regard to the impending danger; in this respect he showed that he had passed his years in Washington to little purpose; he was no reader of men.

Of the total 4,682,069 votes cast November 6, Lincoln received 1,866,452, or nearly forty per cent. of the whole; Douglas, 1,376,957; Breckinridge, 849,781; Bell, 588,879. Of the 303 electoral votes, Lincoln received 180, being every northern vote except 3 of the 7 of New Jersey; Douglas received 3 there and the 9 of Missouri; Bell received the 39 of Virginia, Kentucky, and Tennessee; Breckinridge

[1] Seward, *Works* (ed. of 1884), IV., 416.

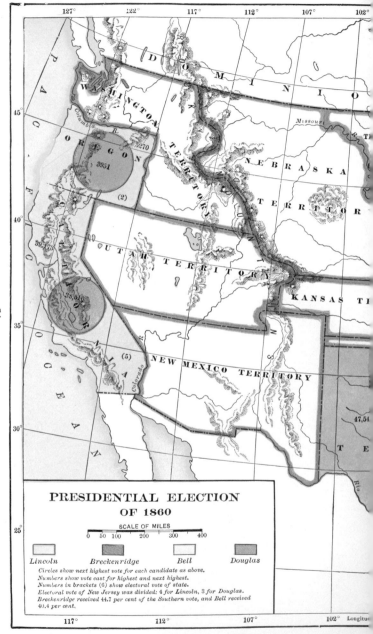

PRESIDENTIAL ELECTION
OF 1860

SCALE OF MILES

0   50 100   200   300   400

Lincoln   Breckenridge   Bell   Douglas

Circles show next highest vote for each candidate as above.
Numbers show vote cast for highest and next highest.
Numbers in brackets (6) show electoral vote of state.
Electoral vote of New Jersey was divided: 4 for Lincoln, 3 for Douglas.
Breckenridge received 44.7 per cent of the Southern vote, and Bell received
40.4 per cent.

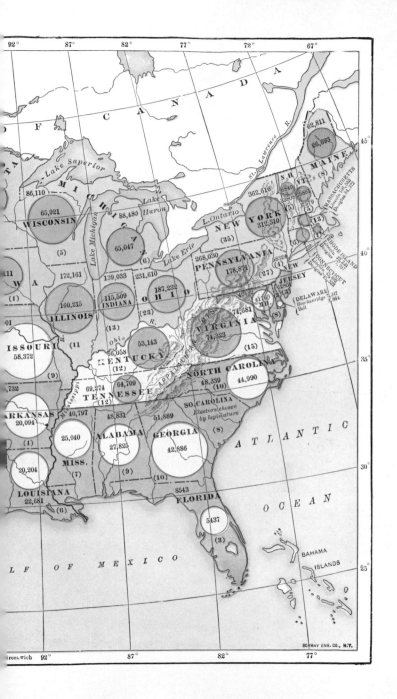

the 72 of the remaining southern states.[1] It is a
remarkable fact that in the southern states, excluding South Carolina, in which the electors were
elected by the legislature, Breckinridge received but
571,051 votes, against 515,973 for Bell; a difference
of less than 60,000, showing that Bell received the
support of almost all of the former Whig party.
The total southern vote for the three candidates
opposed to Breckinridge was 705,928, showing a
majority with unionist sympathies of 134,877. It is
evident that on the day of the election the masses
of the South were not secessionist. The border
states cast 26,430 votes for Lincoln, 17,028 of which
were in Missouri.

But while electing the executive, the Republicans
were clearly to be in a minority in both Senate and
House. Close estimates showed a majority of
8 against the Republicans in the former and 21 in
the latter.[2] Certainly no serious ill could befall the
South in such circumstances.

In Stephens's view, Buchanan was responsible
for the introduction at Charleston of the new dogma
in the party platform which caused the rupture of
the party.[3] It has been supposed, says Stephens,
that the outcome of the movement which led to the
rupture of the Democratic party: the secession at

---

[1] Stanwood, *Hist. of the Presidency*, 297; McKee, *National Conventions and Platforms*, 118, 119.
[2] Rhodes, *United States*, II., 501.
[3] Stephens, *War between the States*, II., 259.

Charleston, the division at Baltimore, the nomination of Breckinridge, was in order to further the ulterior purpose of disunion. No such result was, in Stephens's opinion, anticipated; and speaking for what he thought an overwhelming majority of those who advocated the action which had taken place, the movers were as much disappointed as "men ever were at the consequences of their own acts. They really hoped and expected the final result to be the election of Mr. Breckinridge." Failing election by the popular vote, they were quite assured that he would receive enough electoral votes to carry his name to the House of Representatives, should no one of the candidates receive a majority of votes cast by the electoral colleges. As the majority of the representatives from the majority of states was Democratic, but opposed to Douglas, they considered the election of Breckinridge in such circumstances certain. Even failing this, they looked with confidence to the election of Lane as vice-president either by the electoral colleges or by the Senate, which was Democratic, and to him, they calculated, would fall the presidency should no choice for president be made by the electoral colleges or by the House before March 4, 1861.[1]

In June none of the leaders of the southern wing of the Democrats thought the election of Lincoln and Hamlin possible, and when Stephens, in a speech at Augusta, Georgia, September 1, 1860,

[1] Stephens. *War between the States*, II., 275–277.

said that one need not be surprised to see civil war in less than six months, it was said that the weakness of his body was extending to his head, he was becoming "crazy." As time grew on apprehensions, however, became serious, and many of the leading men and papers supporting Breckinridge declared for secession in case they should not succeed in the elections. When the result came, "**it struck the masses with general consternation.**" [1]

[1] Stephens, *War between the States*, II., 277.

CHAPTER IX

SECESSION ACCOMPLISHED

(October, 1860 – February, 1861)

SEVERAL weeks before the election, steps had been taken in South Carolina looking to secession. A conference was held October 25 at the residence of Senator Hammond, at which were present Governor Gist, ex-Governor Adams, ex-Speaker Orr, and all the delegation of the state to Congress except one who was ill. It was there unanimously resolved to secede in the event of Lincoln's election.[1] The governor called the legislature in special session for November 5, to cast the electoral vote of the state. Before the legislature met there was a caucus called to meet at Columbia, at which were read letters from Pugh, Bullock, Yancey, and others, in reply to categorical questions from Gist in a circular letter of October 5, as to what action it was desired South Carolina should take. The answers counselled that this state should take the lead, pledging the cotton states to support her, and dispelled the idea of jealousy of her leadership. The plea to wait for "cooperation"

[1] Crawford, *Fort Sumter*, 14.

was thus set aside, a fact which largely influenced action later.[1]

Governor Gist's message to the legislature advised that the legislature remain in session and prepare for any emergency, "in view of the probability of the election to the presidency of a sectional candidate by a party committed to the support of measures which if carried out, will inevitably destroy our equality in the Union, and ultimately reduce the southern states to mere provinces of a consolidated despotism, to be governed by a fixed majority in Congress, hostile to our institutions and fatally bent upon our ruin." In the event of Lincoln's election he was constrained to say that the only alternative was the secession of the state. He also recommended the use of all the available means of the state for arming every man between eighteen and forty-five, and that the services of ten thousand volunteers be immediately accepted. To this movement new impulse was given by the refusal of the grand jury of the United States district court, November 7, to make presentments, and by the resignation of Magrath, the judge of the court, who announced that, "feeling an assurance of what will be the action of the state, I consider it my duty, without delay, to prepare to obey its wishes. . . . Let us not forget . . . that he who acts against the wish or

[1] Crawford, *Fort Sumter*, 11; Nicolay and Hay, *Abraham Lincoln*, II., 306–314; cf. Hart, *Am. Hist. told by Contemporaries*, IV., §§ 51, 52.

without command of his State, usurps that sovereign authority which we must maintain inviolate." [1]

The action of the legislature upon Governor Gist's message was the prompt and unanimous passage by the Senate, November 10, of a bill calling for elections December 6, to a convention to be held December 17; two days later it passed the House with like unanimity.

The convention met at Columbia on the day set, and, on account of an epidemic of small-pox, adjourned to Charleston, where, at 1.15 P.M. of the 20th, the ordinance of secession was passed. It was notably brief, as follows: "We, the people of the state of South Carolina in convention assembled do declare and ordain and it is hereby declared and ordained that the ordinance adopted by us in convention on the 23d of May, in the year of our Lord seventeen hundred and eighty eight, whereby the constitution of the United States was ratified and all the acts and parts of acts of the general Assembly of this state ratifying amendments of the said constitution are hereby repealed, and the Union now subsisting between South Carolina and the other states, under the name of the 'United States of America,' is hereby dissolved." [2]

For this momentous action no rashness of youth can be pleaded; more than half of the members of the convention were over fifty years of age; very

[1] Crawford, *Fort Sumter*, 13.
[2] Hart, *Am. Hist. told by Contemporaries*, IV., 185.

many had had large experience of public life, four
as senators, five as governors of the state, nine as
judges; eight as members of the nullification convention of 1832–1833; twenty-eight as members of
the convention of 1852, which affirmed the right of
the state to secede.[1]

South Carolina followed up the ordinance of secession with a declaration of independence which
attempted to justify her action.   It asserted that
"The states of Maine, New Hampshire, Vermont,
Massachusetts, Connecticut, Rhode Island, New
York, Pennsylvania, Illinois, Indiana, Michigan, Wisconsin and Iowa have enacted laws which either
nullify the acts of Congress or render useless any
attempt to execute them."   The non-slave-holding
states "have assumed the right of deciding upon
the propriety of our domestic institutions, and
have denied the rights of property established in
fifteen of the states and recognized by the Constitution; they have denounced as sinful the institution
of slavery."   It complained of the open establishment of abolition societies; of the encouragement
of slaves to escape, or rebel; of the election, by a
section, of one who had declared that the "government cannot endure permanently half slave, half
free"; of the elevation to citizenship of persons
"who, by the supreme law of the land, are incapable
of becoming citizens"; of the announcement that
the South "shall be excluded from the common

[1] Crawford, *Fort Sumter*, 46.

territory; that the judicial tribunals shall be made sectional, and that a war must be waged against slavery until it shall cease." It declared "all hope of remedy is rendered vain by the fact that public opinion at the North has invested a great political error with the sanctions of a more erroneous religious belief."[1] No mention of the tariff as a grievance is made in the document. All of the South Carolina senators and congressmen had voted for the tariff of 1857, and the fiery Keitt himself could say in the secession convention, in reply to a suggestion that it be mentioned, that no tariff since that of 1832 had caused any desire for secession.

Popular feeling in Georgia was so strong against separate state secession, that the legislature was obliged to rescind a resolution of December 7 looking to individual action.[2] A convention was called for January 16, 1861; and December 14 an address, signed by fifty-two members of the legislature, then in session, was issued to the people of South Carolina, Alabama, Mississippi, Florida, and of such other slave states as might hold conventions earlier than that called in Georgia, asking that delegates be appointed to a general convention of the southern states, and that until such convention should meet no final action should be taken by a separate state as to secession.

South Carolina, well knowing the danger to the

[1] Channing and Hart, *Am. Hist. Leaflets*, No. 12.
[2] *Am. Annual Cyclop.*, 1861, p. 337.

secession movement from such a course, and with
an instinctive feeling of the power of sympathy by
which her sister states would be drawn to uphold
actual accomplishment of her own designs, refused
even to receive the message. Throughout, the
leaders in this unfortunate state showed a deep
knowledge of human nature; of its waves of sympathy; its acceptance of actualities; its tendency to
push forward a cause once the Rubicon was passed.
It was Mephistophelian, but none the less effective,
and deceived none more completely than the unhappy president of the United States.

The numerous public meetings in Georgia were
"dignified and conservative in language and clearly
indicated that hostility to the Union was neither
deep-seated nor bitter."[1] Alexander H. Stephens
did much by his powerful speech before the legislature of Georgia, November 14, to fix this temper; he
denied the right to secede because of Mr. Lincoln's
election; he appealed to the people to maintain the
Constitution and not to be its undoers by withdraw-
ing on such a plea; and still more, not to anticipate
a threatened evil. If Lincoln should violate the Constitution, then would be the time to act. "Do not
let us break it, because, forsooth, he may. . . . The
president of the United States is no emperor, no
dictator—he is clothed with no absolute power. He
can do nothing unless backed by power in Congress.
The House of Representatives is largely in the

[1] *Am. Annual Cyclop.*, 1861, p. 338.

majority against him. . . . In the Senate he will also
be powerless. . . . Why, then, I say, should we dis-
rupt the ties of this Union, when his hands are tied
—when he can do nothing against us?" [1]

Stephens was the ablest, wisest, and most far-
seeing man of the South. While strongly pro-slavery, he was not blind to the abyss into which so
many of his fellow-statesmen of his section seemed
bent upon rushing. He had long foretold the war,
and could say in 1850, in a letter to his brother:
"My opinion is that a dismemberment of this Republic is not among the improbabilities of a few
years to come. In all my acts I shall look to that
event. I shall do nothing to favor it or hasten it,
but I now consider it inevitable." [2] The testimony
of no man respecting the true trend of sentiment
in the South is more valuable. It indicates that the
feeling of the mass was not, before the election,
absolutely disunionist; it was a feeling of general
ill-will towards the North which came to be played
upon by the leaders until it developed into a catch-
ing, sympathetic, emotional movement, before which
reason vanished. A few more men of Stephens's type
and ability might have turned the tide; but in the
lower South he stood alone in his class. Having the
general respect of North and South, his Milledgeville
speech had wide circulation and effect. Great numbers of approving letters came from the North, and

[1] Stephens, *War between the States*, II., 279–283.
[2] Johnston and Browne, *Stephens*, 244.

a note was received from Lincoln, dated November 30, asking for a revised copy. Stephens's reply brought three weeks later one of the few letters which at this period Lincoln wrote. It was dated December 22, and asked, "Do the people of the South really entertain fears that a Republican administration would, *directly* or *indirectly*, interfere with the slaves, or with them about the slaves? If they do, I wish to assure you, as once a friend, and still, I hope, not any an enemy, that there is no cause for such fears."[1]

The effect produced in the state by Stephens's speech of November 14 "was a general impression that it had given the quietus to secession in Georgia,"[2] but Stephens himself was not deceived in the trend of affairs. He could write, but two weeks later (November 30): "I am daily becoming more and more confirmed in the opinion that all efforts to save the Union will be unavailing. The truth is, our leaders and public men . . . do not desire to continue it on any terms. They do not wish any redress of wrongs; they are disunionists *per se*, and avail themselves of present circumstances to press their objects"; and December 3: "I fear . . . that it is too late to do anything; that the people are run mad. They are wild with passion and frenzy, doing they know not what."[3]

[1] Lincoln, *Works* (ed. of 1894), I., 660; Stephens, *War between the States*, II., 266, 267 (facsimile).

[2] Johnston and Browne, *Stephens*, 367.

[3] *Ibid.*, 369, 370.

How Georgia wavered, how strong was the Union sentiment of the state, is told at length by Stephens; the wavering scale "was turned by a sentiment, the key note to which" was uttered by T. R. R. Cobb, in a speech before the legislature, November 12: "We can make better terms out of the Union than in it." An idea upon which two-thirds of those who voted for secession acted.[1]

In Alabama, the conservative forces were overturned through the unfortunate action of the legislature in January, 1860, when an act was passed on the heels of the instructions to the delegates to the Charleston convention to withdraw in certain contingencies, requiring the governor, after he should have ascertained the election of a "so-called Republican" to the presidency, to call a convention to meet within forty days; the act also directed the reorganization of the militia and included a vote of two hundred thousand dollars for "military contingencies."[2] But after the election a strong Union sentiment showed itself; "the secessionists were anxious, Unionists suddenly cropped out everywhere."[3] A meeting of prominent secessionists "promptly assembled at Montgomery to consider the duty of the governor" in regard to the resolution of January, and the latter decided that he would call the convention two days after the votes had been cast in the electoral college, and that it should

[1] Stephens, *War between the States*, II., 321.
[2] Du Bose, *Yancey*, 448.   [3] *Ibid.*, 547.

meet January 7, 1861. Jemison, who had led the legislature to pass the resolution requiring the withdrawal from the Charleston convention, was now "an unconditional Unionist," and the members of this party entered the contest with a real recognition of its philosophy. They held that "the day of small governments had passed. . . . If secession succeeds the road to success will require the sacrifice of slavery: if secession fails, anarchy will follow." [1] But Yancey ruled in Alabama by perfervid oratory, much as Calhoun, in South Carolina, by logic. His answer to co-operationists, at a meeting the evening after the presidential election, was: "In the contingency that consultation shall not produce concert, what then? . . . Shall we remain and all be slaves? Shall we wait to bear our share of the common dishonor? God forbid! Let us act for ourselves. I have good reason to believe the action of any state will be peaceable, will not be resisted under the present or any future administration of public affairs. I believe that there will not be power to direct a gun against a sovereign state. Certainly there will be no will to do so during the present administration." [2] The incendiary, he practically said, need fear no punishment. It is not strange that appeals to passion, with the assurance that no harm could befall, should have their effect.

The feeling between the Unionists and secessionists, when the Alabama convention came together,

[1] Du Bose, *Yancey*, 547-549.   [2] *Ibid.*, 539.

January 7, was extreme, and Yancey threatened coercion against the men of the northern part of the state.[1] The prospect of a slave-state convention and a basis of settlement with the North was voted down, by a majority of 10 in a total of 99. "It is touching to read the expressions of regret, of doubt, of protest, with which the opposition members gave in their adhesion"[2] to the final parting.

In Mississippi there was yet a strong Union sentiment, but all gave way before the impulse of the aggressive action of the leaders. An evidently trustworthy correspondent could say, January 2, 1861: "Our country is dying and the people are doing nothing either to accelerate or prevent the death. . . . The convention to assemble Monday next will present an almost undivided front in favor of prompt secession, the people have had but small agency in the movement. In many, perhaps in most of the counties, but a meagre vote has been polled. The people seem stupified, and those who move at all move in obedience to the voice of the extreme leaders."[3]

Though "unbounded enthusiasm" was shown at a New Orleans meeting over the secession of South Carolina, a hundred guns fired and the Pelican flag unfurled, an eminent citizen of Louisiana could say, "I think ninety-nine out of every hundred of the

---

[1] Smith, *Debates of Ala. Convention*, 68–74.
[2] Nicolay and Hay, *Abraham Lincoln*, III., 188.
[3] *National Intelligencer*, January 12.

people sincerely hope that some plan will yet be devised to heal up the dissensions."[1]   And though a militia company could seize the revenue - cutter *General Cass*, January 13, and the collector of the customs arrange, January 18, that the other (the *McClelland*) should be held, the majority for secessionist candidates in New Orleans was but three hundred in a vote of eight thousand, which itself was little more than half the entire vote of the city.[2]

Most significant of all is the fact that in no state of the seven was the question submitted to the people except in Texas.   Here the convention was revolutionary, called as it was by 61 individuals, and not by any constituted authority. Nearly half the 122 counties held no election, and in others an absurdly small minority voted.   The ordinance of secession was passed in the convention by 166 to 7, but when submitted to the people 11,- 235 of the 46,029 votes cast were against it, and only about three-fourths of the usual state vote was cast.[3]

To endeavor to find and detail the concrete grievances which moved the South, with the exception of northern action in the fugitive-slave law, is now a thankless effort.   They did not exist; they were

[1] *Am. Annual Cyclop.*, 1861, p. 428.
[2] *Richmond Whig*, February 5, quoted by Rhodes, *United States*, III., 274.
[3] *Am. Annual Cyclop.*, 1861, pp. 688, 689.

the intangible but no less powerful grievances of sentiment, which found much sympathy even in the North.   Franklin Pierce could write, November 23, 1860, "when you ask me to interpose, then there comes this paralyzing fact that if I were in their places, after so many years of unrelenting aggression, I should probably be doing what they are doing."[1]   The whole was summed in a phrase by Jefferson Davis, "I believe that a sectional hostility has been substituted for a general fraternity."[2]   Men in Congress could not look into one another's eyes with hate for an indefinite period without coming to blows.   There were many northern men who hated slavery and said so.   They accused the southern members of supporting an accursed institution.   The whole North, one may say the whole world, moved largely by Mrs. Stowe's book, *Uncle Tom's Cabin*, had wept itself into a sympathy for the slave which placed the South in moral stocks for the jeering of mankind.   It was not in human nature for the latter, believing as it did that it was morally, politically, and economically in the right, to submit calmly to such an ordeal.   It is but a waste of words to seek further; the subject may be fitly closed by the remark of another distinguished secessionist of the period, which equally with that of Jefferson Davis, just

[1] *Am. Hist. Rev.*, X., 365 (the letter was never sent); cf. The " Pine Street " Resolutions, New York, November, 1860, in Dix, *Dix*, I., 359, 360.   [2] *Cong. Globe*, 36 Cong., 2 Sess., 29.

quoted, completely covers the field. "I look upon it . . . as a war of sentiment and opinion by one form of society against another form of society." [1] The violence of sentiment and opinion had not yet spread from the few to the people; but in the South those "few" were the directing forces.

For throughout the South the movement at first was, in the main, one of the politicians and not of the people. It was impossible that the general mass, densely ignorant, very ill-informed, with no direct interest in slavery extension, should be willing to go to war for a constitutional abstraction. Even in South Carolina a newspaper, later a strong advocate of secession, could print, June 6, 1860, a letter signed by "A Plain Man." "Is there any one desiring to remove to any of the territories and is afraid to go there, and through fear of losing his slaves, asking for protection? No. Is there any of the territories where slave property can be used advantageously, where we are prohibited by Congressional or territorial laws from going? No. . . . Then why are the people, as politicians now call themselves, now demanding of Congress a slave code or 'protection' in the territories? . . . What right is even threatened by the General Government, that we of the South have at this time? None. Does not [the repeal of the Missouri Compromise] make us better off so far as principle and

[1] Mason, of Virginia, in his speech, December 10, 1860, *Cong. Globe*, 36 Cong., 2 Sess., 35.

honor are concerned? Yes. Then what is all this fuss in the democratic party about? I don't know unless there are not offices enough for all. . . . Men who don't want office in the South had better look closely, or they will soon see sights — now mark me." [1]

That the movement soon became a popular one is certain, but the extent of the domination of the politicians and the wide-spread ignorance of the people, the ease with which the feelings of an ignorant and impressionable population can be played upon, the willingness of men to have arms put into their hands to resent an injury or a supposed injury, the *ennui* of southern life, which caused a craving for excitement of any sort, can easily account for the readiness of the southern population, the step of secession once taken, to enroll itself in the military service of their states. It is impossible to think that extreme action was forced upon the leaders by a wave of popular sentiment; the great vote throughout the South for Bell; for the "Constitution, the Union and the enforcement of the laws" is an explicit denial of such an overpowering sentiment.

[1] *Edgefield* (S. C.) *Advertiser*, June 6, 1860.

CHAPTER X

BUCHANAN'S ATTITUDE TOWARDS SECESSION
(NOVEMBER–DECEMBER, 1860)

BUCHANAN was in a large degree the victim of vicious intimate surroundings. Only three of the cabinet had well-defined Unionist opinions: Cass, the secretary of state; Black, the attorney-general; and Holt, the postmaster-general. Toucey, secretary of the navy, was colorless and without weight; Cobb, secretary of the treasury, and Thompson, secretary of the interior, were thoroughgoing secessionists; Floyd, the secretary of war, thought secession unwise, but recognized the right of a state to secede, and was thoroughly opposed to the use of force to restrain such action. His situation and views were complicated by very serious malfeasance in respect to the war department contracts, which did much towards determining his final action.[1] And that his intent was traitorous is shown by his own statement as to the transfer south of large quantities of arms in anticipation of the coming conflict,[2] and

[1] Curtis, *Buchanan*, II., 407.
[2] *N. Y. Herald*, January 17, 1861; cf. Reuben Davis, *Recollections of Miss.*, 395.

in his personal order, December 20, 1860, for the shipment of one hundred and twenty-one heavy guns from Pittsburg to Gulf forts, wholly unprepared to receive them; a shipment only prevented by the vigorous protests of Pittsburg citizens to the president.[1] It is impossible to think of Floyd otherwise than as a traitor and a dishonest man.

An influence of perhaps greater weight than the cabinet was W. H. Trescot, of South Carolina, the assistant secretary of state and acting secretary during General Cass's absence, from June to October, 1860. His relations with the president were close and of the most friendly character, and he was thus able to exercise the insidious and powerful influence of a trusted official friend, called in as an extra-official adviser. He continued his intimacy even after his resignation, which was placed in the hands of the president December 10, but which did not take effect until December 17, because of an interim in the secretaryship of state. On his resignation he became the agent in Washington of his state, and, while intimate with the president, was at the same time taking an active and influential part, through correspondence, in affairs at Charleston. That he should have been able to adjust his action to any known code of honor is one of the amazing characteristics of the situation, though he was so unconscious of dishonor that after his return to

[1] *War Records*, Serial No. 122, pp. 15, 26–46; cf. Rhodes, *United States*, III., 236*n*.–241 *n*.

South Carolina he put on permanent record his
impressions of these events. Cobb and Thompson
were both pronouncedly secessionists; but only the
former had a sense of the proprieties of the situation,
which caused him, December 8, to withdraw from
the cabinet.   Meanwhile, Cass and Black were urgent
for the immediate reinforcement of the Charleston
forts. "The subject," says Trescot, "was one of
constant discussion. Governor Floyd was earnest
in his determination and resolved not to re-inforce,
but he thought if such were his opinions, he ought
to be trusted by the State. . . . He argued on one occasion with great force, 'You tell me that if any
attempt is made to do what under ordinary circumstances is done every day, you will be unable to
restrain your people. . . . Am *I* not bound to enable
them [these garrisons] to resist an unlawful violation
which *you* cannot control?'" Trescot makes a remark thereupon of the deepest significance: "While
I felt the strength of this reasoning, I knew also that
in the then condition of feeling in Charleston anything that could be even misunderstood or misrepre-
sented as reinforcement would lead to an explosion
that would injure the whole Southern cause." [1]

Trescot saw Cobb and explained Floyd's position. Cobb had a conference with Floyd and
Thompson, and Floyd called at once upon Trescot
to express his former convictions, but to say also
that if Trescot thought a collision between the

[1] Crawford, *Fort Sumter*, 26.

people of South Carolina and the Federal forces would be precipitated, he would not consent that a man or a gun should be sent to any of the forts in the harbor of Charleston; and if his sense of duty induced any change in his determination, Trescot should be informed ample time in advance to take such course as he deemed proper.[1]

The president, yielding to the pressure from Cass and Black, informed Floyd of his determination to send reinforcements, but under protests from Floyd suspended his decision to await the arrival, December 12, of General Scott from New York, where were then his headquarters. It then became important to devise means to induce the president to change his purpose. "Floyd," says Trescot, "declared that his mind was made up, that he would cut off his right hand before he would sign an order to send reinforcements to the Carolina forts, and if the president insisted he would resign." Thompson "agreed with him perfectly, and said he would sustain his course and follow him."[2]

The necessity of working upon the president's fears of an act of violence by the Charleston populace was clear, and Trescot set himself this duty, agreeing to go to the president and state Floyd's intention, to submit the reasons, and if he should make no impression he was to say that it was his own duty, however painful, to submit his resignation from the department of state and leave for Colum-

[1] Crawford, *Fort Sumter*, 27.　　　[2] *Ibid.*, 28, 29.

bia next morning, to lay the facts before the executive of South Carolina; that "I would be in Columbia in thirty-six hours, and upon such information there could be no earthly doubt that the forts would be occupied in the following twenty-four."   In place of this, however, it was finally arranged that Trescot should write Governor Gist: "Tell him that the President was under very strong apprehensions that the people of Charleston would seize the forts; that in consequence he felt bound to send re-inforcements. That the Southern members of the Cabinet would resist this policy to resignation, but that they thought that if he [Gist] felt authorized to write a letter assuring the President that if no re-inforcements were sent there would be no attempt upon the forts before the meeting of the convention, and that then commissioners would be sent to negotiate all the points of difference; that their hands would be strengthened, the responsibility of provoking collision would be taken from the State, and the President would probably be relieved from the necessity of pursuing this policy."   Trescot accordingly wrote to Gist, November 26, adding: "I wish you distinctly to understand that there is no possibility of such an order being issued without a dissolution of the Cabinet and your receiving ample notice. . . . I write with the confidence that such an assurance will prevent any hasty and indiscreet movement on the part of the State." [1]

[1] Crawford, *Fort Sumter*, 29, 30.

Gist's reply, November 29, 1860, was such as Trescot expected: "If President Buchanan takes a course different from the one indicated, and sends reinforcements, the responsibility will rest on him of lighting the torch of discord, which will only be quenched in blood. I am under a pledge . . . to use all the military power of the State to prevent any increase of troops in these garrisons, . . . and hope no necessity will arise to compel me to redeem the pledge." [1] The same mail brought Trescot an offer to appoint him the confidential agent of the South Carolina executive so soon as he should resign his Washington office.

The president had now completed his message, and it was decided that a copy should go to Gist by the hands of Trescot, who, "in view of the confidential relations he had held with the President, was thoroughly informed upon the subject of the President's views, . . . and from the relations he held with the authorities in South Carolina could bring back to the President a clear and reliable account of feeling and opinion in the State." [2] Buchanan was assured by Trescot, before leaving, that South Carolina would carry out the right of secession "regularly, peaceably, as a *right*, not as a revolutionary measure; that I [Trescot] really believed it would mortify them to be compelled to resort to force." Buchanan's great hope was, by temporizing, to avoid an issue before the 4th of March; but

[1] Crawford, *Fort Sumter*, 31.   [2] *Ibid.*, 23.

when Trescot arrived at Charleston, December 5, he found that no postponement of the convention to March 4 was now possible.[1]

December 8 came a visit from the five Carolina members of Congress to reiterate and reimpress upon the president the views of the cabal. The president requested a written statement, and their letter, handed to the president December 10, stated the strong convictions of the signers that there would be no attack previous to the action of the convention, adding what could only be construed as a pronounced threat, "provided that no re-enforcements shall be sent." The commissioners stated later that "The impression made upon us was that the President was wavering and had not decided what course he would pursue." The president objected to the word "provided," and made an indorsement of his objection upon the original paper — "as this might be construed into an agreement which I never would make. They said nothing was further from their intention. They did not so understand it and I should not so consider it."[2]

Whatever the president's real views, and it was clearly not his intention absolutely to bind himself, the five South Carolina gentlemen at least satisfied themselves that no change was intended. "One of the delegation, just before leaving the room, remarked, 'Mr. President, you are determined to let things remain as they are, and not to send re-en-

[1] Crawford, *Fort Sumter*, 34.   [2] Curtis, *Buchanan*, II., 377.

forcements; but suppose that you were hereafter to change your policy for any reason, what then?' . . . 'Then,' said the president, 'I would first return you this paper.'" [1]

We have here a full conspiracy: the hesitation of Floyd, whose logic was stronger than his principles; the anxiety of Trescot, assistant secretary of state, lest the forts should escape final seizure, and the assumed fear of mob action, though it would plainly put his state irretrievably in the wrong; the active support of Thompson, secretary of the interior; the concoction of the letter of November 26 to Governor Gist, of South Carolina, urging action upon the lines suggested; the governor's reply, November 29, which, of course, was shown Mr. Buchanan, and an offer of the same date from the South Carolina governor to Trescot to act as confidential agent of his state at Washington; the call of the five members, December 8, to impress, as though independently, these views upon the president. The plan was completely successful, and the passive attitude now taken by the president was adhered to until he had a cabinet which compelled him to a change of opinion.

The immediate result was the resignation of Secretary Cass, in a letter of December 12, upon the ground of the refusal of the president to send reinforcements and a ship of war to aid in the defence of the forts. The president, in his reply, said

[1] *War Records*, Serial No. 1, p. 126

"Your remarks upon the subject were heard by myself and the cabinet, . . . but they failed to convince us of the necessity and propriety, under existing circumstances, of adopting such a measure. The Secretaries of War and of the Navy, through whom the orders must have been issued to reinforce the forts, did not concur in your views; and whilst the whole responsibility for the refusal rested upon myself, they were the members of the cabinet more directly interested." [1]

The remark last quoted is a fit index of the flaccid character which found drifting so much more comfortable than stemming the tide. Had Mr. Buchanan at this time refused to listen to the noisy clamor of South Carolina regarding the forts; had he held firm; had he shaken off the malign influence of Trescot; had he refused to receive the self-appointed delegation of South-Carolinians on the subject of reinforcements; had he, in a word, proceeded to do his simple duty of retaining the control of the property of the Union, the sentiment of Stephens and hundreds of thousands in the South like him might have been solidified, and matters would have had another course.

The president had appealed, November 17, to his attorney-general, Jeremiah Black, of Pennsylvania, a strong Unionist and a lawyer and judge of great distinction, for an opinion on the following points:

1. Whether in case of conflict between the au-

---

[1] Curtis, *Buchanan*, II., 398

thorities of a state and those of the United States
there could be any doubt whether the laws of the
Federal government are supreme? 2. The president's power to collect duties where the revenue
laws are resisted by a force which drives the collector from the custom-house. 3. What right existed to defend public property if assaulted? 4.
What legal means existed for executing United
States laws usually administered through courts
and their officers? 5. Can a military force be used
for any purpose whatever under the acts of 1795
and 1807, within the limits of a state where there
are no judges, marshal, or other civil officers?

The second and third questions were, for the
practical purposes of the moment, first in importance, and to these Black, November 20, gave re-
plies which had no uncertainty. In his opinion the
president could collect the duties anywhere within
the port of entry, ashore or afloat. "Your right to
take such measures as may seem to be necessary
for the protection of the public property is very
clear." He went further, saying, "The right of defending the public property includes also the right
of recapture after it has been unlawfully taken by
another." Whatever exception may be taken to
the opinions expressed by Black in the latter part
of his paper, in which he drew a distinction between
the right of the general government to repel a
direct and positive aggression upon its property or
its officers and what he called "an offensive war to

punish the people for the political misdeeds of their State government or to enforce an acknowledgment that the Government of the United States is supreme," [1] it is clear that there was force enough in the principles just quoted to enable Buchanan to act with a vigor equal to that of Jackson and to bring to his support every loyal man, North and South. He would not only have been within his right as president, but it would have been an acceptance of one of the soundest of principles—to do that which your enemy most wished you should not do; but there was on his part no intention of action; "not in my time; not in my time," was his thought and expression.[2]

The weak, gelatinous state of mind of the president, and of the cabinet as a whole, brings out one of the great weaknesses of American government procedure—viz., the delay in bringing the newly elected authorities to power. Four long months were still to pass—the country practically without a government in the most serious period of its existence. The whole tendency of officialdom on the eve of surrendering its power to new authorities is to maintain the *status quo*. It requires an unusual initiative, boldness, and decision developed by the habit of command to accept the responsibility which Jackson took and Taylor was ready to take,

[1] Cf. Curtis, *Buchanan*, II., 319–324.
[2] Speech of Henry Winter Davis, *National Intelligencer*, February 8, 1861.

but which Buchanan declined. The last was a lawyer wrapped in the technicalities of his profession, with a character developed into the softness which comes with continued success, chiefly the result of encountering no obstacles; Buchanan was pre-eminently the mediocre politician, a being who always seeks to work on the lines of least resistance, and he was determined to leave the management of the terrible storm, of which he should have been the controlling force, to his successor.

His contribution to the issue was a message to the expiring Congress, which met in its second session December 3, 1860, in which the one firm note was a denial of any right of secession, which he declared was "neither more nor less than revolution." All that was necessary to settle the slavery question forever was, according to Buchanan, that the slave states "be let alone and permitted to manage their domestic institutions in their own way"; theirs was the responsibility, and the North had "no more right to interfere than with similar institutions in Russia or in Brazil." The message mentions as "a remarkable fact" that no single act has "ever passed Congress, unless we may possibly except the Missouri Compromise, impairing in the slightest degree the rights of the South to their property in slaves." The president proceeded to declare that the election of any citizen as president could not afford just cause for dissolving the Union; affirmed that the South had never been de-

nied equal rights in the territories, and trusted that
the state legislatures would repeal their unconstitutional and obnoxious enactments regarding the
fugitive-slave law; "Unless this shall be done without unnecessary delay, it is impossible for any
human power to save the Union." Should this be
refused, he held that the injured states "would be
justified in revolutionary resistance to the Government of the Union"; he did not believe that any
attempt would be made to expel the United States
from the Charleston forts by force; "but if in this
I should prove to be mistaken, the officer in command of the forts has received orders to act strictly
on the defensive. In such a contingency the responsibility for consequences would rightfully rest
upon the heads of the assailants."

Much of the remainder of the message was devoted to the question of the power to coerce a seceding state, holding that none such existed; to an invitation to the South to pause and deliberate before
destroying "the grandest temple which has ever
been dedicated to human freedom"; and to the suggestion of an explanatory amendment to the Constitution with, 1, "an express recognition of the
right of property in slaves in the states where it
now exists or may hereafter exist "; 2, "The duty of
protecting this right in all the common territories
throughout their territorial existence"; 3, a recognition of the validity of the fugitive-slave law and
of the unconstitutionality of state laws impairing

or defeating the right of the master to have his slaves.

The discussion of the right of secession, to which, in its constitutional aspect the president devoted a considerable part of the message, was, however able and excellent, out of place; it was the statesmanship of action which was needed, and not glosses on the Constitution. It was in his power to act upon the theories he had announced—to defend the property of the United States and to collect at all ports the customs dues. Instead, he drifted into a policy of supine inaction, while it was clearly apparent that custom-houses and forts were at the mercy of the first attack.

However blameworthy the president, he was, in a way, the victim of his period; of a slovenly *laisser aller* state of mind in which none but secessionists of the Rhett and Yancey type of leadership seemed to have definite views of any sort. The whole government was in a state of sad flabbiness. There was but a nucleus of an army; the navy was moribund; there was a captain afloat in command nearly seventy years of age; the commandant of the Norfolk navy-yard was sixty-eight; the commandant at Pensacola, sixty-seven. The general-in-chief of the army was seventy-four. There was no settled belief or opinion. The *New York Tribune*, which held the position of leadership among Republican journals, and which was a power throughout the North, was proclaiming that "if the Cotton States shall become satisfied that they can do better out of the Union than in it, we insist on letting them go in peace";[1] and, again, that "Five millions of people, more than half of them of the dominant race, of whom at least half a million are able and willing to shoulder muskets, can never be subdued while fighting around and over their own hearthstones"[2] —expressions which had a powerful effect for ill throughout the South.

Nor was Greeley alone in his views; the abolitionists professing anxiety to accomplish the extinction of slavery were arguing that the South should be permitted to secede; Governor Moore, of Alabama, was hailing them as "our best friends." "Northern and southern bigotry . . . stood in such relations of reciprocity that by each the question of preserving the government was ignored and despised. Each set of extremists played into the hands of the other. Though they differed widely in some ways, they agreed perfectly in contempt for the Union and the Constitution."[3]

[1] *N. Y. Tribune*, November 9, 1860 (editorial).
[2] *Ibid.*, November 30 (editorial).
[3] Barnes, *Weed*, 305.

CHAPTER XI

SCHEMES OF COMPROMISE

(DECEMBER, 1860 – JANUARY, 1861)

THE thirty - sixth Congress convened in its second session December 3, 1860, and upon it was thrown the wet blanket of Mr. Buchanan's message.

The reception of the message was followed in the House of Representatives by the adoption, December 4, by a vote of 145 to 38 (the nays all Republican), of a resolution offered by Boteler, of Virginia, for the appointment of a special committee of thirty-three, one from each state, to which was referred "so much of the President's message as relates to the present perilous condition of the country." [1] As Boteler declined being chairman, Corwin, of Ohio, was appointed.

December 6, Powell, of Kentucky, moved in the Senate the appointment of a special committee of thirteen, to which should be referred that part of the message relating to "the agitated and distracted condition of the country, and the grievances between the slave-holding and non-slave-holding states"; and

[1] *Cong. Globe*, 36 Cong., 2 Sess., 6.

(as modified December 10) "to inquire into the present condition of the country and report."[1]

Resolution after resolution was offered looking to propitiation of the South, though it was very evident that no concession whatever was desired by many southern members. Senator Clingman, of North Carolina, the very day of meeting, December 3, said: "It is not . . . merely that a dangerous man has been elected. . . . We know that under our complicated system that might very well occur by accident and he be powerless; but I assert that the President elect has been elected *because he was known to be a dangerous man.* He avows the principle that is known as the 'irrepressible conflict.' He declares that it is the purpose of the North to make war upon my section until its social system has been destroyed and for that he was taken up and elected. That declaration of war is dangerous, because it has been endorsed by a majority of the votes of the free states in the late election. It is this great, remarkable, and dangerous fact that has filled my section with alarm and dread for the future."[2] That this assertion of a sudden crisis, of a danger for the first time encountered, was only a pretext played upon by those in the lead of the secession movement is clear from some of the declarations made in the South Carolina convention. Said Parker there: "It is no spasmodic effort; . . . it has been gradually culminating for a long pe-

[1] *Cong. Globe*, 36 Cong., 2 Sess., 28.   [2] *Ibid.*, 3.

riod of thirty years." Barnwell Rhett asserted that "The secession of South Carolina is not the event of a day. It is not anything produced by Mr. Lincoln's election or by the non-execution of the fugitive slave law. It is a matter which has been gathering head for thirty years."

There could be no mistake about the intention of southern leaders. Both South Carolina senators resigned November 9; and Iverson, of Georgia, the third day of the session, did not hesitate to announce the southern programme: "Before the 4th of March—before you inaugurate your President—there will be certainly five states, if not eight of them, that will be out of the Union, and have formed a constitution and frame of government for themselves. . . . You talk about repealing the personal liberty bills as a concession to the South. Repeal them all to-morrow, sir, and it would not stop the progress of this revolution. It is not your personal liberty bills that we dread; . . . if all the liberty bills were repealed to-day, the South would no more gain her fugitive slaves than if they were in existence. . . . Nor do we suppose there will be any overt act upon the part of Mr. Lincoln. . . . I do not propose to wait for them. . . . We intend, Mr. President, to go out peaceably if we can, forcibly if we must, but I do not believe, with the Senator from New Hampshire [Mr. Hale], that there is going to be any war." [1]

[1] *Cong. Globe*, 36 Cong., 2 Sess., 11.

Such expressions were emphasized, December 14, by an address prepared at the rooms of Reuben Davis, a member from Mississippi,[1] and signed by twenty-three representatives and seven senators, one of whom was Jefferson Davis, saying: "The argument is exhausted. . . . In our judgment the Republicans are resolute in the purpose to grant nothing that will or ought to satisfy the South. We are satisfied the honor, safety, and independence of the Southern people require the organization of a Southern Confederacy—a result to be obtained only by separate State secession." [2]   This action was the outcome of the solid adverse Republican vote, December 13, in the committee of thirty-three, on a resolution offered by Dunn, a Republican member from Indiana, that whether southern "discontent and hostility are without just cause or not, any reasonable, proper and constitutional remedies and additional and more specific and effectual guarantees of their peculiar rights and interests as recognized by the Constitution necessary to preserve the peace of the country and the perpetuation of the Union, should be promptly and cheerfully granted." [3]

Senator Wade, of Ohio, December 17, spoke the mind of the Republican leaders, saying: "I tell you that in that platform we did lay it down that we

---

[1] Reuben Davis, *Recollections of Miss.*, 398.
[2] Nicolay and Hay, *Abraham Lincoln*, II., 436.
[3] *Journal of the Committee* (*House Exec. Docs.*, 36 Cong., 2 Sess., No. 31), p. 7.

would, if we had the power, prohibit slavery from another inch of free territory under this government. I stand on that position to-day; . . . on the other hand our authoritative platform repudiates the idea that we have any right or any intention ever to invade your peculiar institutions in your own States. . . . We hold to no doctrine that can possibly work you an inconvenience. We have been faithful to the execution of all the laws. . . . It is not, then, that Mr. Lincoln is expected to do any overt act by which you may be injured; you will not wait for any; but anticipating that the Government may work an injury, you say you will put an end to it, which means simply, that you intend either to rule or ruin this Government." [1] Viewed in the light of to-day, this most vigorous and most aggressive opponent of the slave power in the Senate spoke the exact truth.

December 18, after nearly two weeks desultory debate, the Senate adopted the Powell resolution, referring to it the same day the so-called Crittenden compromise, as a basis of an understanding which should obtain the hearing of Congress and of the country. The first six articles, in effect as follows, were proposed as constitutional amendments: 1. In all territory now held or to be acquired north of 36° 30' slavery should be prohibited while under territorial government. South of said line slavery should be recognized to exist, and be

[1] *Cong. Globe.* 36 Cong., 2 Sess., 102.

protected as property by the territorial government. In either case the territory, when made a
state, to enter with or without slavery, as the state
constitution should prescribe. (This article was indefinite as to additional territory which might be
acquired south of 36° 30'.) 2. Congress to have no
power to abolish slavery in places under its juris-
diction situated within the limits of a slave state.
3. Congress to have no power to abolish slavery in
the District of Columbia so long as it should exist
in Maryland or Virginia; nor without the consent of
the inhabitants, nor without just compensation to
those who do not consent; members of Congress
and officers of the government to be free to bring
their slaves into the district during official residence.
4. The domestic slave-trade not to be interfered
with. 5. The United States to pay the owner the
full value of a fugitive slave when arrest should be
prevented by force or rescue made. 6. No future
amendment to affect the first five articles or the
present paragraphs of the Constitution affecting
slavery, and no amendment should be made giving
Congress power to interfere with slavery in any of
the states.

Four resolutions were also to be passed jointly
by the Senate and House: 1. That the slave-holding states are entitled to the faithful observance
and execution of an efficient fugitive-slave law.
2. That Congress recommend to the states concerned the repeal of laws in conflict with the fugi-

tive-slave laws.   3. That the fee of the commissioner mentioned in the fugitive-slave act be the same, whether the decision be in favor of or against the claimant, and that the authority to summon the *posse comitatus* by the person holding the warrant be limited.   4. That the laws for the suppression of the African slave-trade be made effectual.[1]

The committee, named December 20, was one of eminent ability and character, including Crittenden, Seward, Toombs, Douglas, Jefferson Davis, and Wade. It met December 21, the day of the reception of the news of South Carolina's secession. On the insistence of Davis that nothing else would answer, it was understood that a majority of the Republican senators and a majority of the other eight should be necessary to the adoption of any report; a necessary precaution if it was to meet with any success in the Senate. The Republican members of the committee voted against all Crittenden's amendments to the Constitution, and against his first and second resolutions, making any compromise impossible. Davis and Toombs also voted against the first article (for the settlement of the slavery question in the territories), but for all the others.

Seward's offer of December 24, in the committee, which originated with Lincoln and was the extreme of compromise to which the latter would go, was made the limit of Republican concession: 1. That

[1] *Cong. Globe*, 36 Cong., 2 Sess., 114.

the Constitution should never be altered so as to authorize Congress to abolish or interfere with slavery in the states (to be a constitutional amendment); 2. that the fugitive-slave law should be amended to grant a jury trial to the fugitive; 3. that the legislatures of the states be requested to review all legislation affecting the rights of persons recently resident in other states, and to repeal or modify such acts as contravene the constitutions or laws made in pursuance thereof. Only the first was accepted;[1] it was clear that the third would not be acceptable to the South, as it plainly bore upon the question of colored seamen entering southern ports. December 31, the committee reported to the Senate that it had "not been able to agree upon any general plan of adjustment."

Crittenden's resolution was undeniably popular in the North, which was now stirred by the realization of a danger to which it had heretofore given but little thought. John A. Dix, of New York, felt "a strong confidence that we could carry three fourths of the States in favor of it as an amendment to the Constitution."[2] Edward Everett, December 23, said, "There is nothing in your resolutions for which I would not cheerfully vote, if their adoption as amendments of the Constitution would save us from disunion, and, what I consider its necessary

[1] Seward to Lincoln, Seward, *Seward*, II., 484.
[2] Letter to Crittenden, December 22, Coleman, *Crittenden*, II., 237.

consequence, civil war, anarchy, desolation at home, the loss of all respectability and influence abroad, and, finally, military despotism." [1] Amos A. Lawrence wrote December 29: "We are all watching with interest your patriotic and vigorous efforts for pacification. . . . One of the elements which produce reaction is disappearing—I mean the scarcity of money.   There is danger that we may lose another; viz: the unwarlike condition of the public mind. The contrast between us and the South in this respect is most striking.   Here, and through the whole North and West, nobody has thought of war or of arms, not a musket or pistol has been *bought* or *sold* for any civil strife.   Nine out of ten of our people would laugh if told that blood must be shed.   This condition of peace which is conducive to calm reasoning and to reaction may, and I fear *will*, be changed suddenly." [2]

One has but to turn to the scores of petitions from men of all parties, praying the adoption of the Crittenden compromises,[3] and to the files of the northern press to be convinced that had the question come to a popular vote it would have been carried by a vast majority, which felt with Thurlow Weed, in a weighty article which appeared in the *Albany Evening Journal* so early as November 30, 1860.   Nothing was easier, in Mr. Weed's view, than to demonstrate the rightfulness of the position of the Repub-

[1] Coleman, *Crittenden*, II., 238.   [2] *Ibid.*, 240.
[3] *Ibid.*, 240–249; *Cong. Globe*, 36 Cong., 2 Sess., passim.

licans, but the issue unfortunately was not to be decided on its merits. "The election of Mr. Lincoln is the pretext for, and not the cause of disunion." As the danger, in his belief, could only be averted "by such moderation and forbearance as will draw out, strengthen, and combine the Union sentiment of the whole country," he would like to see a convention of delegates appointed by the states "to meet, discuss, and determine upon a future."[1]

Such being the popular sentiment, shown later very strongly, why had it not sufficient influence to make itself felt among the Republicans in the committee of thirteen and in the Senate to cause the acceptance of Mr. Crittenden's proposed compromise? All the southern members, if the statements of Senators Douglas and Pugh, and of Toombs himself are to be taken, would have voted for the article respecting territories if it had been supported by the Republican members.[2] Breckinridge, July 16, 1861, said upon the floor of the Senate, "I happened personally to know . . . that the leading statesmen of the lower Southern states were willing to accept the terms of settlement which were prepared . . . by my predecessor." Davis's biographer says, "Despite its unfairness as a measure of settlement, and its great injustice to the South, Mr.

---

[1] Greeley, *Am. Conflict*, I., 360; cf. Barnes, *Weed*, 306, 307.
[2] Toombs, January 7, 1861, *Cong. Globe*, 36 Cong., 2 Sess., 270; Pugh, March 2, *ibid.*, 1390; Douglas, January 3, March 2, *ibid.*, 1391, App., 41.

Davis would have accepted it, as would a large majority of Southern Senators as a finality if the Republican Senators had tendered it." [1]

The difficulty was that the Republican leaders were themselves opposed to any compromise and the southern leaders really desired none. But a few weeks before (December 3), Seward had written Weed: "The Republican party to-day is as uncompromising as the Secessionists in South Carolina. A month hence each may come to think that moderation is wiser." [2] The majority of the Republican party came to this latter view, but the leaders did not. Wilson, Wade, Grimes, Thaddeus Stevens were immovable; and, above all, Lincoln, who wrote: "Entertain no proposition for a compromise in regard to the extension of slavery. . . . The tug has to come and better now than later." He added the important sentence, "You know I think the fugitive-slave clause of the Constitution ought to be enforced—to put it in its mildest form, ought not to be resisted." [3] He was inflexible on the territorial question, and thought that "the Missouri line extended, or Douglas's and Eli Thayer's popular sovereignty, would lose us everything we gain by the election; that filibustering for all south of us and making slave States of it would follow,

---

[1] Alfriend, *Davis*, 214.   [2] Barnes, *Weed*, 308.
[3] To Kellogg, of Illinois, December 11, Lincoln, *Works* (ed. of 1894), I., 657; cf. Grimes to his wife, December 5, 1860, Salter, *Grimes*, 132.

in spite of us, in either case."[1] Greeley's statement in the *Tribune* of December 22, 1860, was definite. "We are enabled to state in the most positive terms that Mr. Lincoln is utterly opposed to any concession or compromise that shall yield one iota of the position occupied by the Republican party on the subject of slavery in the territories, and that he stands now, as he stood in May last, when he accepted the nomination for the presidency, square upon the Chicago platform."

The failure of the Senate committee of thirteen to agree was followed by Mr. Crittenden's insistent and pathetic effort to bring forward in another form his plan of compromise. January 3 he asked that provision "be made by law, without delay, for taking the sense of the people and submitting to their vote" the propositions which were in substance those which had been placed before the select committee. But neither the extreme northern nor the extreme southern leaders favored compromise in any form at this time, and the former declared their stand in the resolution of Mr. Clark, of New Hampshire, pronouncing the provisions of the Constitution ample for the preservation of the Union.[2] In the vote taken January 16, this resolution was passed (six southern senators refusing to vote) by 25 votes to 23, thus killing that of Crittenden.[3]

---

[1] Letter to Weed, December 17, 1860, Lincoln, *Works* (ed. of 1894), I., 660.

[2] *Cong. Globe*, 36 Cong., 2 Sess., 379.   [3] *Ibid.*, 409.

January 14, 1861, the House committee of thirty-three made its report through its chairman, Corwin; there were seven minority reports signed by fourteen members; and as the members from the cotton states had withdrawn on the failure to pass a resolution declaring it the duty of the government to protect slave property, both at sea and on land,[1] the report was in effect that of a minority. It proposed resolutions that all attempts of legislatures to hinder the recovery of fugitive slaves were in derogation of the Constitution; that no authority existed outside a slave state to interfere with slavery in such state; that the justice and propriety of a faithful execution of the laws in regard to fugitive slaves be recognized; that it was the duty of the government to enforce the Federal laws, protect the Federal property, and preserve the union of the states; that each state be requested to revise and if necessary amend its statutes to give the citizens of other states the same protection as citizens of such state enjoy; that each state enact laws to prevent setting on foot the lawless invasion of any state or territory; and, finally, as a joint resolution, that the Constitution be so amended that no subsequent amendment having for its object interference with slavery within the states should originate with any but a slave state, or be valid without the assent of all the states. This last, offered in committee by Charles Francis Adams, was later re-

[1] Reuben Davis, *Recollections of Miss.*, 400.

nounced by him in a minority report of his own in
which he arrived at the conclusion "that no form
of adjustment will be satisfactory to the recusant
States, which does not incorporate into the Constitution of the United States a recognition of the
obligation to protect and extend slavery." [1] The
report also offered draughts of an act for the immediate admission of New Mexico, which then included
Arizona, as a state, with the slave code already
adopted by the legislature; and also an amended
fugitive-slave law, providing that the alleged fugitive be tried in the state from which he was accused of fleeing, and that all offences against slave
property be tried where committed.

The resolutions were adopted in the House by a
majority of 136 to 53, Charles Francis Adams again
changing his mind and voting affirmatively,[2] but
Corwin substituted for the proposed constitutional
amendment one declaring that "no amendment
shall be made . . . which authorize or give to
Congress the power to abolish or interfere, within
any State, with the domestic institutions thereof, including that of persons held to labor or service by the laws of said State." This passed the
House, February 28, by a vote of 133 to 65,[3] and
the Senate, March 2, by a vote of 24 to 12.[4] It
was the sole compromise of the session; was un-

[1] *Report of Select Committee of Thirty-three.*
[2] *Cong. Globe*, 36 Cong., 2 Sess., 1263.
[3] *Ibid.*, 1285.   [4] *Ibid.*, 1403.

necessarily signed by Buchanan; and was accepted by Lincoln himself in his inaugural; but in the upheaval to come received no attention from the states.[1]

Corwin wrote Lincoln, January 16: "If the States are no more harmonious in their feelings and opinions than these thirty-three representative men, then, appalling as the idea is, we must dissolve and a long and bloody civil war must follow. I cannot comprehend the madness of the times. Southern men are theoretically crazy. Extreme Northern men are practical fools. The latter are really quite as mad as the former. Treason is in the air around us everywhere. It goes by the name of patriotism." [2]

How strong the feeling in Congress against compromise had now become is well expressed by Senator Grimes in a letter, January 28, 1861, to Governor Kirkwood, of Iowa: "Let no man in Iowa imagine for a moment that the Crittenden proposition is for a mere restoration of the Compromise line of 1820. It is simply and truly the *application* of the Breckinridge platform to all territory now acquired, or *hereafter to be acquired* south of 36° 30', and would result, if adopted, in the acquisition and admission of new slave States for the ostensible purpose of restoring what is called the equilibrium of the section. . . . There are other pro-

[1] Cf. Blaine, *Twenty Years of Congress*, I., chap. xii.
[2] Nicolay and Hay, *Abraham Lincoln*, III., 218.

visions in the Crittenden resolutions which to my mind are wholly inadmissible, but let them pass. My objection is to any compromise. I will never consent to compromises . . . under threats of breaking up the Government." [1]

If we attempt to measure the right or wrong of the Republican refusal we must recognize that the very existence of the Republican party was based upon its opposition to slavery extension or to giving it a firmer constitutional basis. It could not yield this principle without party stultification. Whether, had they yielded and the compromise been adopted, the situation of the country would have been alleviated, is a subject for limitless thought and argument, with futility as an end.

One of Lincoln's objections, the fear of extension of territory to the south, was, despite the southern attitude on the question, a groundless one. The North by this time was firmly set against such movement, and Cuba could only have been ours by a war in which the North, at that period, would certainly not have allowed the country to engage. The possibility of extension of slavery into the vast western region, despite the onflow of free migration and despite climate and physical conditions, has already been considered. We must, however, believe that had Mr. Lincoln and the other prominent Republican leaders been willing to yield so much, secession would not have gone beyond South Carolina.

[1] Salter, *Grimes*, 134.

But South Carolina was already out of the Union. How, in such circumstances, should she be recalled? It is, of course, not unfair to suppose that, unsupported in her withdrawal by any of the southern states, she would not have resisted the reinforcement of Sumter and thereby engaged against her the North, with the South neutralized to a great extent at least. But the old friction would have remained, accentuated by what had already occurred; the situation of slavery would not have been bettered; the slaves themselves would have been aroused to greater efforts to freedom by the abolitionists, who would have redoubled their efforts through a reaction which must have followed the northern concessions. The whole country by this time was aroused to the subject, and the chief element in the bitterness of the South, the feeling of isolation, of standing apart, a mark for the world to point at, would have grown greater. The only hope of saving the institution, acceptation of its existing geographical limits, and a not too rigid claim of recovery of fugitives—in one word, quietude—was impossible in the state of the southern mind. It was a question of world psychology. Civilized mankind elsewhere had gradually come to that point of moral development which made the further existence of slavery impossible. To have made the compromise finally acceptable, the South had to look forward to yielding slavery by degrees, or the North to its permanent acceptance. The latter, driven by the world impulse towards freedom, could not accede to this; the former was equally driven by the lash of its own conditions to stand firm.

Millson, a member of Congress from Virginia, expressed the only true view of the bone of contention when he said, January 21, 1861: "This territorial question has been settled. The battle has been fought and it has been won by both parties; it has been lost by both parties. . . . You cannot [by the interpretation of the Constitution by the supreme court] . . . prohibit slavery in a Territory . . . but . . . there is not the least probability that slavery will ever be carried into any one of them. Thus, in all that respects practical results, you have gained the battle, and we have lost it. You have lost the principle; we the substance. You have gained the substance; we the principle." [1] Such views apparently had weight in the acts organizing the territories of Colorado, Dakota, and Nevada. These were passed by a Republican majority in both houses, with no reference to the prohibition of slavery, thus vindicating Webster, and practically stamping the fierce agitation of the previous twelve years as a stultification.[1]

[1] *Cong. Globe*, 36 Cong., 2 Sess., App., 77.
[2] Cf. Blaine, *Twenty Years of Congress*, I., 270, 271.

CHAPTER XII

STATUS OF THE FORTS
(OCTOBER 29, 1860–DECEMBER 20, 1860)

GENERAL SCOTT, with his memories of 1832, was one of those who appreciated the danger hanging over the country, and, October 29, 1860, he wrote from New York, where he had his headquarters, a letter of great length to the president, which in pompous phrases, conceding the right of secession, and embodying some absurd ideas, such as allowing "the fragments of the great republic to form themselves into new confederacies, probably four," as a smaller evil than war, gave it as his "solemn conviction" that there was, from his knowledge of the southern population, "some danger of an early act of rashness preliminary to secession, viz: the seizure of some or all of the following posts: Forts Jackson and St. Philip on the Mississippi; Morgan below Mobile, all without garrisons; Pickens, McKee at Pensacola, with an insufficient garrison for one; Pulaski, below Savannah, without a garrison; Moultrie and Sumter, Charleston harbor, the former with an insufficient garrison, the latter without any; and Fort Monroe, Hampton Roads, with an insufficient garrison."

He gave it as his opinion that "all these works should be immediately so garrisoned as to make any attempt to take any one of them by surprise or *coup de main*, ridiculous." He did not state the number of men needed, but in a supplementary paper the next day (October 30) said, "There is one (regular) company in Boston, one here (at the Narrows), one at Pittsburg, one at Baton Rouge—in all five companies only within reach."[1] These five companies, about two hundred and fifty men, were of course absurdly inadequate to garrison nine such posts, but had there been a determination in the president's mind to prevent seizures, enough men could have been brought together to hold the more important points.

For Scott's statement as to the number available was grossly inaccurate, and but serves to show the parlous state of a war department in which the general-in-chief can either be so misinformed or allow himself to remain in ignorance of vital facts. There were but five points in the farther South of primal importance: the Mississippi, Mobile, Pensacola, Savannah, and Charleston; two hundred men at each would have been ample to hold the positions for the time being, and, being held, reinforcement in any degree would later have been easy.

[1] Buchanan, *Administration on Eve of Rebellion*, chap. v.; *National Intelligencer*, January 18, 1861.

There was a total of 1048 officers and men at the northern posts,[1] including Leavenworth, Mackinac, Plattsburg, Boston, New York, and Fort Monroe, who could have been drawn upon. There were already 250 men at Charleston, Key West, Pensacola, and Baton Rouge. It is safe to say that a thousand men were available. There were also some eight hundred marines at the navy-yards and barracks[2] who could have been used in such an emergency. The aggregate of the army, June 30, 1860, was 16,006, of which 14,926 were enlisted men; and it was in the power of the president to increase this total aggregate to 18,626.[3] Recruiting was, in fact, actively going on; almost every man at the posts mentioned could even much after the date of Scott's paper have been safely withdrawn for the object mentioned and quickly replaced.

Scott's inaccurate report gave Buchanan additional reason for the inaction which was his basic thought. He says, in his *apologia* that "to have attempted to distribute these five companies in the eight forts of the cotton States and Fortress Monroe in Virginia, would have been a confession of weakness. . . . It could have had no effect in preventing secession, but must have done much to provoke it." [4] The first part of this statement would have been true

[1] Secretary of war, *Report*, 1860, *Senate Exec. Docs.*, 36 Cong. 2 Sess., No. 1, pp. 214, 216.

[2] Secretary of navy, *Report*, 1860, *ibid.*, 383.

[3] Secretary of war, *Report*, 1860, *ibid.*, 209, 213.

[4] Buchanan, *Administration on Eve of Rebellion*, 104.

had these five companies been the only force available; the second, on the supposition that the president meant that any attempt with a force reasonably large would have provoked secession, was a short-sighted view. To garrison the forts could not have been more obnoxious than to put them in a state of defence. At any time before the secession of a state they could have been garrisoned without bringing on actual conflict. The statesmen of the South were well aware that an attack upon an armed force of the United States, before secession, must place them irretrievably in the wrong. South Carolina did not secede until December 20. To resist the sending of troops before this date to any of these forts would have been unqualified treason, and for this no one in the South was prepared. The safety of the secession movement, the extension of sympathy throughout the South, rested very greatly upon strict compliance with the forms of law and with the theories of the Constitution held by that section. At least one ardent secessionist, Judge Longstreet, recognized this when he appealed to South-Carolinians to refrain from any act of war, "let the first shot," he said, "come from the enemy. *Burn that precept into your hearts.*"[1] It was impossible that the southern leaders should place themselves, or allow their people to place them, in the attitude of waging war against the Union, while even in their own view, their states still remained

[1] *National Intelligencer*, January 11, 1861.

within it. There was, too, still a very large Union
sentiment in the South, though finally swept into
the vortex by the principle of going with the state,
which would not have been averse to a determined
action on the part of the president and might have
upheld it, as in 1833. Such vigor would have given
this sentiment a working basis, through the evidence that the Federal authority was to be upheld;
and it would have caused a pause even in the least
thoughtful of the secessionists had they felt that
their coast strongholds were to be held and all
their ports to be in the hands of the enemy. In
the dearth of manufactures in the South, the holding of their ports was an essential to southern
military success. Their closure by blockade was
equally an essential to the success of the North.
The strategy of the situation was of the clearest
and most palpable; and with their coast forts in
Union hands, warlike action on the part of the
South is not conceivable. One can thus understand the importance of spreading the reiterated
statements of "intense excitement" and "danger
of attack," in the event of reinforcement; statements which, in the circumstances, must be regarded, if the phrase may be used, in the nature of
a gigantic and successful "bluff."

Many people have thought that the awakening
of the North to a willingness for vigorous action had
to be gradual, and that the long delay was therefore necessary to unify Union sentiment. This is

a moot question.   But in any case it is not given to the human mind to follow with certainty every ramification of events under hypothetical conditions; and the subject must be dealt with from the point of view that every emergency should be met as it arises.   There was too much weighing of the political effect of every step taken; the plain path of duty should have been taken and held to, and supposititious political effects left to take care of themselves.

Moreover, on this question the president ignored the psychological power of unchecked action; feelings and prepossessions gravitate to the centre of energy; the acquiescence of the authorities in regard to the southern garrisons was thus an immense element in urging the South to a movement which gathered in weight and sympathy under declamatory appeals to arise and assert its manhood.

The military property of the United States at Charleston consisted of the armory, covering a few acres, where were stored twenty-two thousand muskets and a considerable number of old, heavy guns, and of three forts named for South-Carolinians of Union-wide fame.   The smallest of these, Castle Pinckney, was a round, brick structure, in excellent condition, on a small island directly east of the town and distant from the wharves but half a mile. It completely commanded the town, and had a formidable armament of four forty-two-pounders, fourteen twenty-four-pounders, and four eight-inch sea-coast howitzers. The powder of the arsenal was here stored. The only garrison was an ordnance sergeant, who, with his family, looked after the harbor light which was in the fort.

Almost due east again, and three miles distant, was Fort Moultrie, on the south end of Sullivan's Island, a low sand spit forming the north side of the harbor entrance. The work had an area of one and a half acres, and mounted fifty-five guns in barbette. The drifting sands had piled themselves even with the parapet, and the work was in such condition as to be indefensible against a land attack. The whole was but of a piece with the long-continued neglect arising from many years of peace and the optimistic temperament of a people who never believe that war can occur until it is upon them; it was the natural outcome of the almost entire absence of governmental system and forethought of the time. The fort was garrisoned by two companies, comprising sixty-four enlisted men and eight officers, of the first regiment of artillery; the surgeon, band, a hospital steward, and an ordnance sergeant brought the total to eighty-four.

Almost south of Moultrie was Cummings Point, on Morris Island, forming the southern side of the harbor entrance. Nearly midway between this point and Moultrie, but a half-mile within the line joining them, and distant three and a half miles from the nearest part of the city, was Fort Sumter, begun in 1829, and after thirty-one years not yet

finished. Built on a shoal covered at most stages
of the tide, it rose directly out of the water, with
two tiers of casemates, and surmounted by a third
tier of guns in barbette. In plan it was very like the
transverse section of the ordinary American house,
the apex of the two sides representing the lines of
the roof, looking towards Moultrie. It was intended for a garrison of 650 men and an armament of
146 guns, of which 78 were on hand.

On a report made in July by Captain J. G. Foster,
repairs on Moultrie were begun September 14, and
next day upon Sumter, some two hundred and fifty
men being employed. The sand about the walls of
Moultrie was removed, a wet ditch dug, a glacis
formed, the guard-house pierced with loop-holes,
and the four field-guns placed in position for flank
attack.

At the end of October, Captain Foster, foreseeing
events, requested the issue of arms to the workmen
to protect property, and the secretary of war approved the issue of forty muskets, if it should meet
the concurrence of the commanding officer. Colonel
Gardner, in reply, November 5, doubted the expediency, as most of the laborers were foreigners,
indifferent to which side they took, and wisely
advised, instead, filling up "at once" the two companies at Moultrie with recruits and sending two
companies from Fort Monroe to the two other forts.[1]
The requisition was thus held in abeyance, and the

[1] *War Records,* Serial No. 1, p. 68.

muskets remained at the arsenal. When, only two days later, Gardner, urged by the repeated solicitations of his officers, directed the transfer of musket ammunition to Moultrie, the loading of the schooner was objected to by the owner of the wharf, and the military store-keeper, under apparently very inadequate pressure, returned the stores to the arsenal. A permit, given by the mayor of Charleston next day, for the removal was very properly declined by Gardner, on the ground that the city authorities could not control his actions.[1]

The affair, however, cost Gardner his command, by a process described by the assistant secretary of state, Trescot: "I received a telegram from Charleston, saying that intense excitement prevailed . . . and that if the removal was by orders of the Department of War, it ought to be revoked, otherwise collision was inevitable. Knowing the Cabinet were then in session I went over to the White House. . . . I took Governor Floyd aside, and he was joined, I think, by Messrs. Cobb and Toucey, and showed them the telegram. Governor Floyd replied 'Telegraph back at once; say that you have seen me, that no such orders have been issued, and none such will be issued, under any circumstances.'" Floyd, a day or so later, gave Trescot "his impressions of the folly of Colonel Gardner's conduct, and his final determination to remove him and supply his place with Major Robert Anderson, in whose discretion,

[1] *War Records*, Serial No. 1, p. 69; Crawford, *Fort Sumter*, 57, 58.

coolness and judgment he put great confidence. He also determined to send Colonel Ben. Huger to take charge of the arsenal, believing that his high reputation, his close association with many of the most influential people in Charleston, and the fact of his being a Carolinian, would satisfy the state of the intention of the Government."[1]

That Floyd himself was in an uncertain state of mind is shown by his willingness to begin and continue the work upon the forts; that his mental state did not permit logical action is clear from his temper and attitude regarding the transfer of musket ammunition November 7, though but the week before (October 31) he had authorized the transfer of the muskets themselves.

Major Fitz-John Porter, of the adjutant-general's office, later the able and ill-treated general, was sent to Charleston to inspect the conditions. His report, made November 11, revealed the military inefficiency almost inseparable from a post so neglected and ill-manned, and subject to the lazy peace conditions of the period. He said: "The unguarded state of the fort invites attack, if such design exists, and much discretion and prudence are required on the part of the commander to restore the proper security without exciting a community prompt to misconstrue actions of authority. I think this can be effected by a proper commander without checking in the slightest the progress of

---

[1] *Trescot MS.*, quoted by Crawford, *Fort Sumter*, 58, 59.

the engineer in completing the works of defense."
Major Porter continues with a most significant
phrase, "All could have been easily arranged a few
weeks since, when the danger was foreseen by the
present commander." [1]

November 15, Anderson was ordered to the command. A Kentuckian by birth, his wife a Georgian,
his views in sympathy with those of General Scott,
he appeared to be and, as results proved, was in
many respects particularly fitted for the post; by
November 23 he was able to report that in two
weeks the outer defences of Moultrie would be finished and the guns mounted, and that Sumter was
ready for the comfortable accommodation of one
company, and, indeed, for the temporary reception of
its proper garrison. "This," he said, "is the key
to the entrance to this harbor; its guns command
this work [Moultrie] and could drive out its occu-
pants. It should be garrisoned at once. . . . So important do I consider the holding of Castle Pinckney
by the Government that I recommend, if the troops
asked for cannot be sent at once, that I be authorized to place an engineer detachment [of an officer
and thirty workmen] . . . to make the repairs needed
there. . . . If my force was not so very small I
would not hesitate to send a detachment at once to
garrison that work. Fort Sumter and Castle Pinckney *must* be garrisoned immediately if the Government determines to keep command of this harbor."

[1] *War Records*, Serial No. 1, p. 70.

Anderson proceeded to give advice which sane judgment and every sentiment of national honor demanded. After mentioning his anxiety to avoid collision with the citizens of South Carolina, he said: "Nothing, however, will be better calculated to prevent bloodshed than our being found in such an attitude that it would be madness and folly to attack us. There is not so much feverish excitement as there was last week, but that there is a settled determination to leave the Union, and obtain possession of this work, is apparent to all. . . . The clouds are threatening, and the storm may break upon us at any moment. I do, then, most earnestly entreat that a re-enforcement be immediately sent to this garrison, and that at least two companies be sent at the same time to Fort Sumter and Castle Pinckney." Anderson also stated his belief that as soon as the people of South Carolina learned that he had demanded reinforcements they would occupy Pinckney and attack Moultrie; and therefore it was vitally important to embark the troops in war steamers and designate them for other duty as a blind.[1] Captain Foster, November 24, reported the whole of the barbette tier of Sumter ready for its armament and as presenting an excellent appearance of preparation and strength equal to seventy per cent. of its efficiency when finished.[2] He said, November 30, "I think more troops should have been sent here to guard the

[1] *War Records*, Serial No. 1, pp. 74, 75.   [2] *Ibid.*, 76.

forts and I believe that no serious demonstration on the part of the populace would have met such a course." [1]

The work on the forts was, of course, well known to the people of Charleston, and that at Moultrie, at least, subject to daily inspection by many visitors. There was still no restriction "upon any intercourse with Charleston, many of whose citizens were temporary residents of Sullivan's Island. The activity about the fort drew to it a large number of visitors daily, and the position of the garrison and the probable action of the state in regard to the forts were constant subjects of discussion. There was as yet no unfriendly feeling manifested, and the social intercourse between the garrison and their friends in Charleston was uninterrupted. But as the days went on the feeling assumed a more definite shape, and found expression in many ways. . . . It was openly announced both to the commanding officer and to his officers, that as soon as the state seceded a demand for the delivery of the forts would be made, and if resisted, they would be taken. . . . Meantime, all of the able-bodied men in Charleston were enrolled, military companies were formed everywhere, and drilling went on by night and day, and with the impression among them that they were to attack Fort Moultrie." [2] November 28 and December 1, Anderson again pressed for

[1] *War Records*, Serial No. 1, p. 80.
[2] Crawford, *Fort Sumter*, 64.

troops or for ships of war in the harbor;[1] but his last request was anticipated in a letter of the same date, when he was informed by the war department, "from information thought to be reliable, that an attack will not be made on your command, and the Secretary has only to refer to his conversation with you and to caution you that should his convictions unhappily prove untrue, your actions must be such as to be free from the charge of initiating a collision. If attacked, you are of course expected to defend the trust committed to you to the best of your ability." [2]

A demand being made by the adjutant of a South Carolina regiment on the engineer officer at Moultrie for a list of his workmen, "as it was desired to enroll the men upon them for military duty,"[3] Anderson asked for instructions. The war department replied, December 14, "If the state authorities demand any of Captain Foster's workmen on the ground of their being enrolled into the service of the State . . . you will, after fully satisfying yourself that the men are subject to enrollment, and have been properly enrolled, . . . cause them to be delivered up or suffer them to depart." Banality could go no further, and Anderson, December 18, informed the department that as he understood it, "the South Carolina authorities sought to enroll as a part of their army intended to act against the forces

[1] *War Records*, Serial No. 1, pp. 79–82.   [2] *Ibid.*, p. 82.
[3] Crawford, *Fort Sumter*, 67.

of the United States, men who are employed by and in the pay of that Government, and could not, as I conceived, be enrolled by South Carolina 'under the laws of the United States and of the State of South Carolina.'" No answer was vouchsafed to this, and the request was not complied with.

Anderson's repeated statements of the necessity of the occupancy of Sumter, without which his own position was untenable, led to the despatch of Major Buell, a Kentuckian, and later a major-general of United States volunteers, with verbal instructions which, however, on Buell's own motion, and with the thought that Anderson should have written evidence, were reduced, December 11, to writing. This memorandum is of such importance that it must be given in full.

"You are aware of the great anxiety of the Secretary of War that a collision of the troops with the people of this State shall be avoided, and of his studied determination to pursue a course with reference to the military force and forts in this harbor which shall guard against such a collision. He has therefore carefully abstained from increasing the force at this point, or taking any measures which might add to the present excited state of the public mind, or which would throw any doubt on the confidence he feels that South Carolina will not attempt, by violence, to obtain possession of the public works or interfere with their occupancy. But as the counsels and acts of rash and impulsive persons may possibly disappoint those expectations of the Government, he deems it proper that you should be prepared with instructions to meet so unhappy a contingency. He has therefore directed me verbally to give you such instructions. You are carefully to avoid every act which would needlessly tend to provoke aggression; and for that reason you are not without evident and imminent necessity to take up any position which could be construed into the assumption of a hostile attitude. But you are to hold possession of the forts in this harbor, and if attacked you are to defend yourself to the last extremity. The smallness of your force will not permit you, perhaps, to occupy more than one of the three forts, but an attack on, or attempt to take possession of any one of them will be regarded as an act of hostility, and you may then put your command into either of them, which you may deem most proper to increase its power of resistance. You are also authorized to take similar steps whenever you have tangible evidence of a design to proceed to a hostile act." [1]

These instructions did not come to the president's knowledge until December 21, though a despatch from Washington, December 13, published in the *Charleston Courier*, announced Major Buell's visit; when made known to the president, he directed them to be modified, ordering that if "attacked by a force so superior that resistance would,

[1] *War Records*, Serial No. 1, p. 89.

in your judgment, be a useless waste of life, it will be your duty to yield to necessity, and make the best terms in your power." [1]

December 3, Anderson placed Lieutenant Jefferson C. Davis with thirty men in Castle Pinckney, and began work there. Action upon a request for arms for the workmen at Sumter and Pinckney was deferred by the war department "for the present," but Captain Foster going to the arsenal, December 17, for two gins for hoisting, "to the transmission of which there was no objection," arranged with the store-keeper that the old order of the ordnance department of November 1, for forty muskets, should be complied with, which was done. "Intense excitement" as usual was reported the next day to have occurred; there was the reiteration of great danger of "violent demonstration" from a military official of the state who called upon Foster, and who stated that Colonel Huger had informed the governor that no arms should be removed. Foster declined to return the arms, stating that he knew nothing of Huger's pledge, but was willing to refer the matter to Washington. Trescot was informed by telegraph that "not a moment's time should be lost." The secretary of war was aroused in the depths of the night, and the result was a telegraphic order from Floyd himself to "return [the arms] instantly." [2] The go-between assistant secretary of

[1] *War Records*, Serial No. 1, p. 103.
[2] *Ibid.*, pp. 96–100; Crawford, *Fort Sumter*, 77.

state, so busily engaged with affairs not his own, received from the aide-de-camp of Governor Pickens the telegram: "The Governor says he is glad of your despatch, for otherwise there would have been imminent danger. Earnestly urge that there be no transfer of troops from Fort Moultrie to Fort Sumter and inform Secretary of War." [1] Captain Foster explaining to the war department, December 20, 1860, says, "when in town to see General Schnierle and allay any excitement relative to the muskets, I found to my surprise that there was no excitement except with a very few who had been active in the matter, and the majority of the gentlemen whom I met had not even heard of it." [2]

Pickens, the new governor of South Carolina, December 17, the day after his inauguration, and before the state had passed the ordinance of secession, made a demand on the president for the delivery of Fort Sumter. The letter, drawn in the most offensive terms, and marked "strictly confidential," urged that all work be stopped and that no more troops be ordered. It continued: "It is not improbable that, under orders from the commandant, or, perhaps, from the commander-in-chief of the army, the alteration and defenses of the posts are progressing without the knowledge of yourself or the Secretary of War. The arsenal in the city of Charleston, with the public arms, I am informed,

---

[1] *Trescot MS.*, quoted by Crawford, *Fort Sumter*, 78.
[2] *War Records*, Serial No. 1, p. 101.

was turned over very properly to the keeping and defense of the State force at the urgent request of the Governor of South Carolina. I would most respectfully, and from a sincere devotion to the public peace, request that you would allow me to send a small force, not exceeding twenty-five men and an officer, to take possession of Fort Sumter immediately, in order to give a feeling of safety to the community." [1]

The ever-ready Trescot arranged an interview December 20 with the president for the delivery of the letter. The president stated that he would give an answer the next day. In the mean time Trescot, seeing the difficulties to which it led, consulted both Senators Davis and Slidell, who thought the demand "could do nothing but mischief"; and on consultation with two of the South Carolina delegation in Washington, Governor Pickens was advised by telegraph to withdraw the letter, which was done. Trescot's letter to Governor Pickens, returning that of the latter, after mentioning all that had been done by the executive to refrain from injuring the sensibilities of South Carolina, said: The president's "course had been violently denounced by the Northern press, and an effort was being made to institute a Congressional investigation. At that moment he could not have gone to the extent of action you desired, and I felt confident that, if forced to answer your letter then,

[1] Crawford. *Fort Sumter*, 81–83.

he would have taken such ground as would have
prevented his even approaching it hereafter . . .
you had all the advantage of knowing the truth,
without the disadvantage of having it put on
record. . . . I was also perfectly satisfied that the
status of the garrison would not be disturbed. . . . I
have had this morning an interview with Governor
Floyd, the Secretary of War . . . while I cannot
even here venture into details, which are too confidential to be risked in any way, I am prepared to
say . . . that nothing will be done which will either
do you injury or properly create alarm." [1]

The president's painful weakness is but too clear
in the fact that he had not only given his confidence so largely to such a man, whose position and
attitude he knew, but saw nothing derogatory in
such a letter as that of Governor Pickens, and could
draught a reply (December 20) in which, while
stating that no authority had been given to Governor Gist to guard the Charleston arsenal, he said:
"I deeply regret to observe that you seem entirely
to have misapprehended my position, which I supposed had been clearly stated in my message. I
have incurred, and shall incur, any reasonable risk
. . . to prevent a collision. . . . Hence I have declined for the present to reinforce these forts, relying upon the honor of the South Carolinians that
they will not be assaulted whilst they remain in
their present condition; but that commissioners will

[1] Crawford, *Fort Sumter*, 85, 86.

be sent by the convention *to treat with Congress* on the subject." [1]

If the shades of Andrew Jackson and Zachary Taylor still haunted the White House, they must have wrung their ghostly hands in agony at their impotence. And so the pitiable story proceeds of a weak, well-meaning old man surrounded by false and traitorous counsellors; afraid to do the duty which was before him as plain as the light of day; hoping to fend off the dissolution of the Union during the few short months which remained to him of office; leaving the mighty deluge of woe, so sure to come through his inaction, to his successor.

December 18 the president sent Caleb Cushing with a letter to Governor Pickens, with the idea of inducing the authorities and people of South Carolina to await the action of Congress and the development of opinion in the North as to the recommendation of his message. Governor Pickens told Cushing, December 20, the day of the passage of the ordinance of secession, that he would make no reply to the letter, and stated "very candidly that there was no hope for the Union, and that, as far as he was concerned, he intended to maintain the separate independence of South Carolina." [2]

[1] Curtis, *Buchanan*, II., 385. The emphasis is Buchanan's.
[2] Governor's message to legislature, quoted by Crawford, *Fort Sumter*, 87.

CHAPTER XIII

THE FORT SUMTER CRISIS
(DECEMBER 2, 1860–JANUARY 8, 1861)

THE question of the United States forts was now uppermost, and upon the action regarding them hung war or peace. Three commissioners—Robert W. Barnwell, James H. Adams, and James L. Orr—were appointed by South Carolina to lay the ordinance of secession before the president and Congress, and were empowered as agents of the state to treat for the delivery of the forts and other real estate, for the apportionment of the public debt, and for a division of all the property of the United States.[1]

In apprehension of the occupation of Sumter by Anderson, a patrol by two small steamers, the *Nina* and *General Clinch*, was established, with orders to prevent such action at all hazards and seize Fort Sumter if it should be attempted. A Lieutenant-Colonel Green was sent to Fort Monroe to observe any movements; and one Norris, at Norfolk, was employed to give information of any action at the Norfolk navy-yard. A committee of prominent

[1] *War Records*, Serial No. 1, p. 111.

men was sent to Fort Sumter, which thoroughly inspected the works and reported upon them.

Meantime, Major Anderson had been preparing, with great caution and foresight, to move his command. For some ten days the officers had been apprised that it was advisable to send the families of the men to the unoccupied barracks on James's Island, known as Fort Johnson, a mile and a quarter west of Sumter. The work of mounting guns at Sumter had been discontinued for three days, and the elevating screws and pintle bolts sent to Moultrie so that the guns should not be used if the South-Carolinians should anticipate his action, and also to give the impression that occupancy of the fort was not designed. All stores and provisions at Fort Moultrie which could be carried, and personal belongings, except what the men could carry in their knapsacks, were loaded as for Fort Johnson in the two small sailing-vessels which were to carry the women and children.

Christmas Day had been fixed for the transfer, but heavy rains prevented. The delay might have had other consequences, for, curiously enough, on the morning of December 26, Colonel R. B. Rhett, Jr., waited upon the governor, with a private warning letter from Washington to the effect that Anderson was about to seize Sumter, and urged the governor to secure it.[1]

All was made ready on December 26, and the

[1] Crawford, *Fort Sumter*, 91.

quartermaster who was to have charge of the little
flotilla, loaded with "everything in the household
line from boxes and barrels of provisions to cages
of canary birds," was directed to go to Fort Johnson, but not to land anything. Upon a signal of
two guns from Moultrie he was to go to Sumter on
the plea that he had to report to Anderson that he
could not find accommodations. Five pulling-boats
in customary use were available for the transportation of the men. Only one officer had been thus
far informed, and the men had no suspicion where
they were to go when they fell in at retreat roll-call
with packed knapsacks and filled cartridge-boxes,
carried at parade under a general standing order.
So little was the movement suspected that Captain
Doubleday, second in command, came at sunset to
Anderson in the midst of the officers on the parapet
to invite the major to tea. He was then informed
of Anderson's intentions, and was directed to have
his company in readiness in twenty minutes, an
order met by an "eager obedience." Part of this
time was taken in arranging for the safety of Mrs.
Doubleday in the village outside of the fort, whither
the families of the other officers were also sent.
The men were ready promptly, and the first detachment of twenty, led by Anderson himself,
marched over the quarter of a mile of sand to the
landing-place with the good fortune of encountering no one.

Anderson went in the leading boat. Lieutenant

Meade, the engineer officer in charge of the works at Castle Pinckney, had charge of the second, and Captain Doubleday of the third. When half-way across, Doubleday's boat came unexpectedly in the path of one of the patrol boats, the *General Clinch*, which was towing a schooner to sea. The men were ordered to take off their coats and cover their muskets. The steamer stopped, but in the twilight, and with the resemblance of the boat and its load of men to the usual parties of workmen, suspicion was not aroused, and the steamer resumed her way without questioning. She had been anxiously watched from Moultrie, and had she interfered would have been fired upon by a thirty-two-pounder, two of which had been loaded with that intent. Captain Foster, with Assistant Surgeon Crawford, a Mr. Moall, four non-commissioned officers, and seven privates, had been left at Moultrie to spike the guns, burn the gun-carriages, and hew down the flag-staff.[1]

On reaching Sumter, the workmen, some hundred and fifty, swarmed to the wharf, some feebly cheering, many angrily demanding the reason for the presence of the soldiers; many of the workmen wore the secession cockade; the malcontents (a number of whom shortly returned to Charleston) quickly gave way before the bayonets of Doubleday's men, who at once occupied the main entrance and guard-room; sentries were posted and the fort was under

[1] Crawford, *Fort Sumter*, chap. x.

military control. Boats were now sent back for Captain Seymour's company, which arrived without interference, and the whole force, except the few detailed to remain at Moultrie, was in Sumter before eight o'clock, at which hour Anderson wrote the adjutant-general, reporting that he had "just completed, by the blessing of God, the removal to this fort of all my garrison. . . . The step which I have taken was, in my opinion, necessary to prevent the effusion of blood." [1] On the firing of the signal-guns at Moultrie, Lieutenant Hall left the west side of the bay with the two lighters carrying the men's families and stores, and reached Sumter under sail.

With the help of the engineer's workmen at Moultrie, the boats were loaded during the night with part of the impedimenta of every sort which had to be left in the first crossing, and reached Sumter in the early dawn. The following day, December 27, was passed like the preceding night, in transferring ammunition and other stores to Sumter; but a month and a half's supply of provisions, some fuel, and personal effects, had to be left. All the guns at Moultrie were spiked, and the carriages of those bearing on Sumter burned, the smoke from these bearing to Charleston the first indication of what had happened. At fifteen minutes before noon, the command and one hundred and fifty workmen were formed in a square near the flag-staff of Sumter; the chaplain offered a prayer expressing

[1] *War Records*, Serial No. 1, p. 2.

gratitude for their safe arrival and prayed that the flag might never be dishonored, but soon float again over the whole country, a peaceful and prosperous nation. "When the prayer was finished, Major Anderson who had been kneeling arose, the battalion presented arms, the band played the National Air, and the flag went to the head of the flag-staff, amid the loud and earnest huzzas of the command." [1]

Intense excitement in Charleston was the natural outcome of Anderson's action, and the morning of the 27th the governor sent his aide-de-camp, Colonel Pettigrew, accompanied by Major Capers, with a peremptory demand that Anderson should return with his garrison to Moultrie, to which Anderson replied, "Make my compliments to the Governor and say to him that I decline to accede to his request; I cannot and will not go back." The governor's messenger mentioned that when Governor Pickens came into office he found an understanding between his predecessor (Gist) and the president, by which the status in the harbor was to remain unchanged. Anderson stated "that he knew nothing of it, that he could get no information or positive orders from Washington . . . that he had reason to believe that [the state troops] meant to land and attack him from the north; that the desire of the Governor to have the matter settled peaceably and without bloodshed was precisely his own object in transferring his command . . . that

[1] Crawford, *Fort Sumter*, 112.

he did it upon his own responsibility alone," as safety required it, "and as he had the right to do." He added that, "In this controversy between the North and the South, my sympathies are entirely with the South"; but that a sense of duty to his trust was first.[1] The immediate result was the occupancy by the state forces, December 27, of Pinckney and Moultrie, the seizure, December 30, of the unoccupied barracks known as Fort Johnson, and of the arsenal, with its ordnance and ordnance stores, valued at four hundred thousand dollars.

The news of Anderson's dramatic, bold, and self-reliant act, one for which the country owes a debt to the memory of this upright and excellent commander, brought consternation to the president and secretary of war, who learned it through the indefatigable Trescot, who had, on the 26th, arranged for the three commissioners of South Carolina an interview with the president for December 27, at one o'clock. The news of the morning brought a complete change of circumstances. A telegram to Wigfall was brought by him to the commissioners and to the secretary of war, who at once went to the commissioners Trescot was present, and could not believe in an "act not only without orders but in the face of orders." Floyd at once telegraphed, asking an explanation of the report. "It is not believed, because there is no order for any such movement." A telegram in reply from Anderson assured him of

[1] Crawford, *Fort Sumter*, 110, 111.

the truth, and a written report gave as reasons that "many things convinced me that the authorities of the State designed to proceed to a hostile act. Under this impression I could not hesitate that it was my solemn duty to move my command from a fort which we could not have held probably longer than forty-eight or sixty hours, to this one where my power of resistance is increased to a very great degree." [1]

Trescot sought Senators Davis and Hunter at the Capitol, and went with them to the White House, where they found the president still uninformed. "'Then,' said Davis, 'I have a great calamity to announce to you.'" Having told the story, he added: "'And now, Mr. President, you are surrounded with blood and dishonor on all sides.' The President was standing by the mantel-piece, crushing up a cigar in the palm of one hand—a habit I have seen him practice often. He sat down as Colonel Davis finished, and exclaimed, 'My God, are calamities (or misfortunes, I forget which) never to come singly! I call God to witness, you gentlemen, better than anybody, *know* that this is not only without but against my orders. It is against my policy.'" [2]

The president was urged to restore the previous situation, on the ground that he was so bound in honor and on account of the probability of attack

[1] *War Records*, Serial No. 1, p. 3.
[2] *Trescot MS.*, quoted by Crawford. *Fort Sumter*, 143.

on Sumter. He hesitated; he must call his cabinet
together; he could not condemn Anderson unheard.
"He was told nobody asked that; only say that *if*
the move had been made without a previous attack on Anderson he would restore the status.
Assure us of that determination, and then take
what time was necessary for consultation and information." [1]

With unusual firmness, Buchanan declined com-
mitting himself. The cabinet was called together at
once, and met frequently, from the 27th to the 29th,
in stormy session. Floyd, although his resignation
had been requested by the president December 23,
through Vice-President Breckinridge, on account of
his gross malfeasance which had just come to light,[2]
came uninvited, and, with Thompson and Thomas,
united in severe condemnation of Anderson's action.
But Judge Black, now secretary of state, Holt, postmaster-general, and Stanton, who had succeeded Black
as attorney-general, were a saving triumvirate, and
held the president from inconsiderate action.

Friday, December 28, the three South Carolina
commissioners had their only interview with the
president, who attempted to cover this negotiation
with men who "from being the agents of a conspiracy . . . had now become the emissaries of an
insurrection" [3] by informing them that he could

---

[1] *Trescot MS.*, quoted by Crawford, *Fort Sumter*, 144.
[2] See p. 151, above.
[3] Nicolay and Hay, *Abraham Lincoln*, III., 70.

only recognize them as private gentlemen and not
as commissioners from a sovereign state; that it
was to Congress and to Congress alone that they
must appeal. He expressed, however, his willingness to communicate to Congress any propositions
they might desire to offer. They declared that
they must obtain redress for the removal of Anderson to Sumter before entering upon the negotiation
with which they were intrusted, and insisted not
only upon the immediate withdrawal of the troops
from Sumter but from the harbor as a *sine qua non*.[1]

The commissioners insisted that there had been
a violation of faith; that they could, at any time
after the arrangement was made, have occupied
Sumter and captured Moultrie, and that the faith
of the president and government had been forfeited.
Barnwell said to him at least three times during
the interview, "But, Mr. President, your personal
honor is involved in this matter, the faith you
pledged has been violated and your personal honor
requires you to issue the order." At the third
time the president turned to Barnwell with great
earnestness, saying, "Mr. Barnwell, you are press-
ing me too importunately; you don't give me time
to say my prayers; I always say my prayers when
required to act upon any great State affair." [2]

In their letter to the president the next day they
repeated their demand for the immediate with-

---

[1] Buchanan, *Administration on Eve of Rebellion*, 182.
[2] Letter from Orr to Crawford. Crawford, *Fort Sumter*, 148.

drawal of the troops from Charleston harbor, as a
standing menace, making negotiations impossible
and threatening "to bring to a bloody issue questions which ought to be settled with temperance
and judgment." [1]   This action, if his later statement is to be trusted, was not in Buchanan's mind
for the moment, though he might have considered
a return to Fort Moultrie, on a guarantee that none
of the public property should be molested. [2]

When the cabinet met on the evening of December 29, only one member, Toucey, wholly approved
of the draught of the president's answer; Black,
Holt, and Stanton disapproved altogether as yielding too much; Floyd, Thompson, and Thomas as
yielding too little. The disagreement gave Floyd,
who ought to have been dismissed, an opportunity
to cover his disgrace by resignation the same day.
He embodied in his letter of resignation a paper
which he had read, with a violent and discourteous
manner, to the president and his colleagues, December 27, declaring "that the solemn pledges of
this government have been violated by Major Anderson"; and that "one remedy only is left, and
that is to withdraw the garrison from the harbor of
Charleston altogether." [3]   January 2, Senator Wigfall telegraphed Charleston: "Holt succeeds Floyd.

---

[1] *House Exec. Docs.*, 36 Cong., 2 Sess., No. 26, p. 6; Buchanan,
Administration on Eve of Rebellion, 182.

[2] Buchanan, *Administration on Eve of Rebellion*, 182.

[3] Correspondence of Floyd and Buchanan, Curtis, *Buchanan*,
II., 409.

It means war. Cut off all supplies from Anderson and take Sumter soon as possible." [1]

The exact contents of the president's draught of reply to the commissioners have never been made known; but it may be gathered from the memorandum prepared by Judge Black that it was very compromising, and Buchanan held firmly to it until the three Union members of the cabinet threatened resignation. Black insisted that the whole paper should be recast, which was done by Black himself. "As fast as the sheets were written, they were handed to the Attorney General who copied them in his own hand, the original being sent directly to the President." Black's memorandum demanded that every word implying that the president could treat with South Carolina should be stricken out, as well as all expression of regret that the commissioners were unwilling to proceed with the negotiations. Above all things it was objectionable to intimate that the possession of a military post could be a subject of negotiation. "The forts in the harbor of Charleston belong to this Government, are its own and cannot be given up. . . . Sumter is impregnable and cannot be taken if defended as it should be. It is a thing of the last importance that it should be maintained if all the power of this nation can do it." A flat denial of bargain, pledge, or agreement assumed by the commissioners to exist should be made; the remotest expression of doubt about An-

[1] *War Records*, Serial No. 1, p. 252.

derson's perfect propriety of behavior should be carefully avoided. "He has," said Black, "saved the country, I solemnly believe, when its day was darkest and its peril most extreme.[1] He has done everything which mortal man could do to repair the fatal error which the administration have committed in not sending down troops enough to hold *all* the forts. He has kept the strongest one. He still commands the harbor. We may still execute the laws if we try. . . . It is a strange assumption of right on the part of . . . [South Carolina] to say that the United States troops must remain in the weakest position they can find in the harbor. It is not a menace . . . it is simply self-defense."

Judge Black added: "But there is one thing not to be overlooked in this terrible crisis. I entreat the President to order the *Brooklyn* and the *Macedonian* to Charleston without the least delay, and in the mean time send a trusty messenger to Major Anderson to let him know that his Government will not desert him. The reinforcement of troops from New York or Old Point Comfort should follow immediately. If this be done at once all may yet be, not well, but comparatively safe. If not, I can see nothing before us but disaster and ruin to the country." [2]

The president's answer to the commissioners, December 31, was a weak accord with Black's

[1] Cf. Crawford, *Fort Sumter*, 155 *n.*
[2] *Ibid.*, 153–155.

draught. "The Executive," he said, "has no authority to decide what shall be the relations between the Federal Government and South Carolina." He denied that he had bound himself by any pledge. As to Anderson, he said: "My first promptings were to command him to return to his former position. . . . But before any steps could possibly have been taken in this direction, we received information, dated the 28th instant, that 'The Palmetto flag floated out to the breeze at Castle Pinckney and a large military force went over last night (the 27th) to Fort Moultrie.' Thus the authorities of South Carolina, without waiting or asking for any explanation, and doubtless believing, as you have expressed it, that the officer had acted not only without, but against my orders, on the very next day after the night when the removal was made, seized by a military force two of the three Federal forts in the harbor of Charleston. . . . On the very day . . . ," he continued, "the Palmetto flag was raised over the Federal custom house and post office in Charleston; and . . . every officer of the customs . . . resigned. . . . It is under all these circumstances that I am urged immediately to withdraw the troops from the harbor of Charleston, and am informed that, without this, negotiation is impossible. This I cannot do; this I will not do."[1]

The reply next day (January 1, 1861) of the com-

---

[1] Curtis, *Buchanan*, II., 386-390; *War Records*, Serial No. 1, pp. 115-118.

missioners was so insulting in temper and character
that the president declined to receive it.   Buchanan
must have read with bitterness the stinging résumé
of what he had failed to do.   "You did not re-enforce
the garrisons in the harbor of Charleston.   You removed a distinguished and veteran officer from the
command of Fort Moultrie because he attempted
to increase his supply of ammunition.   You refused
to send additional troops to the same garrison when
applied for by the officer appointed to succeed him.
You accepted the resignation of the oldest and most
efficient member of your Cabinet rather than allow
these garrisons to be strengthened.   You compelled
an officer stationed at Fort Sumter to return immediately to the arsenal forty muskets which he had
taken to arm his men.   You expressed not to one
but to many of the most distinguished of our public
characters . . . your anxiety for a peaceful termina-
tion of this controversy, and your willingness not
to disturb the military status of the forts, if commissioners should be sent to the Government, whose
communications you promised to submit to Congress." [1]

It was a new light to the president.   For a time he
was another man, in so far that he now placed himself in the hands of the Unionist members of the
cabinet, which was soon to become wholly of Unionist complexion.   The presidency thenceforward may
be said to have been in commission, the commission-

[1] *War Records*, Serial No. 1, pp. 121, 122.

ers executing the office hampered, however, by the irrepressible tendency of the president to treat with his ancient friends of the South on a footing of friendliness, with the hope apparently of winning them back by softness both of word and conduct. January 2 he gave an indication of his new trend of intention in the appointment of Peter McIntire, a Pennsylvanian of character and force, as collector of the port of Charleston; the Senate never acted upon the nomination.[1]

Anderson's conduct met with enthusiastic approval in the North. The country felt that it had finally found a man of action, and there was an immense patriotic rebound from the depression of the previous two months. The House of Representatives gave emphatic approval in a resolution, January 7, commending Anderson's "bold and patriotic" act, by a vote of 124 to 53.[2] The support of Anderson by the administration, the changes in the cabinet, and the ill success of the South Carolina commissioners created a new phase of the issue.

January 8 the president sent a message showing his own changed state of mind. With it he submitted the correspondence with the South Carolina commissioners. Throughout the message ran a note of despair. Hope of amicable adjustment had "been diminished by every hour of delay"; and as evidence of this no responsible bidder had offered

[1] Curtis, *Buchanan*, II., 483.
[2] *Cong. Globe*, 36 Cong., 2 Sess., 280.

to take any considerable sum of the ten millions of treasury notes authorized December 17, 1860, at a lower rate of interest than twelve per cent. He recognized that the country was "in the midst of a great revolution." On Congress, and on Congress alone, he said, rested the responsibility for adjustment, or for the authorization of the employment of a military force. Could the question be transferred to the ballot-box, "the people themselves would speedily redress the serious grievances which the South had suffered." He recommended that Congress devote itself exclusively to the question of the preservation of the Union. "Action, prompt action, is required." [1]

The reading of the president's message in the House, January 9, was immediately followed by a resolution offered by Howard, of Michigan, passed after a short debate by a vote of 136 to 62, for the appointment of a special committee to inquire whether any executive officer of the government was holding any communication with any persons concerning the surrender of public property; whether any pledge or understanding had been entered into regarding reinforcement of the Charleston forts; why such reinforcements had not been furnished; and to inquire in general into the situation of public property at Charleston.[2] This same day the *Star*

---

[1] Curtis, *Buchanan*, II., 433-436; Richardson, *Messages and Papers*, V., 655-659.
[2] *Cong. Globe*, 36 Cong., 2 Sess., 295.

of the West, with the much-needed reinforcements, turned from the weak Confederate batteries, the guns of Sumter silent.

While the president had come slowly to a recognition of his duty to reinforce Sumter, and could not but see in the changed attitude of the northern mind towards himself a thorough appreciation of his action in regard to Anderson and Sumter, his political instincts should have enabled him to recognize that to lean upon Congress for readjustment was, in the temper of both parties, hopeless.

CHAPTER XIV

EPISODE OF THE *STAR OF THE WEST*
(JANUARY, 1861)

BLACK'S insistence upon reinforcing Sumter eventually had effect, but there was a fatal divergence, due to Scott, from his wish to send the *Brooklyn*, then lying ready for sea at Norfolk, with trained troops from Fort Monroe. Scott, December 28, sent a memorandum to Floyd, still his superior, expressing the hope that Sumter should not be evacuated; that one hundred and fifty recruits should be immediately sent as reinforcement from Governor's Island, and that one or two armed vessels be sent to support the fort. He also hoped that his previous recommendations regarding "Forts Jackson, St. Philip, Morgan, and Pulaski, and particularly in respect to Forts Pickens and McRee and the Pensacola navy - yard, in connection with the last two named works, may be reconsidered by the secretary." [1] Two days later, December 30, he sent a memorandum to the president asking permission to send, without reference to the war department, two hundred and fifty re-

[1] *War Records*, Serial No. 1, p. 112.

cruits from New York to Sumter, together with extra arms, ammunition, and subsistence. He also hoped "that a sloop - of - war and cutter may be ordered for the same purpose as early as to-morrow." The president, now so much more alive to the situation, and probably upon the insistence of Black, preferred to send the *Brooklyn*. "He thought that a powerful war steamer with disciplined troops on board would prove more effective than a sloop of war and cutter with raw recruits." [1] The morrow, Monday, December 31, began well. Holt, who had taken over the war department, at once sent for Scott; and Colonel Dimick, commandant of Fort Monroe, was ordered to put aboard the *Brooklyn*, then at Norfolk ready for sea, as soon as she could receive them, "four companies, making at least two hundred men," and subsistence for ninety days.[2] Had General Scott adhered to this wise plan, there would have been a different story.

With the orders given for Sumter's relief came an unfortunate delay on the part of the president, who felt it necessary to give the commissioners of South Carolina time to reply to his letter, just sent (December 31). Scott, who was called in for consultation, agreed in the propriety of the delay as being "gentlemanly and proper." [3] Later in the

[1] Buchanan, *Administration on Eve of Rebellion*, 189.
[2] *War Records*, Serial No. 1, p. 119.
[3] Buchanan, *Administration on Eve of Rebellion*, 190.

same evening Buchanan promised the disunion secretary of the interior, Thompson, that the orders for the reinforcements should not be renewed "without being previously considered and decided in the cabinet." Two days later, on receiving the commissioners' caustic reply, he exclaimed, "It is now all over, and reinforcements must be sent." [1] But the delay was fatal. In the meantime Scott became convinced, "after advising with an individual believed to possess much knowledge and practical experience in naval affairs, that the better plan to secure both secrecy and success" would be to send recruits in a merchant steamer from New York. The *Star of the West*, of the New Orleans line, on the insistence of Scott and against the judgment of the president,[2] was thus chosen; and "two hundred well instructed men with, say, three officers," were ordered to be embarked as secretly as possible from Governor's Island,[3] thus substituting a weak, unarmed, side-wheel merchantman and lately recruited men for the powerful man-of-war and seasoned soldiers.

To suppose such a change more conducive to secrecy was perfectly vain, as was shown by its publication broadcast. The details left to General Scott were carried out at New York by Lieutenant-

[1] Buchanan to Thompson, January 9, 1861, Curtis, *Buchanan*, II., 402.

[2] Buchanan, in *National Intelligencer*, October 28, 1862; Curtis, *Buchanan*, II., 447; Buchanan, *Administration on Eve of Rebellion*, 189, 190. [3] *War Records*, Serial No. 1, p. 128.

Colonel Lorenzo Thomas, the assistant adjutant-general on his staff. The ship was cleared as if for her regular trip, the provisions bought as for the ship's account, and at 5 P.M., January 5, an hour of darkness at this season, she left her wharf, stopped off Staten Island, received aboard from a tug four officers and two hundred men, and stood to sea. A New York paper of the same afternoon announced the movement.[1] The news appeared also in the *Constitution* (of Washington), January 8, a fact upon which Secretary Thompson based his right to telegraph the news the same day to Charleston. Senator Wigfall also telegraphed on the 8th, so that Charleston was fully informed the evening before the ship's arrival. Colonel Thomas sent a letter from New York, January 5, to Anderson, of general advice regarding the movement, which directed him, "should a fire, likely to prove injurious, be opened upon any vessel bringing reinforcements or supplies, or upon tow boats within reach of your guns, they may be employed to silence such fire; and you may act in like manner in case a fire is opened upon Fort Sumter itself." [2]

This letter, which should have been sent by a special messenger in the inception of the arrangement, did not reach Anderson in time, his only intimation of the ship's coming being a paragraph in a Charleston evening paper of January 8, which

[1] Crawford, *Fort Sumter*, 176.
[2] *War Records*, Serial No. 1, p. 132.

was not believed, as Anderson had not thought it
possible that any but a ship of war would be sent.
Thus no special arrangements at Sumter were made
or orders given to meet this most important emergency.[1]

Few things reflect more discredit upon American
administration than the failure of the *Star of the
West* to render the service intended. Arriving off
Charleston at 1.30 in the morning of January 9, the
harbor lights were found extinguished, and it was
not until 4 A.M. that a light, supposed to be on
Sumter, was made. At daybreak a vessel inshore
fired colored signals and steamed up the channel.
As soon as the leading marks could be made out, the
Star of the West, with colors at the peak, moved up
the channel. When abreast Cummings Point (the
northern end of Morris Island) and "within one
and three quarter miles of Forts Sumter and Moultrie,"[2] fire was opened by the battery there, one
shot from which struck abaft the port fore-channels
and one near the rudder, doing no important damage. A large American ensign was now hoisted at
the fore, put aboard at New York by Colonel
Thomas with instructions to be so used if fired
upon, and with the statement that "Major Anderson would understand it and protect the ship under the guns of Sumter." As the ship approached

---

[1] Crawford, *Fort Sumter*, 185.
[2] Report of Lieutenant Woods, commanding troops, *War
Records*, Serial No. 1, p. 10.

Moultrie, which had to be passed at about three-quarters of a mile, "a steamer was seen approaching with an armed schooner in tow, and the battery on the island firing on us all the time and having no cannon to defend ourselves from the attack of the vessels, we concluded that to avoid certain capture or destruction, we would endeavor to get to sea, consequently we wore round and steered down the channel, the battery firing upon us until the shot fell short." [1] The ship was back at New York Saturday, January 12.

Captain (later General) Doubleday's account is so graphic that it must be given in his own words: "Soon after daylight on the morning of the 9th I was on the parapet with my spyglass; for I fancied from a signal I had observed the previous evening on a pilot boat that something must be coming. As I looked seaward I saw a large steamer pass the bar and enter the Morris Island channel. It had the ordinary United States flag up; and as it evidently did not belong to the navy, I came to the conclusion it must be the *Star of the West*. . . . Anderson himself was still in bed. When the vessel came opposite the new battery which had been built by the cadets, I saw a shot fired to bring her to. Soon after an immense United States garrison flag was run up at the fore. . . . I dashed down to Anderson's room. . . . He told me to have the long roll beaten, and to post the men on the parapet.

[1] Captain McGowan's report, *N. Y. Times*, January 14, 1861.

. . . It took but a few minutes for men and officers to form at the guns. . . . The battery was still firing, but the transport had passed by and was rapidly getting out of range. At the same time it was approaching within gunshot of Fort Moultrie. The latter immediately opened fire from one or two guns. Anderson would not allow us to return this fire; and the captain of the vessel, wholly discouraged by our failure to respond, turned about. . . . We had one or two guns bearing on Fort Moultrie; and as that was within easy range we could have kept down the fire there long enough to enable the steamer to come in." [1]

Fine as Anderson's conduct in general was, it here fell short both of duty and the traditions of the service. The moment was one for action which would have covered his name with highest honor; he hesitated, the ship fled, and what might have become a great turning-point of the time became a ridiculous fiasco. Anderson listened to advice which tallied too much with his own feelings. Of those proffering it, no doubt with good intentions, was Lieutenant Meade (who later joined the South), who earnestly advised that fire should not be opened, as it would at once "initiate civil war," [2] and that the governor would repudiate the act. The attack was war; and there should have been not a moment's hesitancy in treating it as such.

[1] Doubleday, *Sumter and Moultrie*, 102–104.
[2] Crawford, *Fort Sumter*, 186.

The fault was in the ineptitude of the government itself: in its not giving Anderson in the outset of preparation full and definite information of its intention; in its repeated admonitions to preserve the peace; in not sending the troops in a man-of-war, or, if sent in a merchant vessel, in not placing the ship under the direction of a naval officer. The duty under the circumstances was one which it was scarcely possible to expect the merchant captain to fill successfully. To give its leadership to one unaccustomed to war, whose whole life had been an education merely in the navigation and preservation of his ship, was an act of bad judgment which it is difficult to criticise too harshly. But had he received any support; had his signals, made by lowering and hoisting the ensign at the fore, been noticed in any way (the fort halyards unfortunately fouled);[1] above all, had Sumter fired a single gun to hearten him, the captain and the officer in command of the troops aboard would probably have held to their duty and run all risks.

The risks were not great. The raw volunteers in the batteries had never been trained to use the guns; the results of the two shots which struck the ship showed no more, in fact, than that the powder used was of a very deteriorated sort, and any vessels of the port which might have attempted to pass in the narrow waters between Sumter and Moultrie

[1] Crawford, *Fort Sumter*, 186.

would have been quickly sunk by the guns of the former in expert hands.

But the chief personal blame must fall upon Scott, in changing from the *Brooklyn* and the trained men at Fort Monroe to the *Star of the West* and raw recruits. Even if the batteries had dared to fire upon the former, which was most unlikely, her own heavy battery of twenty - two 9 - inch guns would have quickly silenced their feeble efforts; no naval commander could have hesitated a moment to return such fire; Sumter would have been reinforced, and the ship herself would have been a powerful fort in the harbor to resist future attack, even had Moultrie and the Morris Island battery been left undestroyed. There would have been no future question of holding Charleston harbor. It was, however, an era of failure; it required the rough school of defeat and humiliation to teach the way of moral courage and success.

Scott, says Lincoln's secretaries, "had never favored the plan of sending the *Brooklyn*. Two insuperable objections to it appeared to his professional judgment. It was affirmed that the vessel, by reason of her deep draft, could not cross the Charleston bar, unless under circumstances exceptionally favorable. Her arrival at low tide, or during a storm, would delay and most likely defeat her entrance by giving notice of her approach and time to organize resistance. But the second objection was even more imperative. Fort Monroe was one

of the two most important strongholds on the whole
Atlantic coast. . . . To strip it of two hundred men
. . . would be to place it in extreme jeopardy." [1]
Neither of these was a valid reason.   The *Brooklyn*,
with everything she could conveniently carry, drew
but sixteen feet three inches.   She could have been
made easily to draw but fifteen and a half feet.[2]
There was no need for loading her deeply, as coal
and stores could have been sent separately.   As to
the defence of Fort Monroe, the two hundred men
withdrawn could have been simultaneously replaced by the recruits from New York as easily as
they were sent to Charleston.   It, in fact, only
needed efficiency in the war department, backed by
a resolute president, to have saved and completely
altered the situation.

Even when it was decided to send the *Brooklyn*
to aid the *Star of the West* in case of injury to the
latter, and to convey an order of recall to Hampton
Roads should she fail, the orders were not issued
until January 7, two days after the ship had left
New York, and did not reach the *Brooklyn* until
January 9, the day the *Star of the West* reached
Charleston.   The *Brooklyn* left Norfolk at 11.20
A.M. the same day the orders were received, and arrived off Charleston the 12th.   Speaking a schooner
leaving Charleston for New York, Captain Walker,
of the *Brooklyn*, heard of the ill success of the *Star*

[1] Nicolay and Hay, *Abraham Lincoln*, III., 94.
[2] From official data.

of the West. His orders required him not to attempt to cross the bar, and there was nothing to do but return to Hampton Roads, as his orders directed.[1]

Immediately after the disappearance of the *Star of the West*, Anderson called a council of his officers, who were much divided in opinion as to the question of closing the port and firing upon vessels or batteries.[2] The milder course was adopted of sending by an officer a letter to the governor demanding to know if the firing was without his sanction, for "under that hope, and that alone," said Anderson, "did I refrain from opening fire upon your batteries. . . . If it be not disclaimed . . . I must regard it as an act of war, and . . . shall not, after a reasonable time for the return of my messenger, permit any vessels to pass within range of the guns of my fort." Anderson, in closing, expressed a hope, however, that the answer might be such as to justify a further continuance of forbearance on his part.[3]

It was scarcely possible that Anderson could expect a disavowal; the same day brought from the governor an elaborate rehearsal of the situation, which said, in closing: "The act is perfectly justified by me. In regard to your threat to vessels in the harbor, it is only necessary to say that you must

---

[1] *Naval War Records*, IV., 220, 221.
[2] Crawford, *Fort Sumter*, 187.
[3] *War Records*, Serial No. 1, p. 124.

judge of your own responsibilities." [1] This reply, insulting in tone and substance, was really a declaration of war; and, if not regarded as such by Anderson, should have been so taken by the government to the extent at least of reinforcing the fort at all hazards.

Anderson informed Governor Pickens that he would refer the matter and await instructions. Lieutenant Talbot left the same evening for Washington, with a safe-conduct as bearer of despatches. The reply of the secretary of war was not sent until January 16. Anderson was then informed that the president fully approved his forbearance to return the fire; but the most important sentence was: "Whenever in your judgment additional supplies or re-enforcements are necessary for your safety or for a successful defense of the fort, you will at once communicate the fact to this Department and a prompt and vigorous effort will be made to forward them." [2]

How much this meant can be known only by taking as a context a despatch sent by Anderson December 31, and received in Washington January 5, in which he said: "Thank God we are now where the Government may send us additional troops at its leisure; . . . we can command this harbor as long as our Government wishes to keep it." [3] Acting on this information, a telegram was actually sent from

---

[1] *War Records*, Serial No. 1, 135.
[2] *Ibid.*, 140.   [3] *Ibid.*, 120.

Washington countermanding the sailing of the *Star of the West;* but she had already left.[1] The result of Anderson's statement was most unhappy; in the future the responsibility, technically, was on Anderson and not on the war department, to which he had given so strong an assurance of his ability to hold his own. Nevertheless, there should have been, and there was, ability enough in the department to recognize that sixty men could not work the forty-eight heavy guns already mounted. Deep incapacity and ignorance seem to have ruled, despite the well meaning of an able and thoroughly energetic secretary of war, supported by a secretary of state whose memorandum to General Scott, January 16, shows the stress of mind under which labored these two loyal civilians, groping for military advice and eager for action. Black asked: " 1. Is it the duty of the Government to re-enforce Major Anderson? 2. If yes, how soon is it necessary that these re-enforcements should be there? 3. What obstacles exist to prevent the sending of such re-enforcements at any time when it may be necessary to do so?" Black then proceeded to expound at length his own views, in substance as follows:

I. It seems settled that Anderson is to be withdrawn; his position is so nearly impregnable that attack at present is improbable, and he had provisions for two months. The fort is now in a state of siege: in the course of a few weeks it will be

[1] Buchanan, *Administration on Eve of Rebellion,* 191.

very difficult for him to hold out; the men will be exhausted; his surrender is a question of time only; unless ordered to surrender at once, relief must be sent him.

II. Can we justify delay? The South Carolina authorities are increasing their ability to prevent reinforcement every hour; it is certain Anderson could have all he needs with very little risk, if the effort be made immediately; but it is impossible to predict cost in blood and money if postponed two or three months.

III. I am persuaded the difficulty of relief is much magnified by some. From you I shall be able to ascertain whether I or they be mistaken. A pirate or slaver assured of five hundred dollars would laugh the danger to scorn. But suppose it impossible for an unarmed vessel, what is the difficulty of sending the *Brooklyn* or *Macedonian* in? The *Brooklyn* draws ordinarily only sixteen and a half feet, and her draught can be reduced eighteen inches by putting her on an even keel. The shallowest place will give her eighteen feet at high tide. In point of fact, she has crossed the bar more than once. But the government has three or four smaller steamers of light draught and great speed which could be armed and at sea in a few days, and would not be troubled by any opposition they might meet at the entrance. Your opinion, of course, will be conclusive with me.[1]

[1] *War Records*, Serial No. 1, pp. 140–142.

The only answer made to this was a memorandum in General Scott's best turgidity of style: "Lieutenant - General Scott received the Hon. Mr. Black's communication yesterday at too late an hour and in the midst of too complexing engagements to attend to it. The moment he is released by the War Department this morning, General Scott will seek Mr. Black, and repeat his efforts till he has had the pleasure of finding him at the Department of State Thursday morning."[1] The question, so far as official records show, ended here: the general did not meet the secretary;[2] there was no advice given, no action taken.

Nor were other offers of effective plans of relief wanting. Commander Ward, of the navy, proposed to employ four or more coast-survey steamers. Scott had no doubt this would succeed, but the president would not allow the attempt.[3] Another plan, which was later to receive attention, was presented by G. V. Fox, an ex-officer of the navy, who became assistant secretary of the navy in the next administration: "From the outer edge of the Charleston bar in a straight line to Sumter through the Swash Channel the distance is 4 miles, with no shoal spots having less than 9 feet at high water. The batteries on Morris and Sullivan's islands are about 2600 yards apart, and between these troops and supplies must pass. I proposed to anchor three small men-of-war off the entrance to the

[1] Crawford, *Fort Sumter*, 240.   [2] *Ibid.*
[3] *War Records*, Serial No. 1, p. 197.

Swash Channel as a safe base of operations against any naval attack from the enemy, the soldiers and provisions to be carried to the Charleston bar in the Collins steamer *Baltic*, all the provisions and munitions to be put in portable packages easily handled by one man, the *Baltic* to carry 300 extra sailors and a sufficient number of armed launches to land all the troops at Fort Sumter in one night. Three steam tugs of not more than 6 feet draft of water . . . were . . . to be used for carrying in the troops and provisions in case the weather should be too rough for boats. With the exception of the men-of-war and tugs, the whole expedition was to be complete on board the *Baltic*, and its success depended upon the possibility of running past batteries at night, which were distant from the center of the channel 1300 yards." [1]

This plan, undoubtedly feasible,[2] was presented February 4, and, on the 7th, Scott, who approved the plan, presented Fox to Holt, who agreed to present the matter to the president that evening. February 8, however, the day after the election of Davis to the presidency of the Confederacy, Scott informed Fox that probably no effort would be made to relieve Sumter. Scott "seemed much disappointed and astonished." [3]

[1] *Naval War Records*, IV., 245, 247.
[2] Chisholm, "Notes on the Surrender of Fort Sumter," in *Battles and Leaders of the Civil War*, I., 83.
[3] *Naval War Records*, IV., 246.

Anderson's hesitancy and overcaution quickly bore further fruit. January 11, four hulks were sunk across the harbor entrance, and shortly after noon of the same day a boat brought Magrath, secretary of state of South Carolina, and Jamison, secretary of war, to demand the delivery of Sumter. Anderson again assembled the officers and put to them the question of acceding or not to the demand. They were unanimously opposed, though a marked impression was made upon them, long kept as they had been in ignorance of the intentions of the government. Judge Magrath, addressing the improvised council, said "that President Buchanan was in his dotage; that the Government at Washington was breaking up; that all was confusion, despair, and disorder there; and that it was full time for us to look out for our own safety, for if we refused to give up the fort nothing could prevent the Southern troops from exterminating us. He ended this tragical statement by saying, 'May God Almighty enable you to come to a just decision.'" [1]

Anderson, asking why they did not first attempt diplomacy, offered, if the South Carolina authorities would send a commissioner to Washington to present their claims, to send an officer "to represent the condition of the fort, and the Government could then form its own judgment and come to some decision." Again, of course, it was playing the secessionists' own game of delay, and in a way which

[1] Doubleday, *Sumter and Moultrie*, 107, 108.

could not have better suited their purposes. This truce, for such it practically was, was eagerly accepted.[1] The South-Carolinians were but too well aware of their weakness; they had, on January 1, but three 24-pounders on Morris Island, manned by a force "not a man of whom probably ever saw a 24-pounder manipulated or fired."[2] At this time it has been truly said, "The Charleston insurrection was as weak and defenseless as a new born infant."[3]

The governor's envoy, I. W. Hayne, the attorney-general of South Carolina, and Major Anderson's messenger, Lieutenant Hall, left Charleston January 12, the former bearing the demand of Governor Pickens for the delivery of Sumter. They arrived at Washington the next day, and then began a conspiracy for a delay which could only tie the hands of the Federal government, and give time to complete the full scheme of secession and to prepare for the capture of Sumter.

On advice, in a note to Hayne from nine southern senators, Jefferson Davis at the head,[4] Governor Pickens's letter was not delivered. Instead, the president was called upon by various persons, especially by Senator Clay, of Alabama, January 16, who pressed for a withdrawal from Sumter. He was informed by the president that this would not

[1] Doubleday, *Sumter and Moultrie*, 109.
[2] Report of General James Simons to Governor Pickens, in *S. C. House Journal*, 1861, pp. 177–179.
[3] Nicolay and Hay, *Abraham Lincoln*, III., 121.
[4] Buchanan, *Administration on Eve of Rebellion*, 197.

be done under any circumstances. Clay, mentioning that he had come from the seceding senators,
said they wanted Hayne to remain a few days and
submit a proposition to the government of South
Carolina to agree that Anderson should be placed
in his former position, the government to have free
access to him; that he should be free to buy all the
provisions needed, and that he should not be disturbed if not reinforced. He injected the remark
that "there was a truce agreed upon so long as
Hayne was" in Washington. Buchanan replied
that he "had understood that there had been."
Clay went on to say that the truce might be continued even until the 4th of March, and Buchanan
replied that the truce would continue until Colonel
Hayne left, which "he supposed would be in a few
days." "I told him," says Buchanan, "I could
say nothing further on the subject of the truce, nor
could I express any opinion on the subjects to
which he had referred, unless the proposition were
reduced to writing, and presented to me in a distinct form. He said I need be under no apprehensions as to the security of the fort. He had just
come from Jefferson Davis, who said it could not be
taken; and Lars Anderson had informed him that
Major Anderson said he did not require reinforcements." Clay thereupon "got up and said he
would go to those who had sent him, and it would
be for them to decide upon the proposition." [1]

[1] Curtis, *Buchanan*, II., 452–454.

Many writers have deprecated applying the word "conspiracy" to the secession movement; but if the word is suitable for a secret, long-continued, and concerted movement, the term is just. On January 5, Senators Davis and Brown, of Mississippi; Hemphill and Wigfall, of Texas; Slidell and Benjamin, of Louisiana; Iverson and Toombs, of Georgia; Johnson, of Arkansas; Clay, of Alabama; Yulee and Mallory, of Florida, met in Washington and passed resolutions for the immediate secession of their respective states, and for a convention at Montgomery, Alabama, to meet not later than February 16, to organize a southern confederacy; they requested instructions from their friends as to whether the delegations were to remain in Congress until March 4, so as to defeat threatened hostile legislation.[1] As one of them privately expressed it, "By remaining in our places . . . it is thought we can keep the hands of Mr. Buchanan tied and disable the Republicans from effecting any legislation which will strengthen the hands of the incoming administration."[2] Extraordinary ethics which could permit men sworn to support the Constitution, and paid out of the Federal treasury, to use their official position to conspire for the downfall of their government!

The fact that the action of this cabal was almost at once published, and that it was openly mentioned in southern conventions, does not divest it of its

[1] *War Records*, Serial No. 1, p. 443.
[2] Yulee to Finegan, January 7, 1861, in *ibid.*

true character. It is impossible in our country to keep secret proceedings of a character designed to influence many widely separated individuals; but the intent of secrecy undoubtedly existed. Even the southern leaders were not so disregardful of place and circumstances as to flaunt willingly such action in the face of the president, or such designs upon legislation in the face of their northern colleagues.[1]

Mr. Davis, twenty years later, indignantly proclaimed the absurdity of the statement;[2] but it is very difficult to accept this opinion in face of the resolutions of January 5, which he signed, and of a letter to Governor Pickens, January 13, in which he said: "I take it for granted that the time allowed to the garrison of Fort Sumter has been diligently employed by yourselves, so that before you could be driven out of your earthworks you will be able to capture the fort which commands them"; and, January 20, "The occurrence of the *Star of the West* seems to me to put you in the best condition for delay, so long as the Government permits that matter to rest where it is. Your friends here think you can well afford to stand still, so far as the presence of a garrison is concerned, and if things continue as they are for a month, we shall then be in a condition to speak with a voice which all must hear and heed." [3] Nor can it be reconciled with the

---

[1] Contemporary opinion, *National Intelligencer*, January 14, 1861.   [2] Davis, *Confederate Government*, I., 200–202.

[3] Crawford, *Fort Sumter*, 263–265.

action of such men as Senators Wigfall and Mallory, who bristled with telegrams and advice to the secession leaders in the South, crowned as such action was by that of Floyd and Thompson in the cabinet.

In weighing Davis's statement one must consider his peculiarly sophistical mental make-up. No man could more easily deceive himself. He could constantly declare himself no disunionist while instigating secession in the strongest terms. A memorable instance is a speech of 1858, in which he said: "Neither in that year [1852], nor in any other, have I ever advocated a dissolution of the Union, or a separation of the State of Mississippi from the Union, except as the last alternative. . . . I hold . . . that whilst occupying a seat in the Senate, I am bound to maintain the Government of the Constitution, and in no manner to work for its destruction; that the obligation of the oath of office, Mississippi's honor and my own, require that as a Senator of the United States, there should be no want of loyalty to the Constitutional Union." [1] In almost the next words of this speech he is able to declare that if an abolitionist be chosen president (and the word abolitionist in the southern view included every Republican), whether by the House of Representatives or by the people, the state of Mississippi should provide for its safety outside the

[1] *Daily Mississippian*, November 15, 1858, quoted by Nicolay and Hay, *Abraham Lincoln*, III., 210.

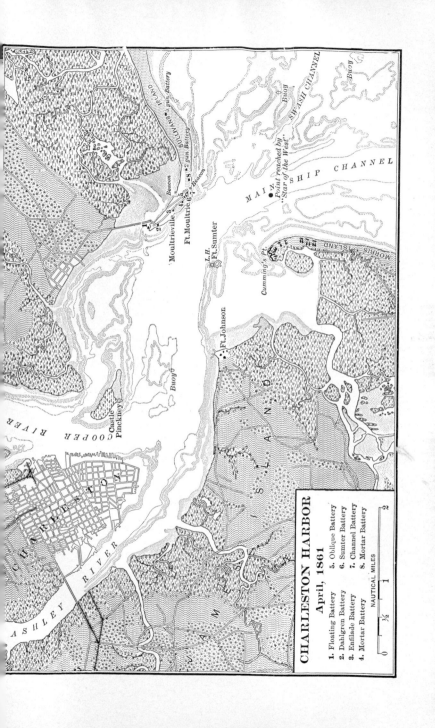

CHARLESTON HARBOR
April, 1861

1. Floating Battery   5. Oblique Battery
2. Dahlgren Battery   6. Sumter Battery
3. Enfilade Battery   7. Channel Battery
4. Mortar Battery   8. Mortar Battery

NAUTICAL MILES

Union, and "as when I had the privilege of address-ing the Legislature a year ago, so now do I urge you to the needful preparation to meet whatever contingency may befall us" by the establishment of an arsenal for the manufacture and repair of arms. And by January 5, 1861, we find him doing that which "his oath, Mississippi's honor and his own," demanded he should not do.

There was at least one beneficial result of the mission of the *Star of the West*, in the resignation of the secretary of the interior, Thompson, January 7, and that of Thomas, of the treasury, January 11. The former was guilty of traitorous action in send-ing information to Charleston of the mission of the *Star of the West*. He offered the excuse that honor compelled him to keep promise with a friend,[1] as if such promise could take precedence of his oath of office and his duty to the government of which he was a minister! The resignation of Thomas was forced by information from Wall Street to the president, that not a dollar would be forthcoming until he should place men in the cabinet upon whom the Union could depend.[2] John A. Dix, then postmaster at New York, was named by a meeting of leading men as one whose appointment would be required. The president offered him the war department, of which until now Holt was only acting secretary; but Dix, knowing that the under-

[1] Thompson's letter, *National Intelligencer*, January 11, 1861.
[2] Dix, *Dix*, I., 362.

standing of the meeting mentioned was that he should be secretary of the treasury, declined. The resignation of Thomas was then, January 11, placed in the hands of the president. Dix was appointed the next day, and Holt confirmed at the same time as secretary of war, the vacancy in the department of the interior remaining unfilled. There was an immediate reversal of the attitude of the money power; the ominous financial deadlock was at once broken, and the government put in possession of the funds it so much needed.[1]

From the time of his appointment to the end of the administration, Dix was a resident of the White House. How different an atmosphere was brought into it is shown in his action regarding the revenue-cutters at the Gulf ports. On January 18 he sent a treasury official to New Orleans with orders to provision the cutters and send them to New York. January 29 he received a despatch advising him that the captain of the *McClelland* refused to obey the order. Dix at once sent a telegram ordering his arrest and the command to be turned over to a lieutenant. The despatch ended with a phrase which was to become a Unionist watchword: "If any one attempts to haul down the American flag, shoot him on the spot."[2] Notwithstanding, however, the two cutters at New Orleans remained in secessionist hands, and were burned a year later to prevent their falling into the hands of Farragut.

[1] Dix, *Dix*, I., 362, 363.   [2] *Ibid.*, 371.

CHAPTER XV

FORT PICKENS AND THE CONFEDERACY
(JANUARY, 1861–FEBRUARY, 1861)

THE long show of diplomatic etiquette caused
by the visit of Hayne had one break, in the
occupancy, by Lieutenant Slemmer and his company of forty-eight men, of Fort Pickens, a large
and important work at the western end of Santa
Rosa Island, which forms the south side of the
extensive bay of Pensacola. Slemmer acted under
orders of the war department, of January 3, 1861,
to do his utmost to prevent the seizure of either of
the forts in Pensacola harbor by surprise or assault,
issued when the president found himself in a more
courageous spirit through the resistance to the
South Carolina commissioners. With the assistance
of the gun-boat *Wyandotte* and store-ship *Supply*,
after spiking the guns at forts Barrancas and McRee,
and destroying ten tons of powder by pouring it
into the sea, he transferred the rest of the powder
and stores during January 9, 10, and 11.[1] But the
Pensacola navy-yard, seven miles west of the town,
with its great store of guns and other material, was

[1] *War Records*, Serial No. 1, pp. 334–336.

sacrificed under circumstances to deserve the deepest condemnation, no attempt at resistance being made to the three or four hundred Florida militia who appeared January 12, two days after the secession of the state, at the yard gates, although there was at the yard a guard of forty marines and some sixty other men who could have been armed, besides the steamer *Wyandotte*, with a crew of sixty men and an armament of four 32-pounders, and the ship *Supply*, with a crew of thirty-five, a force ample, supported as it was by the *Wyandotte's* guns, to repel any number of militia brought against it.[1]

Equal culpability and folly was shown by the secretary of the navy, who did at last act, but too late. For many weeks a strong squadron had been lying at Vera Cruz, for the protection of American interests, including the steamer *Powhatan*, flag-ship, the steam-gunboat *Pocahontas*, the sailing frigates *Sabine* and *Cumberland*, and the sloop-of-war *St. Louis*. It was not until December 24 that orders were issued for the *St. Louis*, and January 5 for the *Sabine*, to proceed to Pensacola. With the slow mail service of the day, it was not until January 21 that the orders were received by Commodore Pendergrast, who at once despatched the two ships, but, under instructions, retained the most useful and necessary of all, the *Powhatan*, whose mere presence would have held the place beyond the possibility of attack. Had orders been sent to Vera Cruz by

[1] *Naval War Records*, IV., 16–56.

the *Wyandotte* even so late as January 3, the *Powhatan* could have been in Pensacola by January 10, the sailing distance being but eight hundred miles. The president's spasm of energy lasted, however, sufficiently to enable orders to be given, January 21, 1861, for the *Brooklyn* to carry from Fort Monroe to Fort Pickens Captain Vogdes's company of artillery, with orders for Vogdes to take over the command at Pickens, "as well as that of other forts and barracks which it may be in your power to occupy and defend, with the co-operation of any naval commander or commanders at hand, though it is understood that Fort Barrancas and probably Fort McRee are already in the hands of the seceders." But a postscript nullified the whole spirit of the order: "You are to understand that you are not to attempt any reoccupation or recapture involving hostile collision, but that you are to confine yourself strictly to the defensive." [1]

Ex-President Tyler, who had but just arrived in Washington as one of the commissioners from Virginia to the "Peace Conference," heard, January 25, of the despatch of the *Brooklyn*, and at once sent a note to the president questioning him in the matter. He received reply that the *Brooklyn* was "on an errand of mercy and relief," and that her movement was in no way connected with South Carolina. But this was not enough for the self-constituted secession committee of senators. Not

[1] *War Records*, Serial No. 1, p. 352.

knowing the passive orders given, there was in the *Brooklyn's* errand a possibility in their minds of a reoccupation of the Pensacola navy-yard, an easy task for such a ship; and Senator Mallory was hurried there to arrange that nothing should occur. All happened as they desired.   Despite his repeated declarations that he would make no pledge, which he had but repeated in his message of January 28 commending the Virginia resolution to Congress, the president, on January 29, gave orders in a despatch signed by both the secretary of war and the secretary of the navy that, "In consequence of the assurances received from Mr. Mallory in a telegram of yesterday to Messrs. Slidell, Hunter, and Bigler . . . that Fort Pickens would not be assaulted, and an offer of such an assurance to the same effect from Colonel Chase for the purpose of avoiding a hostile collision, upon receiving satisfactory assurances from Mr. Mallory and Colonel Chase [commanding the Florida forces] that Fort Pickens will not be attacked you are instructed not to land the company on board the *Brooklyn* unless said fort shall be attacked or preparations shall be made for its attack.   The provisions necessary for the supply of the fort you will land. . . . The commissioners of different States are to meet here on Monday, the 4th February, and it is important that during their session a collision of arms should be avoided. . . . Your right . . . to communicate with the Government by special messenger, and its right in the

same manner to communicate with yourselves and
them, will remain intact as the basis on which the
present instruction is given." [1]

How one-sided was the truce will be seen by
the preparations continued at Charleston, where
batteries were strengthened and extended, a float
built carrying a battery protected with railway
iron, and, while the place was rendered unattack-
able by any force at the government's command,
and the eventual fate of Sumter made certain, the
now powerful naval force off Pensacola, reinforced
by the *Brooklyn*, the frigates *Macedonian* (ordered
from Portsmouth, New Hampshire, January 5),
Sabine, and *St. Louis*, idly looked on the desolate
sand-beaches which mark the entrance to Pensacola
Bay, which it had but to enter, and the navy-yard,
with its hundreds of guns, later to go to arm
the batteries of Port Hudson and Vicksburg, would
have been again in possession of the United States
government. The hands of the president were indeed tied, but by himself.

On February 4, 1861, the delegates of six states
—South Carolina, Mississippi, Florida, Alabama,
Georgia, and Louisiana—met at Montgomery, Alabama. The states had passed ordinances of secession in the order named; the first, December 20,
1860; the others, January 9, 10, 11, 19, and 26,
1861. The delegates were apportioned as were the
senators and representatives in the Congress of the

[1] *Naval War Records*, IV., 74.

Union, but voting by states as units. The date of meeting had been advanced from February 15, on a resolution of the Mississippi legislature of January 29, urged by the governor of South Carolina; and it is "another evidence of the secret and swift concert of secession leaders, that in six days thereafter the delegates" of every cotton state but Texas (which was represented provisionally February 14) were thus assembled.[1] Howell Cobb, of Georgia, was elected permanent chairman. As it was impossible that it should remain, with any efficacy, as a convention, it was determined that it should declare itself, on its own authority, the congress of a provisional government; and it thus exercised for the time all the functions of government, executive as well as legislative. In the opinion of Alexander H. Stephens, the congress, taken all in all, was "the ablest, soberest, most intelligent and conservative body" he "was ever in. . . . Nobody looking on would ever take this Congress for a set of revolutionists."[2]

Four days after the convention assembled a "Constitution for the Provisional Government of the Confederate States of America"[3] was adopted, a speed which again indicated the intimate working together of the leaders.

[1] Nicolay and Hay, *Abraham Lincoln*, III., 197.
[2] Johnston and Browne, *Stephens*, 392.
[3] See Davis, *Confederate Government*, I., 640–648; compared with U. S. Constitution, *Am. Annual Cyclop.*, 1861, p. 155.

The next day the officers and members of the congress were sworn to support the provisional constitution, and proceeded to elect a president. States had one vote each, and Jefferson Davis received the whole six; Alexander H. Stephens was elected vice-president. A considerable number had favored Howell Cobb and Toombs, both of Georgia, and particularly the latter, for the presidency. Toombs is stated to have been the choice of the South Carolina, Florida, Louisiana, and possibly the Alabama delegations, and in the opinion of Stephens had qualifications for the presidency superior to those of any other connected with the secession movement. His name was, however, not brought forward in the convention, apparently through a misunderstanding as to the preference of Georgia for Cobb.[1] The laws of the United States in force November 1, 1860, which were not inconsistent with the provisional constitution were continued; committees were appointed on all principal subjects, and also a committee of two from each state to report a permanent constitution, which was submitted to the states a month later.

Though Mississippi had seceded January 9, Florida on the 10th, and Alabama on the 11th, and in their own theory were foreign countries, it was not until January 21 that the senators from these states received official notification; and meanwhile

[1] Johnston and Browne, *Stephens*, 389–391; Stephens, *War between the States*, II., 329–333.

they defiantly retained their places in the Senate. Davis, January 21, took leave in a speech of much pathos and sensibility,[1] and left for home shortly after. It was there that he received the news of his election as president of the newly organized Southern Confederacy, news which, he mentions, surprised and disappointed him. He had, he says, thought himself "better adapted to command in the field, and Mississippi had given me the position which I preferred to any other—the highest rank in her army." He regarded the presidency as temporary, and expected "soon to be with the army of Mississippi again." On his way to Montgomery, and while waiting for the train at Jackson, the capital of the state, he met Chief-Justice Sharkey, who was looking for him to ask if he believed there would be war. Davis's "opinion was freely given, that there *would* be war, long and bloody, and that it behooved every one to put his house in order."[2]

The organization of the machinery of the Confederate government proceeded rapidly. Executive departments were created, and by March 7 an army of 100,000 men was authorized; bills were passed for a loan of $15,000,000, payable in ten years at eight per cent., for which an export duty after August 1, 1861, of one-eighth of a cent per pound on cotton was pledged; all questions between the states of the Confederacy and the United

[1] Alfriend, *Jefferson Davis*, 225–230.
[2] Davis, *Confederate Government*, I., 230.

States as to forts and other property were taken over; a declaration was made, February 15, that "immediate steps should be taken to obtain possession of forts Sumter and Pickens," and authorizing President Davis to carry the resolution into effect; the United States tariff of 1857 was continued in force, and a national flag adopted.

President Davis was inaugurated February 18, with all the pomp and ceremony attainable in the small town which was the temporary capital. In his inaugural speech he claimed the right of secession as undeniable, and denied that it was revolution; he announced that if "we may not hope to avoid war, we may at least expect that posterity will acquit us of having needlessly engaged in it. Doubly justified by the absence of wrong on our part and by wanton aggression on the part of others, there can be no cause to doubt that the courage and patriotism of the people of the Confederate States will be found equal to any measures of defense which honor and security may require."[1] He declared reunion neither practicable nor desirable.

President Davis appointed in his cabinet Robert Toombs, of Georgia, as secretary of state; C. G. Memminger, of South Carolina, secretary of the treasury; L. P. Walker, of Alabama, secretary of war; S. R. Mallory, of Florida, secretary of the navy; J. H. Reagan, of Texas, postmaster-general;

[1] Stephens, *War between the States*, II., 340 – 344; Alfriend, *Jefferson Davis*, 241.

and Judah P. Benjamin, of Louisiana, as attorney-general. To negotiate friendly relations and to settle all questions of disagreement between the Confederate States "and their late confederates of the United States in relation to the public property and the public debt," as called for by Article VI. of the provisional constitution, Davis appointed A. B. Roman, of Louisiana, Martin J. Crawford, of Georgia, and John Forsyth, of Alabama, with plenary powers for such adjustment.

The permanent constitution, adopted March 11 (but which did not go into force until 1862), followed closely the phraseology of the Constitution of the United States. The essential differences were as follows: legislative powers were *delegated*, not granted; the word *slaves* was used instead of *other persons;* any judicial or other federal officer resident and acting solely within the limits of any state might be impeached by a vote of two-thirds of both branches of the legislature; congress could grant to the heads of the executive departments seats upon the floor of either house, with the privilege of discussing any measures pertaining to their departments; the president could approve any appropriation and disapprove any other appropriation in the same bill; no bounties could be granted or protective duties laid; congress could not appropriate money for internal improvement except for aids to navigation, improvement of harbors, and removal of obstructions in river navigation; to defray the costs and expenses of these, duties were to be laid on the navigation facilitated; the importation of slaves, except from the slave-holding states or territories of the United States, was forbidden; and congress was also given the power to prohibit the introduction of slaves from any state not a member of, or any territory not belonging to, the Confederacy; no law denying or impairing the right of property in negro slaves could be passed; no duty could be laid on exports except by a vote of two-thirds of both houses; no appropriation of money could be made unless asked and estimated for by heads of departments, and submitted to the president; all bills were to specify the exact amount of each appropriation; every law must relate to but one subject, expressed in the title; the president and vice-president were to hold office for six years, but the president was not re-eligible; all civil officers of the executive departments could be removed by the president when their services were unnecessary, or for certain sound reasons, and, when so removed, the removal, except in the case of principal executive and diplomatic officers, was to be reported to the senate with the reasons therefor; new territory could be acquired, and, in all such, negro slavery as it exists in the Confederate States was to be recognized and protected by congress and by the territorial government, and the inhabitants of the Confederate States and territories had the right to take slaves to such territory; when five states should have ratified the constitution it should take effect.

This constitution was, in some respects, a distinct advance upon our own.   1. In enabling heads of departments to have seats upon the floor of either house, and the privilege of discussing any measures affecting their several departments—a privilege enjoyed during the provisional congress, but never confirmed by statute under the "permanent" government.   (Stephens would have gone further, and have required that they should be selected from the senate and the house.[1])   2. In enabling the president to disapprove appropriation bills in part.   3. In prohibiting bounties or protective legislation.   4. In limiting money appropriations, except by a two-thirds vote of both houses, to those asked for by the heads of departments.   5. In making the term of office of the president six years and making him non-re-eligible.

But the constitution was stamped throughout with slavery.   It was a direct throwing-down of the gauntlet before the civilized world, and a placing of the Confederacy across the road by which all other nations were travelling towards humane dealing and recognition of the inherent right of every man, in the words of Lincoln, "to eat the bread without the leave of anybody else, which his own hands earn." [2]   Stephens had foreseen this outcome, and

[1] Johnston and Browne, *Stephens*, 395.
[2] Nicolay and Hay, *Abraham Lincoln*, II., 149.

one ground of his opposition the previous year to
secession was that he foresaw that the policy was not
to leave the way open to the admission of some of
the non-slave-holding states; thinking some of the
western communities would be so inclined. He
urged that "We should be known as the 'Black
Republic,'" and as such should be without sympathy from any of the world outside.[1]

The organization of the Confederate government,
in February, transferred the question of Sumter
from Charleston to Montgomery. Toombs, then
acting, and later to be actual, secretary of state of
the Confederacy, wrote the governor of South Carolina not to attack "without the sanction and juris-
diction of our joint Government."[2] The governor
pressed the necessity of attack at the earliest possible moment, and it was to avoid this action that,
February 12, a resolution was passed by the Montgomery congress taking over "all questions and
difficulties . . . relating to the occupation of forts
. . . and other public establishments." State sus-
ceptibilities entered keenly into the question, and
the South Carolina authorities chafed at leaving
action in hands other than their own. When Governor Pickens was informed by telegraph of this
move, he replied, February 13, at length as to the
right of the state to act, and said that he was satisfied that the welfare of the new confederation, as

---

[1] Johnston and Browne, *Stephens*, 392.
[2] Crawford, *Fort Sumter*, 266.

well as the necessities of the state, required "that Fort Sumter should be reduced before the close of the present administration at Washington." Pickens held that if action be so taken, "Mr. Buchanan cannot resist, because he has not the power. Mr. Lincoln may not attack, because the cause of quarrel will have been, or may be considered by him; as past." [1]

Though but few of the southern leaders, in the earlier stages of secession, could bring themselves to think war even possible, they had now come to a clear view of its imminency and even certainty, unless the commissioners sent to Washington should succeed in negotiating an agreement. Beauregard, who had resigned from the United States service February 8, and was now a brigadier-general in the provisional army of the Confederacy, was thus summoned to Montgomery, February 22, and was ordered thence to Charleston to report to the governor of South Carolina for military duty in that state; he was authorized to receive not over five thousand men into the service of the Confederacy. He arrived at Charleston March 3, inspected the several works, including the floating battery, and on the 6th, by authority of the departments of war of both the Confederacy and the state of South Carolina, assumed command of all the forces now organized in South Carolina, amounting to ten

[1] Pickens to president of provisional congress, *Journal of Congress of Confederate States*, I., 56–58.

regiments with 8835 rank and file.[1]   Beauregard, in
his report to Walker, the Confederate secretary of
war, detailing the arrangement and armaments of
the batteries, said: "If Sumter was properly garrisoned and armed, it would be a perfect Gibraltar
to anything but constant shelling night and day
from the four points of the compass. As it is, the
weakness of the garrison constitutes our greatest
advantage, and we must, for the present, turn our
attention to prevent it from being re-enforced." [2]

Work on the batteries commanding Fort Sumter
was vigorously progressing, and fairly accurate accounts of its progress were sent almost daily to
Washington by Anderson and Foster, the engineer
officer.[3]   Anderson asked, February 16, the course
it would be proper for him to take if, without a
declaration of war, he should see the floating battery approaching the fort.[4]   The secretary of war
informed him, February 23, that he held Sumter as
he had held Moultrie, under the verbal orders communicated by Major Buell December 11; he was
ordered to remain strictly on the defensive as a
redemption of the implied pledge to Hayne in the
letter written by the secretary on behalf of the
president. The news that the question of the forts
had been taken over by the Confederate congress,
and that the decision "would probably be preceded
in its settlement by negotiation with the Govern-

[1] *War Records*, Serial No. 1, pp. 260, 265–267.
[2] *Ibid.*, 26.   [3] *Ibid.*, 158–195.   [4] *Ibid.*, 175.

ment of the United States, has impressed the President with a belief that there will be no immediate attack on Fort Sumter, and the hope is indulged that wise and patriotic counsels may prevail and prevent it altogether. The labors of the Peace Congress have not closed and the presence of that body here adds another to the powerful motives already existing for the adoption of every measure, except in necessary self-defense, for avoiding a collision with the forces that surround you." [1]

Simultaneous with Beauregard's arrival at Charleston was the advent of Crawford, one of the Confederate commissioners, at Washington. He at once wrote Toombs that he would have nothing more to do with Buchanan, because "his fears for his personal safety, the apprehension for the security of his property, together with the cares of State and his advanced age, render him wholly disqualified for his present position. He is as incapable now of purpose as a child." [2] This same impression was made upon a distinguished financier of New York, who came to Washington on the president's request, for consultation on the national finances, and found the unfortunate president anxious chiefly about his investments. [3] February 28, Anderson was informed by the war department that the Confederate commissioners were expected,

[1] *War Records*, Serial No. 1, p. 182.
[2] Crawford, *Fort Sumter*, 316.
[3] Alexander Duncan, personal statement to author.

and that "The Secretary [of war] entertains the hope that nothing will occur now of a hostile character."[1]

One can but wonder at the extraordinary blindness of the administration of which such documents are evidence; for Secretary Holt was not one of those who condoned in any wise the action of the South; and the press of the country called for action throughout the whole of this early period. How completely Buchanan had now yielded to the impression that matters might still be adjusted is shown by a spirit which it is scarcely too harsh to term grovelling, in countermanding the customary parade of the troops on Washington's birthday. The rumor of a plot to seize the capital caused the transfer, at the instigation of General Scott, of several companies from Fort Monroe, which, with those already at hand, made a force of nearly seven hundred regular troops. Scott had made careful arrangements for all contingencies, and the city was regarded as safe from an attack of which baseless rumors were afloat.[2] So much does imagination enhance men's fears that it was even supposed that the official presidential count might be interfered with; but this passed, February 13, with perfect quietude, and Vice-President Breckinridge announced Lincoln as the elected president.

As usual on Washington's birthday, the troops

---

[1] *War Records*, Serial No. 1, p. 187.
[2] *House Reports*, 36 Cong., 2 Sess., No. 79.

were intended to form part of the usual parade of February 22, and the orders for the arrangements were published, when Ex-President Tyler, president of the Peace Convention, intervened and influenced Mr. Buchanan to give orders, late in the evening of February 21, to the secretary of war to countermand the parade. This, coming next morning to the knowledge of Representative Daniel E. Sickles, who had introduced a resolution for the observance of the day, caused Sickles to call upon and remonstrate with the president, who then requested the secretary of war to again add the regular troops to the militia, the appearance of which the order had not affected; and the parade, shorn somewhat of its proportions through want of time to restore the arrangements, took place.[1]

[1] Crawford, *Fort Sumter*, 273–275.

CHAPTER XVI

BORDER STATES AND SECOND EFFORT AT COMPROMISE

(JANUARY, 1861–FEBRUARY, 1861)

THE attitude of the border states, and particularly that of Virginia, was a question of momentous interest. The influence of Virginia was still great, especially in the South, where the great traditions of the state, blood relationship, and the common bond of slavery gave her easy primacy. Washington, Jefferson, and Madison were not in such a distant past but that there were still some living men who had known them all. Though the state had sunk to much less than the second rank politically and commercially, the glamour of her ancient ascendency still remained. Reversing Marshal Lefevre's dictum concerning himself, she was truly a descendant, no longer an ancestor. John Brown's attempt at Harper's Ferry had been used to arouse the blood of the state, which had acted upon Wise's call in his message of December 5, 1859, to "organize and arm"; half a million was voted for arms in the winter of 1859–1860; muskets were distributed, volunteer companies formed, and the antiquated militia organization brought into such working order as it was capable of.

Leaving aside about sixteen thousand votes cast for Douglas and 1929 for Lincoln, the remaining vote of the state (about 149,000) had been almost equally divided between Bell and Breckinridge, the former having but 218 plurality. While strongly Unionist in general, the sympathy of the state was warmly southern, except in the northwest counties, where every other feeling gave way before that for the Union. Union meetings were held in nearly every part of the state, but more especially in the valley of Virginia and "across the mountains" in what is now West Virginia. In the latter region, talk of secession was not tolerated, and it was not long before threats of separation in case the state should secede became too frequent to be lightly regarded.

The Virginia legislature met January 7, 1861, in extra session. Governor Letcher, in his message, charged the non-slave-holding states with the responsibility for affairs; declared that any attempt of Federal troops to pass through Virginia for the purpose of coercing a southern state would be repelled, and advised that New England and western New York be "sloughed off" and allowed to ally themselves with Canada.[1] Although he opposed a state convention, one was called for February 4, also the date of the meeting of the Confederate provisional congress.

[1] *National Intelligencer*, January, 8, 1861.

The resolutions passed by the legislature of New York, January 11, tendering the president "whatever aid in men and money may be required to enable him to enforce the laws and uphold the authority of the Federal Government,"[1] were ordered, January 17, by the Virginia legislature, to be returned to Governor Morgan of that state, with an expression of indignation with the policy of coercion thus countenanced. On this same day, in the lower house, an amendment bringing up the right, and the present policy, of secession was lost by 96 to 36. In the state senate, however, a resolution that, if efforts to reconcile differences should prove abortive, "every consideration of honor and interest demands that Virginia shall unite her destinies with her sister slave-holding states," was passed unanimously. January 23 was passed an appropriation for one million dollars for the defence of the state. As indicative of the influence of the environment of Congress, ten of the Virginia members of Congress at this time sent an address declaring that it was "vain to hope for any measures of conciliation and adjustment from Congress which the people of Virginia could accept"; and that it was the design of the Republican party to coerce the southern states under the pretext of enforcing the laws.[2]

The Virginia convention met at Richmond, February 13, with 152 delegates. Of these only twenty-

[1] *Am. Annual Cyclop.*, 1861, p. 519.　　[2] *Ibid.*, pp. 729, 730.

five were classed as secessionists,[1] but not more than six were "actual submissionists—that is, men in favor of the preservation of the Union under any and all circumstances."[2]   Kentucky, though Governor Magoffin was in close affiliation with his seceding colleagues, would have no convention; Governor Hicks, of Maryland, was firm in resisting a call of the legislature, and state sentiment gradually crystallized in favor of the Union.

In North Carolina the convention bill provided also for putting at the time of the election of delegates the question whether or not there should be a convention.   In the 90,000 votes cast there was a majority of 651 opposed.   Of the 120 delegates elected, but 38 were secessionists.   In Tennessee the election, February 9, showed a strong Union majority in every part of the state and a majority of nearly 12,000 against holding a convention. The election in Missouri gave a Union majority of 80,000, and not a secession delegate was chosen. Even in Arkansas, in the election of delegates to a convention, the Union majority was 5699.[3]

The action of the Virginia legislature, January 19, in calling what came to be known as the Peace Conference, strengthened the influence of Hayne and his senatorial advisers to continue the truce

---

[1] Tyler, *Tylers*, II., 621.

[2] *Richmond Whig*, February 8, 12, quoted by Rhodes, *United States*, III., 309.

[3] *Am. Annual Cyclop.*, 1861, pp. 22, 395, 443, 538, 677.

with regard to Sumter. The resolution extended an invitation to all states "willing to unite with Virginia in an earnest effort to adjust the present unhappy controversies in the spirit in which the Constitution was originally formed" to meet in Washington, "to consider, and, if practicable, to agree upon some suitable adjustment." The basis proposed was the Crittenden resolution, with the first article modified to apply to all territory "now held or hereafter acquired" south of latitude 36° 30', and to protect slavery therein during the continuance of territorial government, and with a new provision that slave-owners should have the right of transit with their slaves through non-slave-holding states and territories.[1] Ex-President Tyler and Judge Robertson, the latter already a commissioner of peace to the seceding states, were appointed to request President Buchanan to agree to abstain, pending the proposed proceedings, "from any and all acts calculated to produce a collision of arms." Tyler, on this errand, met Buchanan January 24, and the latter promised to refer the mission of the former to Congress, with a recommendation "to avoid the passage of any hostile legislation."

South Carolina's answer to Virginia's proposal was complete and emphatic. January 28, on the reception by the legislature of the governor's message transmitting the resolution, it was resolved

[1] *Am. Annual Cyclop.*, 1861, p. 178.

that it was not deemed "advisable to initiate negotiations, when they had no desire or intention to promote the ultimate object in view"; that the separation of the state was final, and that she had "no further interest in the Constitution of the United States."[1]

The Peace Convention met February 4, with representatives from fourteen states—New Hampshire, Vermont, Connecticut, Rhode Island, New Jersey, Pennsylvania, Delaware, Maryland, Virginia, North Carolina, Kentucky, Ohio, Indiana, Iowa; delegates from Maine, Massachusetts, New York, Illinois, Tennessee, Missouri, and Kansas were shortly added, so that about two-thirds of the states of the whole Union were represented. The convention, in the character of its 153 delegates, was in every way worthy of the impressiveness and importance of its object. But the very terms of its call, the instructions of many of the legislatures appointing delegates, as well as the heterogeneous views of the members, made any valuable result impossible.

The convention was organized by the unanimous election of Ex-President Tyler as chairman, who made a rhetorical opening address destitute of any thought or suggestion, except to lament that the Constitution should not have arranged for a convention every fifty years to amend and reform it. In all questions each state was to have one vote.

[1] *National Intelligencer*, January 29, 1861; resolutions of legislature, *S. C. Exec. Docs.*, No. 4; Crawford, *Fort Sumter*, 245.

Immediately after organization, resolutions sent in by the several states, to be considered by the conference, were laid before it.   Massachusetts authorized its seven commissioners "to confer with the General Government or with the separate States, or with any association of delegates from such States," and report their doings.   Rhode Island directed her commissioners to meet such "as may be appointed by other States, . . . to consider, and, if practicable, to agree upon some amicable adjustment of the present unhappy national difficulties upon the basis and in the spirit of the Constitution."   New York resolved that it did not approve of the Virginia propositions, but would not reject an invitation holding out the possibility of an honorable settlement. New Jersey declared the Crittenden propositions acceptable, and earnestly urged their support upon its senators and representatives.   Pennsylvania declared that no reasonable cause existed for the extraordinary excitement, and, while willing to unite with Virginia in the effort to restore peace, did not desire any alteration or amendment of the Constitution; she would unite in the adoption of any constitutional measures to secure a more faithful observance of the second section of the fourth article of the Constitution regarding the privileges and immunities of the citizens of the several states and the return of fugitive slaves.   Delaware was ready to sacrifice "all minor considerations on the altar of the Union."   Ohio, while not prepared to assent to the

Virginia proposals, and satisfied that a fair interpretation of the Constitution would amply provide for the evils complained of, was induced by a sincere desire to adjust all differences to appoint a commission as requested. The views of Indiana and Illinois were similar to those of Ohio. Missouri's delegates were "to endeavor to agree upon some plan of adjustment" which would "secure the honor and equal rights of the slaveholding States." The instructions of Kentucky and Tennessee were practically framed upon the Crittenden resolutions.[1]

The committee of one from each state brought in a report, February 15, which was discussed and amended until February 26. The most important section, relating to slavery in the territories, was passed, after previous failure, by but one vote. The general purport of the seven sections submitted as a thirteenth amendment to the Constitution[2] was less favorable to the South than the Crittenden propositions; and this, combined with the want of anything approaching unanimity, and the certainty that it would not be regarded with general favor, north or south, made its defeat a certainty. It suffered from like opposition to that against the Crittenden compromise; there were those of both sides who would have no compromise.

On February 27, the day the report of the convention was transmitted to Congress, two letters

[1] *Am. Annual Cyclop.*, 1861, pp. 564, 565.
[2] *Senate Misc. Docs.*, 36 Cong., 2 Sess., No. 20.

were read in the Senate by Powell, of Kentucky, from Bingham and Chandler, the senators from Michigan, to the governor of the state; the former regarded the conference "as another effort to debauch the public mind, and a step towards obtaining that concession which the imperious slave power so insolently demands." The latter said: "Governor Bingham and myself telegraphed you, ... at the request of Massachusetts and New York, to send delegates to the peace or compromise Congress. They admit that we were right and that they were wrong; that no Republican State should have sent delegates. ... I hope you will send *stiff-backed* men or none. The whole thing ... will end in thin smoke. Still, I hope as a matter of courtesy to some of our erring brethren, that you will send the delegates." In a postscript he added: "Some of the manufacturing States think that a fight would be awful. Without a little blood - letting this Union will not, in my estimation, be worth a rush." Chandler's reply to the reading was an iteration of the sentiments of the letter.[1] In the last hours of the session, Crittenden, after a pathetic speech, brought forward the resolutions of the Peace Conference; but with such a feeling prevalent among the Republicans, there was no hope. It received but seven votes, of which two were those of Crittenden and Douglas.[2]

However much the failure of the Peace Conven-

---

[1] *Cong. Globe*, 36 Cong., 2 Sess., 1247.   [2] *Ibid.*, 1405.

tion and of the Crittenden compromise was in accord with the wishes of the leaders in Congress, the country at large was bitterly disappointed. Hope had run high, in the border states particularly, and the continuance of "palaver," as it was termed by Lowell,[1] did much to withhold these states from precipitate action. Many of the public men, of whom Crittenden and Powell were excellent types, were strongly Unionist, and it was true of the border population in general, as has been said of the people of Kentucky, that they "almost without exception shrank from a dissolution of the Union with a real horror."[2] But they were torn by a conflict of emotion that those farther north could not feel; the severance of the Union meant to them the severance of nearly all the ties, social and sympathetic, which bound them with other states. It cost much more, from every point of view, to be a Union man in the southern border-land than it did in Massachusetts or Michigan.

The president was about to give up his now so unpleasant office. Seven states had declared themselves out of the Union and had formed a new and, as it proved, an effective governmental organization. Every fort south of Virginia had been seized, with the exception of Sumter, Taylor (Key West), Jefferson (Tortugas), and Pickens, at Pensacola. Nineteen sea-coast fortifications, which had been built

---

[1] *Atlantic Monthly*, VII., 758 (June, 1861).
[2] Shaler, *Kentucky*, 235.

at a cost of about seven million dollars, and armed with over thirteen hundred guns, were thus in possession of the secessionists. All had been occupied without resistance, as, with the exception of those still retained by the government, the only force was a fort-keeper or a few workmen; it was but necessary to walk in and the place was theirs.[1] Very few of the forts seized were, even if garrisoned, in a condition for any defence against attack by men-of-war; Pulaski, at Savannah, had but half its armament; and Clinch, Cumberland Sound, Florida, was in no condition even for occupancy. Ship Island, designed for one of the most important defences of the South, had no guns, and was not yet in readiness for any. General Beauregard reported, February 13, to the military board of Louisiana that forts Jackson and St. Philip, the passage of which was later to make Farragut famous, could be passed by any steamer in broad daylight.[2] Seven arsenals had been seized, with over two hundred thousand muskets, many of the highest standard, and with a large quantity of heavy ordnance. The value of the property at the ordnance depot at San Antonio, Texas, alone, was twelve hundred thousand dollars.

The situation in this last state was one of special aggravation. The department of Texas had been

[1] For list, condition, etc., see *War Records*, Serial No. 122, pp. 47-51; also *House Reports*, 36 Cong., 2 Sess., No. 85.
[2] *War Records*, Serial No. 1, p. 501.

placed in command of General Twiggs only in November, 1860. He asked almost immediately after his arrival what was to be done with the army property in case of the secession of Texas. "My course," he said, "as respects myself will be to remain at my post and protect this frontier as long as I can, and then, when turned adrift, make my way home, if I have one." The inquiry in this letter (of December 13) was repeated two weeks later. An answer to his first, from General Scott, had gone the same day the second was written. It contained no advice, but left everything in Twiggs's hands, "in full confidence" of his discretion and patriotism. January 15 he asked to be relieved, as he must follow his native state, Georgia. The war department now proceeded to act, and on January 28, Holt now being secretary, orders were despatched relieving Twiggs and placing Colonel Waite in command. But the order was too late. February 9, Twiggs, at San Antonio, ordered a commission of three officers "to meet the commissioners on behalf of the Convention of the People of Texas, . . . to transact such business as relates to the disposition of the public property upon the demand of the State of Texas." Formal sessions were held to discuss the questions involved, until February 16, when the invasion of San Antonio by armed bodies of Texans, who seized the property of the United States, made such further action useless, and the record of these extraordinary proceedings to that date were submitted to the commanding general. The next day the convention committee made a formal demand for the surrender of all posts and property, to which Twiggs acceded, provided that the troops should retain their arms, clothing, subsistence, etc., and such means of transportation as might "be necessary for an efficient and orderly movement of the troops from Texas, prepared for attack or defense against aggression from any source," which was accepted.[1] The result was one of the few displays of energy made by this unhappy administration. Twiggs was dismissed, by order of March 1, "for his treachery to the flag of his country."[2] But the fault was primarily with the administration itself; Twiggs's pleas for instructions had passed unheeded. He had under his command a force of 2479 officers and men, which, if concentrated, could probably have held the whole state. Scattered as they were over a vast extent, the individual posts were powerless. This General Scott, as well as every officer in the war department, knew, but no step was taken, not an intimation given as to action. The supineness, the folly, shown go far to support the theory of the necessity of an occasional war to revamp the human mind and character.

[1] *War Records*, Serial No. 1, pp. 503–514.   [2] *Ibid.*, 597.

CHAPTER XVII

LINCOLN'S ATTITUDE
(DECEMBER, 1860–FEBRUARY, 1861)

LINCOLN, after his election, remained at home in such quiet as the anxiety of friends regarding his own course would allow. No period of this wonderful man's career exhibits more complete greatness than that of this trying four months' waiting to take up the burden which day by day was being made heavier by those who, under a more reasonable system, should have surrendered their authority as soon as possible into the hands now made responsible for the government of the country.

Lincoln clearly defined his course in a letter of December 21, 1860, which is of the utmost importance as showing his mind to have been long made up, and that any apparent want of decision later was due to the influence of his cabinet. Thanking Washburn for an account of an interview with General Scott, he says: "Please present my respects to the general, and tell him, confidentially, I shall be obliged to him to be as well prepared as he can to either hold or retake the forts, as the case may

require, at and after the inauguration." [1] December
17 he wrote Thurlow Weed, whose paper, the *Albany
Evening Journal*, had strongly leaned to compromise,
of the character of that brought forward by Crittenden: "My opinion is that no State can in any way
lawfully get out of the Union without the consent
of the others; and that it is the duty of the President
and other government functionaries to run the ma-
chine as it is." [2] He steadily resisted any compromise in Congress, and equally and against very strong
pressure refused to make any special announcement
of his views, holding, in his own words: "I could say
nothing which I have not already said, and which is
in print, and accessible to the public. . . . If I thought
a repetition would do any good, I would make it.
But in my judgment it would do positive harm.
The secessionists *per se*, believing they had alarmed
me, would clamor all the louder." [3]

In nothing does Lincoln appear to better advantage than in an admirable, frank, and wise letter to Gilmer, of North Carolina, in response to a
similar request, December 15, 1860: he disclaimed
any thought of recommending the abolition of
slavery in the District of Columbia, or the slave-
trade among the slave states; he had never in his
life thought of the question of the employment of
slaves in arsenals and dock-yards; as to patronage

[1] Lincoln, *Works* (ed. of 1894), I., 660.
[2] *Ibid.*
[3] Lincoln to Paschal, in *ibid.*, 655.

in the slave states, he did not expect to inquire as to the politics of the appointee or whether he owned or did not own slaves. "I intend in that matter to accommodate the people in the several localities, if they themselves will allow me to accommodate them. In one word, I never have been, am not now, and probably never shall be in a mood of harassing the people either North or South. On the territorial question I am inflexible. . . . On that there is a difference between you and us; and it is the only substantial difference. You think slavery is right and ought to be extended; we think it is wrong and ought to be restricted. For this neither has any just occasion to be angry with the other." He had never read one of the state laws regarding fugitive slaves, mentioned by Gilmer. "If," he says, "any of them are in conflict with the fugitive-slave clause, or any other part of the Constitution, I certainly shall be glad of their repeal; but I could hardly be justified, as a citizen of Illinois or as President of the United States, to recommend the repeal of a statute of Vermont or South Carolina." [1]

Early in December, Thurlow Weed, regarded as the most astute politician of the day, and Seward's most intimate friend, was invited by Lincoln to Springfield for consultation as to the coming cabinet. With him also came Judge David Davis and Leonard Swett (both of Illinois), and all stayed for two days. Lincoln had already decided to offer

[1] Lincoln. *Works* (ed. of 1894), I., 659.

the position of secretary of state to Seward, which
he did in a wise and kindly letter of December 8.[1]
Weed's account makes it clear, however, that Lincoln had also practically made up his mind as to
most of the others: Chase, of Ohio, for the treasury;
Cameron, of Pennsylvania, for the war department;
Welles, of Connecticut, for the navy; Blair, of
Maryland, for postmaster-general; Bates, of Missouri, for attorney-general; only one place, that of
secretary of the interior, was, apparently, undeter-
mined, and for this Caleb B. Smith, of Indiana, was
mentioned. Lincoln, in thus recognizing the varied
elements which had gone to make Republican success, had acted on the principle which he had mentioned in his letter to Seward just mentioned: "In
regard to the patronage sought with so much eager-
ness and jealousy, I have prescribed for myself the
maxim, 'Justice to all'; and I earnestly beseech
your coöperation in keeping the maxim good."

Weed was eager for a representation in the cabinet of at least two from the slave states, and
named Henry Winter Davis, of Maryland; Botts, of
Virginia; Gilmer, of North Carolina; and Peyton, of
Tennessee, as men for whose loyalty under the most
trying circumstances he could vouch. Lincoln met
half the demand in naming Bates, of Missouri, who
was undeniably a fitting selection. He raised the
objection of taking men from states which might
secede, and made the pregnant remark that "he did

[1] Lincoln, *Works* (ed. of 1894), I., 657.

not quite like to hear Southern journals and Southern speakers insisting that there must be no 'coercion'; that while he had no disposition to coerce anybody, yet after he had taken an oath to execute the laws, he should not care to see them violated." Yielding to the united suggestion of his three visitors, Weed was commissioned to carry an offer of a cabinet post to Gilmer, which the latter declined on account of the attitude of his native state.[1] The vacant place went to Caleb B. Smith, of Indiana, who had from the first been in Lincoln's mind.

Lincoln left Springfield February 11, timed to reach Washington February 23. The journey "embraced two weeks of official reception by committees, mayors, governors, and legislatures; of crowded evening receptions and interminable handshakings; of impromptu or formal addresses at every ceremony; of cheers, . . . and imposing processions and miles of spectators." [2] It was an ovation which indicated that the tide of northern feeling was rapidly rising, and that there would be no want of support to the incoming president.

As he was leaving Springfield he made a short and touching address at the railway station, fine in thought, and in diction such as made Lincoln one of the great masters of our language. "I now leave," he said, "not knowing when or whether ever I may return, with a task before me greater than that

---

[1] Weed, *Autobiography*, chap. lxii.
[2] Nicolay and Hay, *Abraham Lincoln*, III., 291.

which rested upon Washington. Without the assistance of that Divine Being who ever attended him, I cannot succeed. With that assistance, I cannot fail. Trusting in Him who can go with me, and remain with you, and be everywhere for good, let us confidently hope that all will yet be well. To His care commending you, as I hope in your prayers you will commend me, I bid you an affectionate farewell." [1]

The next day, February 12, addressing the legislature at Indianapolis, he defined "coercion" and "invasion," and gave a hint of the trend of his intention. "Would the marching of an army into South Carolina without the consent of her people, and with hostile intent toward them, be 'invasion'? I certainly think it would; and it would be 'coercion' also if the South Carolinians were forced to submit. But if the United States should merely hold and retake its own forts and other property, and collect the duties . . . or even withhold the mails from places where they were habitually violated, would any or all of these things be 'invasion' or 'coercion'?" [2]

It is clear that in his view the federation of the United States had become a nation, and that it was for the preservation of nationality that he was about to struggle. In the same speech he asked: "On what rightful principle may a State, being not

---

[1] Lincoln, *Works* (ed. of 1894), I., 672.
[2] *Ibid.*, 673.

more than one fiftieth part of the nation in soil and population, break up the nation and then coerce a proportionally larger subdivision of itself in the most arbitrary way? What mysterious right to play tyrant is conferred on a district of country with its people, by merely calling it a State? Fellow-citizens, I am not asserting anything; I am merely asking questions for you to consider." [1]   In Cincinnati, February 12, he repeated a phrase of his speech made in the same city September 17, 1859, addressed more particularly to Kentuckians, and now having a much weightier meaning: "We mean to treat you, as near as we possibly can, as Washington, Jefferson, and Madison treated you. We mean to leave you alone, and in no way to interfere with your institutions; to abide by all and every compromise of the Constitution." [2]   Between this date and his arrival in Washington he made twenty-four speeches, some of but a few words. His route included Columbus, Pittsburg, Cleveland, Buffalo, Albany, New York, Trenton, Philadelphia, and Harrisburg, and in each of the capitals of the states through which he passed he addressed the legislatures.

The last hours of Lincoln's journey were complicated by a sudden announcement of a plot to assassinate him as he passed through Baltimore in the night. Against his will, and conscious of the

---

[1] Lincoln, *Works* (ed. of 1894), I., 674.
[2] *Ibid.*, 675.

probable effect upon the public, he was induced to leave the party and travel the short remainder of the journey incognito. The step was justified by warnings which, whether well or ill based, were so authoritative as to leave no other proper course.[1] No untoward incident occurred, and at six o'clock on the morning of February 23 Lincoln reached Willard's Hotel in Washington.

Calls were exchanged with President Buchanan. The Peace Conference, headed by their chairman, Ex-President Tyler, called in a body, in pursuance of a unanimous resolution. He received visits from Douglas and Breckinridge, from the mayor, the municipal council, and many high functionaries. To the mayor's address he made a felicitous reply, assuring all that he had not now, and never had, "any disposition to treat you in any respect otherwise than as my own neighbors. I have not now any purpose to withhold from you any of the benefits of the Constitution, under any circumstances, that I would not feel myself constrained to withhold from my own neighbors." [2]

The inaugural address should have assured the country that no mistake had been made in the selection of its new president; it stands among the glories of Anglo-Saxon literature and thought, a witness to the possibilities of democracy. The defeated Douglas held Lincoln's hat during the speech,

[1] Nicolay and Hay, *Abraham Lincoln*, III., chap. xx.; Lamon, *Lincoln*, 512.   [2] Lincoln, *Works* (ed. of 1894), I., 694.

and the author of the Dred Scott decision administered the oath.   The coming wreck of the theories
with which their lives were bound up must have
been visible to both.   The most momentous declaration of the speech was as follows: "The power con-
fided to me will be used to hold, occupy, and possess
the property and places belonging to the government,
and to collect the duties and imposts; but beyond
what may be necessary for these objects there will
be no invasion, no using of force against or among
the people anywhere."   Touching upon the proposed
amendment to the Constitution which had passed
Congress, to the effect that the Federal government
should never interfere with the domestic institutions
of the states, including that of persons held to service, he said: "Holding such a provision to be implied constitutional law, I have no objection to its
being made express and irrevocable."   He ended
with words which should have brought calm to any
southern mind not distempered by passion.   "In
your hands, my dissatisfied fellow-countrymen, and
not in *mine*, is the momentous issue of civil war.
The Government will not assail *you*.   You can have
no conflict without being yourselves the aggressors.
You have no oath registered in heaven to destroy
the Government, while *I* shall have the most solemn
one to 'preserve, protect, and defend it.' " [1]

Few souls in this world can have undergone a

[1] The speech, and Seward's proposed or accepted emendations,
in Nicolay and Hay, *Abraham Lincoln*, III., 327-344.

more dramatic and solemn hour than did Lincoln when he found himself a few hours later at the end of these four volcanic months, in the falling shades of a gloomy March day, in the White House, the guide and master, as he was soon to show himself, of his country's future.

Next day, March 5, the names of the members of the cabinet, which were as forecasted during the visit of Davis, Swett, and Weed to Lincoln in December, were confirmed by the Senate in extra session.

A consultation of secessionist leaders was held March 4, immediately after the delivery of the inaugural address, at which were present Crawford, Garnett, Pryor, De Jarnette, Wigfall, and L. Q. Washington, who wrote to Walker: "We all put the same construction on the inaugural. . . . We agreed that it was Lincoln's purpose at once to attempt the collection of the revenue, to re-enforce and hold Fort Sumter and Pickens, and to retake the other places. He is a man of will and firmness. His Cabinet will yield to him with alacrity, I think. Seward has, of course, agreed to the inaugural, and the pretenses of his conservatism are idle. We believe that these plans will be put into execution immediately. I learn five or six United States ships are in New York Harbor, all ready to start." He concludes: "There is a general concurrence in the opinion that if any attack is made on Sumter it should be by order of the Government of the Con-

federate States and not by South Carolina alone."
A postscript adds: "I fear the present Virginia Convention will not pass an ordinance of secession unless a collision or war ensues; then public feeling
will force them to it." [1]

[1] *War Records*, Serial No. 1, pp. 263, 264.

CHAPTER XVIII

THE LAST NEGOTIATION
(MARCH 4, 1861–APRIL 12, 1861)

LINCOLN found himself with a cabinet the great majority of whom were inclined to give way before the storm and withdraw from Sumter. But their chief was of different mould from his predecessor. He clearly saw, what apparently few, if any, of his cabinet were able to see, that to yield Sumter voluntarily would be to sacrifice the vantage-ground of his constitutional position, and throw upon the Federal government the onus of beginning a war or else admitting the independence of the Confederacy. Lincoln saw, as every one now must see, that eventually war was in any case inevitable; and, with the wisdom and firmness which made him one of the greatest of men, he determined that the South should not have the advantage of beginning it after its independence should have been recognized. Should the secessionists begin it now, the question of the constitutional right of secession would still be indeterminate, and the Union would be in the undeniably constitutional position of defending its own. To hold Sumter at every hazard was thus vital.   From the beginning, every expression by Lincoln upon the question showed his recognition of this necessity and his determination to act in accord with this conviction.

The question was brought forward in an unexpectedly acute phase by the reception at the war department, March 4, of a report from Anderson of February 28, that he had provisions for only about a month. Accompanying were separate opinions of the officers of the garrison as to the force necessary to relieve the garrison, varying from two thousand men, aided by a naval force, to Anderson's estimate of twenty thousand.[1]

The startling fact was the shortness of provisions. The inaction of the previous administration and its ineptitude in the case of the *Star of the West* now bore their fruit.   Time had worked for the secessionists both by strengthening their power of attack and by weakening the powers of the defence; not a gun need be fired to attain their object.   Yet the situation could not be laid wholly at the door of Mr. Buchanan and his recent cabinet.   Anderson himself was largely responsible through his failure to support the *Star of the West* with his fire, through the establishment of the fatal truce, and through his repeated asseverations of safety.   In answer to a private letter written him April 5, Anderson says: "Justice . . . compels me . . . to take upon myself the blame of the Government's not having sent to

[1] *War Records*, Serial No. 1, pp. 197, 202.

my rescue. Had I demanded reinforcements while
Mr. Holt was in the War Department I know that
he would have despatched them at all hazards. I
did not ask them, because I knew that the moment
it should be known here that additional troops
were coming, they would assault me and thus inaugurate civil war. My policy, feeling—thanks be
to God!—secure for the present in my stronghold,
was to keep still, to preserve peace, to give time for
the quieting of the excitement, . . . in the hope of
avoiding bloodshed. There is now a prospect that
that hope will be realized, that the separation which
has been inevitable for months, will be consum-
mated without the shedding of one drop of blood." [1]

This letter reveals the fixed belief in Anderson's
mind that secession must succeed, and his sense of
responsibility for keeping it from swelling to the
dimensions of war. Able, high-minded, patriotic as
he was, he had no true conception of the mighty
movement of which for the moment he was the
pivot, nor was there any attempt on the part of the
authorities at Washington to enlighten him. Nevertheless, the administration had its own means of
judging the situation; both Anderson's and Foster's
reports as to the batteries were full and accurate,
and military men in Washington could forecast the
outcome as well as Anderson himself. In reading
between the lines it would seem that the authorities
at Washington merely salved their consciences for

Crawford, *Fort Sumter*, 290.

inaction with the fact that no official documents had been put before them as to the impossibility of a lengthened resistance. But the thing was self-evident; Black's memorandum to Scott, January 16, covered the situation completely.[1]

Lincoln's own mind as to the course of action had, as we know from his message early in December to Scott, been long made up, and every utterance thereafter, whether public or private, including his inaugural address, showed that he had not swerved from his early intention. He thus referred the information received March 4 back to General Scott for more thorough investigation, and transmitted to him through the secretary of war, as soon as the latter was in office, a memorandum draughted by himself, as follows: "I am directed by the President to say he desires you to exercise all possible vigilance for the maintenance of all the places within the military department of the United States, and to promptly call upon all the departments of the Government for the means necessary to that end."[2] But Lincoln was leaning upon a broken reed. Scott, who was now on terms of intimacy with Seward, to whom he apparently looked as the directive force of the nation, wrote, March 3, a letter which seems inspired by Seward,[3] or at any rate was the outcome of a previous conversation. In it Scott said

[1] See above, p. 235.
[2] Nicolay and Hay, *Abraham Lincoln*, III., 379.
[3] Bancroft, *Seward*, II., 96 n.

to Seward: "I beg leave to repeat in writing what I have before said to you orally." Leaving untouched the field of military duties, the aged general became the politician advising conciliation; and he ended with, "Say to the seceded States— *Wayward Sisters, depart in peace!*" [1]

Scott now gave an emphatic opinion that to relieve Sumter was impracticable. The president, March 9, asked him in substance: "(1) To what point of time can Anderson maintain his position in Sumter? (2) Can you with present means relieve him within that time? (3) What additional means would enable you to do so?" Scott replied that he would need a naval fleet and transports which could not be collected in less than four months, 5000 additional regular troops, and 20,000 volunteers. To raise, organize, and discipline such an army (not to speak of necessary legislation) would require from six to eight months. "As a practical military question, the time for succoring Fort Sumter with any means at hand had passed away nearly a month ago. Since then a surrender under assault or starvation has been merely a question of time." Scott also submitted the draught of an order for the evacuation of the fort. [2]

Postmaster-General Blair, however, knew of the proposal made by Fox in February, and March 12

---

[1] Scott, *Autobiography*, II., 625–628.   The italics are Scott's.
[2] Nicolay and Hay, *Abraham Lincoln*, III., 379–381; *War Records*, Serial No. 1, p. 197.

sent the latter a telegram which brought him from New York to Washington the next day. Accompanied by Blair, Fox at once went to the White House to lay his project before the president, whence, after its presentation, adjournment was made to General Scott's office, where a renewed discussion took place, Scott informing the president that, while the plan was practicable in February, the increased number of batteries now made it impossible.[1] The outcome was a memorandum from the president to each member of the cabinet: "Assuming it to be possible to now provision Fort Sumter, under all the circumstances is it wise to attempt it?"[2] Seward, Cameron, Welles, Smith, and Bates, in lengthy opinions filed March 15, were against it. The first argued the political issue at length. His paper is of great importance, as showing how fully Seward at the time was committed to the policy of non-resistance. Under the influence of the impression made upon him by the great Unionist vote of the South in November, he believed that disunion stood upon an unreasoning popular excitement "arising out of a simple and harmless disappointment in a presidential election"; if it should find no new ailment, it would quickly subside; that everywhere, even in South Carolina, there was a profound and permanent national senti-

[1] *Naval War Records*, IV., 246.
[2] Lincoln, *Works* (ed. of 1894), II., 11–22; *War Records*, Serial No. 1, p. 196.

ment, which, if encouraged, could be relied upon to cause the seceding states to reverse their action. Conciliation which should deny to disunionists any new provocation was the true policy, and a perseverance in that policy was the only peaceful means of assuring the continuance of the remaining slave states, or most of them, in the Union. He denied the usefulness of holding Sumter, even if it could be done: "I would not provoke war in any way now." [1]

Cameron's reply, quoting that of Scott on the 9th, approved the latter's conclusions, saying, "As the abandonment of the fort in a few weeks, sooner or later, appears to be an inevitable necessity, it seems to me that the sooner it is done the better." [2] The reply of the secretary of war included several memoranda and communications rehearsing the various plans submitted and the opinions; these were read by General Totten, chief of engineers, the author of one of very pessimistic character, before the president and cabinet, General Scott, Commodore Stringham, and Mr. Fox. [3]

Only two members of the cabinet, Chase and Blair, answered the president's inquiry affirmatively, and even the former hesitatingly on account of the financial difficulties in case of war. There was no doubt, however, in the opinion of Blair, who was supported in his views by his father, Francis P.

[1] Nicolay and Hay, *Abraham Lincoln*, III., chap. xxiii.; Bancroft, *Seward*, II., 99–101 ; Crawford, *Fort Sumter*, 348–353.
[2] *War Records*, Serial No. 1, pp. 196–198.   [3] *Ibid.*, 198–205.

Blair, an intimate friend and counsellor of Jackson's.[1] The powerful opposition of three-fourths of the cabinet, of the general-in-chief, and of the whole of the war department could not but give Lincoln reason to ponder.

Seward's extreme optimism, his belief that his own views would be those which must necessarily be adopted by Lincoln, his confidence that he was to be the leading spirit of the government, now led to the first of three extraordinary endeavors to usurp the direction of affairs, and caused him to place the administration in a false light. He even went so far when Senator Gwin showed him a telegram which he was about to send to Montgomery, mentioning Chase's appointment to the cabinet, declaring that the war policy was in the ascendant, and advising the South to look out for itself, that he substituted over Gwin's signature the statement that the outlook was peaceable and that matters had never looked so encouraging.[2] He went still further by giving out to the press the information that Fort Sumter would shortly be evacuated, and requesting the editor of the *National Intelligencer* to communicate the fact to George W. Summers, "the recognized leader of the Union majority in the Virginia Convention."[3]

All this was, of course, known to the Confeder-

[1] Crawford, *Fort Sumter*, 358–361.
[2] Gwin to Crawford, in *ibid.*, 320.
[3] Welling, in *Nation*, XXIX., 383 (December 4, 1879).

ate commissioners, of whom, through the arrival of
Forsyth, there were now two in Washington.
Hunter, of Virginia, agreed to be their instrument
in establishing an understanding with the secretary
of state, whom Hunter found urgent for delay.
While this was wholly in accord with the views of
the Confederate authorities so long as the "military
status should be maintained and no advantage
taken of the delay," they were desirous that their
willingness should not appear. A memorandum
was prepared by the commissioners defining the
terms upon which they "would consent to and
stipulate for a brief respite." They agreed to post-
pone the consideration of the subject of their mission for twenty days on a positive pledge that the
military status should be preserved in every respect.[1]

It is not at all surprising, as reported by the commissioners, that Seward "was perceptibly embar-
rassed and uneasy" on Hunter's presenting the
paper, March 11, and asking if he would consent to
an informal interview, when it is understood that
Scott received the same day instructions, of which
Seward must have been aware, to issue orders to
Vogdes to land his company of artillery at Fort
Pickens. Seward informed Hunter that he must
consult the president, and the next day, March 12,
informed him by note that it was not in his power

[1] *Confederate Correspondence*, in U. S. Treasury Department,
cited by Crawford, *Fort Sumter*, 322, 323.

"to receive the gentlemen of whom we conversed yesterday." The commissioners thereupon, March 13, formally requested an official interview at an early day. No formal reply was made to this, but a memorandum, with instructions to furnish the commissioners a copy if called for, was placed in the files of the department, defining the position of the government and showing that the interview was declined.[1]

Justice Nelson, of New York, and Justice Campbell, of Alabama, who had convinced themselves "that an inflexible adherence to a policy of moderation and of peace would inevitably lead to the restoration of the Union," and were equally convinced of the unconstitutionality of any coercion, now appeared on the scene in an endeavor to urge their views. They finally recommended to the secretary of state to reply to the letter of the commissioners and announce the earnest desire of the government for conciliation and peace. Seward rose with a forcible gesture. "I wish I could do it. See Montgomery Blair, see Mr. Bates, see Mr. Lincoln himself; . . . convince them—no, there is not a member of the cabinet who would consent to it. If Jefferson Davis had known the state of things here, he would not have sent those commissioners; the evacuation of Sumter is as much as the administration can bear." Seward authorized Campbell, on the latter's request to know what he should say

[1] In full in Moore, *Rebellion Record*, I., Doc. 47, pp. 42–44.

to Davis, "to say that before that letter could reach him, he would learn by telegraph that the order for the evacuation of Sumter had been made." [1]

Campbell now, March 15, had an interview for the first time with Commissioner Crawford, and urged upon him a delay of five days in demanding a response to the commissioners' note, as in that time he was confident Sumter would be evacuated. Crawford at once said: "You come from Seward; those are his views?" Campbell declined giving his authority, but said that "Justice Nelson was aware of all that I was, and would agree that I was justified in saying to him what I did." [2]

On Crawford's demand that the information should be in writing, Campbell drew up a note, which received the approval of Justice Nelson, who had also been in communication with the secretary of state, and, its contents having been communicated to the latter, it was given the commissioner, who at once advised the Confederate government. This note expressed perfect confidence that Sumter would be evacuated in the next five days, that no measure changing the status prejudicially to the Confederacy was at present contemplated, and that an immediate demand for an answer to the commissioners would do evil. A delay "until the effect of the evacuation of Sumter could be ascertained—

---

[1] Davis, *Confederate Government*, I., 268; Campbell's account, in Crawford, *Fort Sumter*, 328.

[2] Campbell's account, in Crawford, *Fort Sumter*, 329.

or at least for a few days, say ten days "—was earnestly asked.[1]

On the same day, March 15, the important cabinet meeting mentioned seemed to Seward to justify his sanguine hopes, as a large majority, as well as the general-in-chief and chief of engineers, were in favor of evacuation. Meantime the agreed five days of waiting passed; the commissioners learned by telegraph from Charleston that there were no indications of change at Sumter, and that work on the defences was still in progress. This word was carried by Campbell and Nelson to Seward, who assured them all was right, and arranged for an interview the next day. Campbell left with the commissioners another reassuring note. The interview with Seward the next day, March 22, resulted in a "full and satisfactory" conversation, in which Campbell was informed that the delay was accidental, and "that there was nothing in the delay that affected the integrity of the promise or denoted any intention not to comply." The status of Pickens was not to be altered, or, if so, Campbell should be informed. Campbell thereupon left a third note with the commissioners, stating that he had unabated confidence. Justice Nelson withdrew from the negotiations after March 22, and left Washington.[2]

[1] *Confederate Correspondence*, in U. S. Treasury Department, cited by Crawford, *Fort Sumter*, 330; correspondence of Campbell with Seward, in Moore, *Rebellion Record*, I., Doc. 267, pp. 427, 428.
[2] Crawford, *Fort Sumter*, 330–333.

Seward held to his views, and impressed the commissioners with the idea that his will would be carried out; he permitted himself to express his opinions freely to Stoeckl, the Russian minister, who carried them, March 24, to the commissioners in the statement that "the peace policy would prevail in time, the Secretary thought, and the difficulties surrounding him should be considered." [1] The Russian minister advised the commissioners that he thought Seward had been overruled in his policy, but this the commissioners did not believe; nevertheless, March 26, they advised the Montgomery government to make active preparations for defence, to display a strong force at Pickens in order to give the administration "an excuse for evacuating that fort." They also stated that the Russian minister had that day told Seward that he need not hesitate to recognize the Confederacy, for the European powers would certainly do so. [2]

The Montgomery authorities were, of course, kept fully informed, and March 28 replied to the commissioners that, while relying upon the representations of Justice Campbell, the same confidence was not placed in the good faith and sincerity of those from whom Campbell drew his convictions. They were directed to urge with firmness the evacuation of all the forts in the Confederacy, and to ask an

---

[1] Crawford, *Fort Sumter*, 334.
[2] *Confederate Correspondence*, in U. S. Treasury Department, cited in *ibid.*, 335.

explanation of the unusually large naval force now in the United States ports.[1]

In the reflections of the Confederate authorities upon Campbell's source, injustice was done Seward, who, listening only to the promptings of his own mind, was perfectly sincere, however unwise. His ear at the moment was attuned to catch only such words as those of Douglas, who, in the Senate, March 15, was proclaiming that peace was "the only policy that can save the country or save your [the Republican] party," and was calling for the withdrawal of Anderson from Sumter as demanded by "duty, honor, patriotism, [and] humanity."[2] Neither Douglas nor Seward, however, measured the mind of Lincoln or of the country. Wrote Dix to Buchanan, March 14: "The people are now agitated by the intelligence that Fort Sumter is to be abandoned. . . . The disappointment will be very great, and it will go far to turn the current against the new administration."[3] And the true sentiment of the Republican leaders in the Senate, still in extra session, was in the resolution offered March 27 by Trumbull, of Illinois, "that . . . the true way to preserve the Union is to enforce the laws of the Union . . . that it is the duty of the President to use all the means in his power to hold and protect

[1] *Confederate Correspondence*, in U. S. Treasury Department, cited by Crawford, *Fort Sumter*, 333.

[2] *Cong. Globe*, 36 Cong., 2 Sess., 1461.

[3] Curtis, *Buchanan*, II., 533.

the public property of the United States and enforce the laws," as well in the seceding states as in the others.[1]

The commissioners asked, March 26, "whether we shall dally longer with a Government hesitating and doubting as to its own course or shall we demand our answer at once?" To this Toombs replied, April 2, giving President Davis's views at length. "He thought the policy of Mr. Seward would prevail. He cared nothing for Seward's motive or calculations. So long as the United States neither declare war nor establish peace, 'it affords the Confederate States the advantage of both conditions, and enables them to make all the necessary arrangements for the public defense, and the solidifying of their Government, more safely, cheaply, and expeditiously than they could were the attitude of the United States more definite and decided.'"[2]

Fox, with the president's permission, had left Washington, March 19, for Charleston, to look over the ground himself. He arrived on the 21st. Through a Captain Hartstene, formerly of the Federal navy, he was presented to the governor, and, after some demur, was allowed "expressly upon the pledge of 'pacific purposes'"[3] to proceed to Sumter, which he reached after dark, and where he remained

[1] *Cong. Globe*, 36 Cong., 2 Sess., 1519.
[2] *Confederate Correspondence*, in U. S. Treasury Department, cited by Nicolay and Hay, *Abraham Lincoln*, III., 413.
[3] Message of Pickens to legislature, November, 1861, in Davis, *Confederate Government*, I., 272.

about two hours. Fox reported that "Anderson seemed to think it was too late to relieve the fort by any other means than landing an army on Morris Island. He agreed with General Scott that our entrance from the sea was impossible; but as we looked out upon the water from the parapet it looked very feasible, more especially as we heard the oars of a boat near the fort, which the sentry hailed; but we could not see her through the darkness until she almost touched the landing. . . . It was agreed that I might report that the 15th of April at noon, would be the period beyond which the fort could not be held unless supplies were furnished. I made no arrangement with Major Anderson for reenforcing or supplying the fort nor did I inform him of my plan." [1]

The insistence of Seward upon the existence of a strong Union feeling South caused at this same time with the consent of the president the visit to Charleston of S. A. Hurlbut, of Illinois (later a major-general of volunteers), ostensibly to see a sister, and of Ward H. Lamon, a former law partner of the president, who gave out that he was upon business for the post-office. The result was, so far as South Carolina was concerned, a complete denial of Seward's views. Hurlbut met James L. Petigru, one of the most distinguished jurists of South Carolina and the only avowed Unionist of prominence. The result was Hurlbut's report that there was " posi-

[1] *Naval War Records*, IV., 247.

tively nothing to appeal to." [1] Lamon, remaining in Charleston, obtained an interview with the governor as the "confidential agent" of the president, and informed him, wholly without the authority of Lincoln, that he had come to "arrange for the removal of the garrison." [2] He was sent to Sumter, accompanied by one of the governor's aides. He took his leave of Anderson after an hour and a half's interview, making an impression "upon Major Anderson, as well as upon the officers and men of the garrison," that the command was to be withdrawn. [3]

On the return of Fox from Charleston, Lincoln became convinced that his scheme was feasible, and several times called Fox before the members of the cabinet, to whom he criticised the objections of the military authorities. He had the support of Commodore Stringham, who confirmed his views in the presence of Scott, reinforcing them with those of Commodore Stewart, who had declared to Stringham that Sumter could be easily reinforced and provisioned by boats at night. [4] The president, March 28, caused Fox to prepare a memorandum for the war and navy departments directing the organization of the expedition. The same day Lincoln was startled by a memorandum from General

[1] Nicolay and Hay, *Abraham Lincoln*, III., 390–392.

[2] Governor's message, November, 1861, in Davis, *Confederate Government*, I., 272; Crawford, *Fort Sumter*, 374.

[3] Crawford, *Fort Sumter*, 374.

[4] *Naval War Records*, IV., 247.

Scott, forwarded by the secretary, advising the evacuation of Pickens as well as Sumter, on the ground that as the abandonment of Sumter in a few weeks would appear to be a sure necessity, and as it was doubtful whether its voluntary evacuation would have a decisive effect upon the states now wavering between Union and secession, and as continuing to hold Pickens would support the view of necessity, "our Southern friends . . . are clear that the evacuation of both forts would instantly soothe and give confidence to the eight remaining slave-holding States, and render their cordial adherence to this Union perpetual." [1]

Before the state dinner that evening (the first given by Lincoln) this memorandum was shown to the members of the cabinet, who were all present and were called into an adjoining room for consultation. Without any formal votes there was a unanimous expression of dissent from Scott's suggestion, and, under the president's request to meet in formal council the next day, the cabinet retired. [2] At this meeting, March 29, there was a marked change of mind in the members, due to the persistency of Fox and his naval supporters; secretaries Seward and Smith were now the only two who opposed the holding and provisioning of Sumter. The former said, in his memorandum: ". . . I do not think it wise to provoke a civil war begin-

[1] *War Records*, Serial No. 1, p. 200.
[2] Nicolay and Hay, *Abraham Lincoln*, III., 394.

ning at Charleston and in rescue of an untenable position. Therefore I advise against the expedition in every view. Second, I would call in Captain M. C. Meigs forthwith. Aided by his counsel, I would at once, and at every cost, prepare for a war at Pensacola and Texas, to be taken, however, only as a consequence of maintaining the possessions and authority of the United States." [1] The mention of Meigs shows that Seward had already made up his mind to an extraordinary interference with the expedition upon which the president had determined.

But Lincoln's resolve, shown in his directions to Fox the day previous, was not to be moved, and he signed, on the day of this meeting, an order to the secretary of the navy, which read as follows: "Sir: I desire that an expedition to move by sea be got ready to sail as early as the 6th of April next, the whole according to memorandum attached; and that you cooperate with the Secretary of War for that object." The memorandum sent the navy department was as follows: "The *Pocahontas*, at Norfolk, *Pawnee* at Washington, and revenue cutter *Harriet Lane* at New York, to be ready for sea with one month's stores. Three hundred seamen to be ready for leaving the receiving ship at New York." That to the war department ran: "Two hundred men at New York, ready to leave garrison. One year's stores to be put in a portable form." [2]

[1] Nicolay and Hay, *Abraham Lincoln*, III., 430.
[2] *Naval War Records*, IV., 228.

The first steps had thus been taken when, March 30, Justice Campbell came to the secretary of state with a telegram from the governor of South Carolina, giving to the Confederate commissioners the facts of Lamon's visit and his misrepresentations of the president's views. Campbell, April 1, questioning Seward, was told that "the President was concerned at the contents of the telegram"; that the question involved a point of honor; that Lamon had no commission or authority "nor any power to pledge him by any promise or assurance"; and so desirous was the president that Governor Pickens should be satisfied of this that Campbell was requested to question Lamon, who was in the next room. This Campbell declined to do, and, asking what he was to say as to Sumter, received from Seward a written memorandum to the effect "that the president may desire to supply Fort Sumter, but will not undertake to do so without first giving notice to Governor Pickens." "There is no intention," said the secretary, "to reinforce it." Campbell now became apprehensive that the question of holding Sumter was still an open one, and he pressed for something more explicit. Seward replied, "I must see the president"; and on his return he modified the paper to say, "I am satisfied the Government will not undertake to supply Fort Sumter without giving notice to Governor Pickens." [1]

How completely Seward's unwise consultations

[1] *Campbell MS.*, cited by Crawford, *Fort Sumter.* 337-339.

with Campbell had been in accord with Confederate
wishes is shown by Campbell's correspondence with
Davis. "The great want of the Confederate States,"
says Campbell, "is peace." Mentioning that his own
course would depend upon circumstances, he proposed continuing his present relation with the government, and deferring his own final action "until
the chance of being of service at this critical period
has terminated," for all of which he received Davis's
cordial thanks.[1]

Seward's attitude convinced both Campbell and
the commissioners that delay in evacuation, and
only delay, was meant; and Crawford, April 1, wrote
that they had secured "an explicit promise" that
no hostile movement would be made, and that
meanwhile the Confederate states "were not bound
in any way" and were free to go on and organize
their army and concentrate their forces at discretion.[2] Events, however, were moving much too
forcibly to go unnoticed, and the commissioners,
judging from a telegram from the secretary of war
to Beauregard, April 3,[3] undoubtedly had information from subordinates within the departments.
The commissioners thus forestalled the information
in the peaceful letter of April 1, by telegrams of reported movements of ships and troops. They re-

[1] Nicolay and Hay, *Abraham Lincoln*, III., chap. xxiii.
[2] *Confederate Correspondence*, in U. S. Treasury Department
cited by Crawford, *Fort Sumter*, 339.
[3] *War Records*, Serial No. 1, p. 286.

ported, April 5, that the preparation of "a formidable military and naval force is certainly on foot";
the same telegram said, "Having no confidence in
the administration, we say, be ever on your guard." [1]
Justice Campbell was requested to ask an explanation, which he did April 7; the next day Campbell
received an envelope containing a paper without
date or signature, with the words, "Faith as to
Sumter fully kept; wait and see; other suggestions
received, and will be respectfully considered." [2]

Governor Pickens, inundated with telegrams, telegraphed, April 7, wanting to know the truth of
the report that Sumter was to be reinforced.   The
commissioners replied that they thought Sumter
would be evacuated and Pickens provisioned; but
Crawford telegraphed Beauregard the same day
that they had no faith in the assurance given. [3]
Crawford's doubts were amply justified; for Lincoln
had prepared, April 6, with his own hand, instructions to Chew, a clerk of the department of state, to
proceed to Charleston and inform Governor Pickens
that an attempt would be made to supply Sumter
with provisions only, and, if not resisted, no effort
would be made "to throw in men, arms, or ammunition" without further notice, "or in case of an
attack upon the fort." If, on arrival, he should find

---

[1] *Confederate Correspondence*, in U. S. Treasury Department,
cited by Roman, *Beauregard*, I., 34.

[2] *Campbell MS.*, cited by Crawford, *Fort Sumter*, 340; Davis,
Confederate Government, I., 273.

[3] Crawford, *Fort Sumter*, 341.

Sumter already evacuated, surrendered, or attacked, he was to return without seeking an interview.[1]

It was only now, April 8, when there was no longer room for doubt, that Seward's memorandum of March 15, declining to receive the commissioners, was called for by those gentlemen. The memorandum, explicit and forcible in denial of the claims of the commissioners as representing an independent power, brought from them next day a reply which accused the secretary of state of not meeting the issues they presented with "frankness and manliness," and saying, "You are dealing with delusions . . . when you seek to separate our people from our government and to characterize the deliberate, sovereign act of the people as a 'perversion of a temporary and partisan excitement.' If you cherish these dreams you will be awakened from them and find them as unreal and as unsubstantial as others in which you have recently indulged."[2]

Though the Federal administration has been severely attacked by Confederate authorities for want of honest dealing, the attack is unjust. The commissioners were the victims of Justice Campbell's belief in Seward as the actual head of affairs, which Seward thought himself to be. The president was unaware of Seward's assurance that Sumter would be evacuated, and never sanctioned the

---

[1] Nicolay and Hay, *Abraham Lincoln*, IV., 34.
[2] In full in Moore. *Rebellion Record*, I., Doc. 51, pp. 49–51.

statement.[1] One can understand Seward's extraordinary hallucination by reference to his equally extraordinary action in laying, April 1, before Lincoln "Thoughts for the President's Consideration," so erratic in character as to be now scarcely conceivable. Seward practically proposed that he should take over the president's duties and direct the administration of the government, suggesting at the same time a foreign policy which could only have been fatal. Lincoln's reply, a model of kindliness, reserve, and power, settled the question of mastership between them forever.[2]

The *Powhatan* returned, March 13, to New York from the Gulf, and was ordered out of commission for repairs only the day before the writing of the president's memorandum of March 28. The navy department telegraphed, April 1, countermanding its order for repairs and ordering the ship to be ready for sea at the earliest possible moment,—a duty complicated by the fact that she had gone out of commission at 2 P.M. of that day, that her crew was transferred to the receiving-ship, and her officers detached and mostly gone home on leave of absence. When it is understood that "going out of commission" means the detachment of all officers, the transfer of the crew, the landing of stores, and the partial dismantling of the ship, it will be

[1] Welles, *Lincoln and Seward*, 56.
[2] Lincoln *Works* (ed. of 1894), II., 29, 30; Nicolay and Hay, *Abraham Lincoln*, III., 448.

seen how much the delay by the navy department in sending its telegram meant. Captain Foote, the acting commandant, promised, however, by working day and night, to have the ship ready in four days.

Orders were issued, April 5, to Captain Mercer of the *Powhatan*, placing under his command, for the purposes of Fox's expedition, the *Powhatan*, *Pocahontas*, *Pawnee*, and *Harriet Lane*. If the authorities at Charleston should permit Sumter to be provisioned, the ships were to return north. Should they attempt to prevent the vessels with supplies from entering the harbor, Mercer was to protect them, "repelling by force, if necessary, all obstructions towards provisioning the fort and reinforcing it; for in case of resistance to the peaceable primary object of the expedition a reinforcement of the garrison will also be attempted." [1] The *Powhatan* failed to accompany the expedition; the cause brings into startling prominence Seward's disregard of the president's views, and the fixedness of his own impression that he was the true head of the administration.

On the evening of April 1, Lieutenant David D. Porter was having his last dinner with his family prior to departure for New York to take the steamer for California, with the determination to resign and go into the employ of the Pacific Mail Steamship Company. A note from the secretary of state requested his presence. Arriving at the latter's resi-

[1] *Naval War Records*, IV. 225.

dence, he was asked if he could devise a plan by which Fort Pickens could be saved, and he opened out a plan, which he had already discussed with Captain Montgomery Meigs of the engineers, of taking a military force in a transport, convoyed by a ship-of-war, and landing them under the protection of the latter's guns. He proposed entering the harbor, supported by the other ships of the powerful naval force present, and engaging the Confederate batteries if necessary. Captain Meigs, who had but a short time before returned from duty as the engineer officer in charge of the works at the Dry Tortugas, and was much impressed with the necessity of holding the Gulf forts still in the hands of the United States authorities, had suggested sending for Porter. Meigs having joined the party, the three went to the White House and explained the plan, which the president thereupon adopted. It was decided that the *Powhatan* should be chosen, that Porter should command, "and that the orders should be issued directly by the President without the intervention of the Secretary of the Navy, and even without his knowledge. The President expressed doubt as to the propriety of such a course, but being pressed by Mr. Seward, who reassured him on that point, with Porter's concurrence, he acquiesced and signed the necessary orders." [1]

Probably none of the four knew of the orders already issued to the *Powhatan*, but this was no

[1] Soley, *Porter*, 101.

extenuation of this gravely improper procedure; the secretary of the navy was quite as worthy of the president's confidence as any of the others, and it was in the power of the president as commander-in-chief to overrule Welles should he object to the use of the *Powhatan*, which undoubtedly the latter would have done. The intense secrecy insisted upon has a bad look, and the whole proceeding reflects discredit upon all three of the men involved in misleading the president, but most of all upon the secretary of state.

Orders were prepared by Porter, copied by Meigs, and signed by the president. The order to Porter was as follows: "You will proceed to New York, and with the least possible delay assume command of any naval steamer available. Proceed to Pensacola Harbor, and at any cost or risk prevent any expedition from the mainland reaching Fort Pickens or Santa Rosa [island]. You will exhibit this order to any naval officer at Pensacola, if you deem it necessary after you have established yourself within the harbor, and will request cooperation by the entrance of at least one other vessel. This order, its object, and your destination will be communicated to no person whatever until you reach the harbor of Pensacola.

"ABRAHAM LINCOLN.

"Recommended: Wm. H. Seward."

The second order was to Captain Mercer, detaching him from the command of the *Powhatan*, as it was "necessary to place in command . . . and for a special purpose, an officer who is duly informed and instructed in relation to the wishes of the Government."

The third directed the commandant of the navy-yard at New York to fit out the *Powhatan* without delay. "Lieutenant Porter will relieve Captain Mercer in command of her. She is bound on secret service, and you will, under no circumstances, communicate to the Navy Department the fact that she is fitting out."

A fourth order, a commission of plenary powers to Porter, was also signed by the president. "Lieutenant D. D. Porter will take command of the steamer *Powhatan*, or any other United States steamer ready for sea, which he may deem most fit for the service to which he has been assigned by confidential instructions of this date. All officers are commanded to afford him all such facilities as he may deem necessary for getting to sea as soon as possible. He will select the officers who are to accompany him." Again appeared the somewhat foolish subscription, "Recommended: Wm. H. Seward."[1]

When Porter and Meigs left the White House, the former believed that he was to command an expedition the main purpose of which was to recover the harbor of Pensacola.[2] But Meigs had other views. The two went to Scott's headquarters to

[1] Soley, *Porter*, 102–104.   [2] *Ibid.*, 105.

arrange regarding the army force to be taken, but Porter "was refused admission and went home." He thus knew nothing of orders other than his own until he arrived at Pensacola. These other orders, signed by Scott, were countersigned "Approved" by the president the next day, and thus had full force as from the latter. They placed Colonel Harvey Brown in general command, and were accompanied by a memorandum signed by the president and which must have been prepared the evening previous at Scott's headquarters, as it bore date April 1. It was as follows: "All officers of the Army and Navy, to whom this order may be exhibited, will aid by every means in their power the expedition under command of Col. Harvey Brown, supplying him with men and material and cooperating with him as he may desire."[1] One can well believe that had Porter been admitted to Scott's headquarters, and had he known the result of Meigs's visit there, he would have thrown up the command, have returned to his earlier intention, and the navy would thus have lost one of its greatest officers.

Although the commandant at the New York yard reported, April 4, a call by Captain Meigs showing authority to have certain preparations made, it apparently had not attracted the attention of the navy department. Not until April 6 were matters understood by Welles, who at once

[1] *War Records*, Serial No. 1, pp. 365–367.

protested to the president. Lincoln immediately directed the return of Mercer to the *Powhatan* and the ship's restoration to her previous assignment. Though Seward remonstrated, and claimed that she was essential to reinforce Pickens, the president was decided, and ordered that a telegram be sent covering his directions, which reached the navy-yard at 3 P.M. The *Powhatan* had, however, left the yard at 2.30, preceded by the transports *Atlantic* and *Illinois*, with Colonel Brown, Captain Meigs, and the troops. A fast tug overhauled her at Sandy Hook and delivered the telegram. Unfortunately this was signed by the secretary of state, reading as follows: "Give the *Powhatan* up to Captain Mercer. Seward." But Porter had the president's order; he was not subordinate to Seward, and he was in nowise bound to acknowledge his authority. He replied to Seward: "I received my orders from the president and shall proceed and execute them." [1]   The victory, such as it was, was thus still with Seward.

The final result at Pensacola was a scandalous inaction. Brown, on April 17, the day after his arrival, wrote to Bragg, the Confederate commander, practically declaring a truce, and making any movement, whether of army or navy, impossible.[2] Porter, on his arrival, April 17, at once proceeded to carry out his orders to "establish himself within the

[1] Soley, *Porter*, 110–112.
[2] *War Records*, Serial No. 1, p. 380.

harbor," and was only prevented by the *Wyandotte's* placing herself, at Meigs's request, across the *Powhatan's* course. Brown's authority from the president of a later date could not be disputed, and Pensacola remained long in the hands of the Confederates undisturbed, though Bragg's report to his secretary of war—"I am not prepared with my batteries for anything more than a feeble defense " [1]— shows how easily Porter would have succeeded. It is a sad history from the improper beginning to the thoroughly abortive end.

The story is not complete without giving the results of the *Mohawk's* mission, which, as mentioned, was sent March 12 from New York to Pensacola with orders to Vogdes to land his company from the *Brooklyn*. With the inefficiency so rife at the time, and with the general want of correlation, these orders were signed by General Scott only. The *Mohawk* arrived April 1. Captain Adams, the senior naval officer, refused to recognize Scott's authority to set aside the truce, signed conjointly January 29 by the secretaries of war and of the navy, and Vogdes was not landed. A courier was sent by Adams to explain, who arrived at Washington April 6. That same night Lieutenant (later Rear-Admiral) Worden left with verbal instructions to Adams to land Vogdes and his men. He arrived at Pensacola April 10, and, after some demur, was able to get out to the *Sabine*, the senior officer's

[1] *War Records*, Serial No. 1, p. 457.

ship, April 12. The troops were landed the same night without opposition. On Vogdes's request, Adams landed some of his marines, and held in readiness five hundred seamen and marines to go if needed.[1]

Despite the conviction of the chief of engineers, General Totten, expressed in an elaborate paper of April 3 upon the situation at Sumter and Pickens, "that neither these measures nor any others now within our reach will in my opinion prevent the loss of Fort Pickens,"[2] there was, after April 12, no danger whatever; nor would there, with any display of energy and initiative, have been danger at any time. The despatch of the *Powhatan* was thus a perfectly useless measure unless Pensacola was to be taken, which it should have been, as Porter proposed and intended. Worden, it should be said, attempted to return by land, was taken prisoner and kept in confinement seven months, returning in time to command the *Monitor* in 1862.

[1] Meigs to Seward, in *War Records*, Serial No. 1, p. 375.
[2] *War Records*, Serial No. 1, pp. 232–235.

CHAPTER XIX

THE FALL OF FORT SUMTER

(APRIL, 1861)

LAMON'S officiousness resulted in giving both to Anderson and to the Confederate authorities an impression that Sumter would surely be evacuated; hence Beauregard, March 26, wrote to Anderson offering facilities for removal, but asking his word of honor that the fort would be left without any preparation for its destruction or injury. This demand deeply wounded Anderson, and he resented it in a letter of the same date, saying, "If I can only be permitted to leave on the pledge you mention, I shall never, so help me God, leave this fort alive." [1] Beauregard hastened to state that he had only alluded to the "pledge" on account of the "high source" from which the rumors appeared to come, and made a full amend, which re-established their usual relations.

Anderson had informed Fox that, by placing the command on a short allowance, he could make the provisions last until after April 10; but not receiving instructions from the war department that it was

[1] *War Records*, Serial No. 1, p. 222.

desirable to do so, it had not been done.[1]   He had already reported, March 31, that his last barrel of flour had been issued two days before.[2]

Anderson's little command, as he explained to Washington April 1, would now face starvation should the daily supply of fresh meat and vegetables, still allowed from Charleston, be cut off.   Being in daily expectation, since the return of Colonel Lamon to Washington, of receiving orders to vacate the post, he had, to the great disadvantage of the food supply, kept the engineer laborers as long as he could.   He now asked permission to send them from Sumter; but the request, referred to Montgomery April 2 by Beauregard, was refused, unless all the garrison should go.[3]

April 1 an ice-laden schooner bound for Savannah entered Charleston harbor by mistake, and was fired upon by a Morris Island battery.   Again the Sumter batteries were manned and a consultation held, at which five of the eight officers declared in favor of opening fire, but no action was taken by Anderson beyond sending an officer to the offending battery, from which word was returned by its commanding officer that he was simply carrying out his orders to fire upon any vessel carrying the United States colors which attempted to enter.

On April 4, Anderson assembled his officers, and for the first time made known to them the orders of

[1] *War Records*, Serial No. 1, p. 230.
[2] *Ibid.*, p. 228.   [3] *Ibid.*, pp. 284, 285.

January 10 and February 23, directing him to act strictly on the defensive. As Lieutenant Talbot had just been promoted captain and ordered to Washington, Anderson determined to send by him his despatches. In order to arrange for his departure, Talbot, April 4, accompanied Lieutenant Snyder, under a white flag, to call the attention of the governor to the fact that the schooner fired upon had not been warned by one of their own vessels, as had been arranged. It developed that the guard-vessel on duty had come in on account of heavy weather, and the commanding officer was consequently dismissed. The request to allow Talbot to proceed brought out the fact that orders had been received from Montgomery not to allow any portion of the garrison to leave the fort unless all should go,[1]—which, however, Beauregard construed, for the benefit of Talbot, to apply more particularly to laborers and enlisted men,[2]—and also that the following telegram from Commissioner Crawford had reached Charleston April 1: "I am authorized to say that this Government will not undertake to supply Sumter without notice to you. My opinion is that the President has not the courage to execute the order agreed upon in Cabinet for the evacuation of the fort, but that he intends to shift the responsibility upon Major Anderson by suffering him to be starved out. Would it not be

[1] *War Records*, Serial No. 1, p. 285.
[2] Crawford, *Fort Sumter*, 377.

well to aid in this by cutting off all supplies?" [1]
Beauregard had, the same day, sent the message
to the Confederate secretary of war, with the remark, "Batteries here ready to open Wednesday or
Thursday. What instructions?"

The knowledge of these telegrams called from
Anderson, April 5, a pathetic despatch to the war
department: "I cannot but think Mr. Crawford
has misunderstood what he has heard in Washington, as I cannot think the Government could abandon, without instructions and without advice, a
command which has tried to do all its duty to our
country." He ended a fervent appeal for this act
of justice with, "Unless we receive supplies I shall
be compelled to stay here without food, or to abandon this post very early next week." [2] "At this
time," says Doubleday, "the seeming indifference of
the politicians to our fate made us feel like orphan
children of the Republic, deserted by both the State
and Federal administration." [3]

Two days later Anderson received a letter of April
4 from the secretary of war, informing him of the
government's purpose to send the Fox expedition,
and hoping that he would be able to sustain himself
until the 11th or 12th. [4] The same day he was informed by the Confederate authorities that the supply of provisions had been stopped, and late that

[1] War Records, Serial No. 1, p. 283.   [2] Ibid., p. 241.
[3] Doubleday, Sumter and Moultrie, 98.
[4] War Records, Serial No. 1, p. 235.

evening that no mails coming or going would be allowed to pass. The fort was to be "completely isolated." This action was undoubtedly taken at this moment in consequence of a telegram from Washington sent Magrath April 6, as follows: "Positively determined not to withdraw Anderson. Supplies go immediately, supported by naval force under Stringham if their landing be resisted." This telegram, signed "A Friend," was, as later became known, from James E. Harvey, who was about to go as United States minister to Portugal. It was sent to Montgomery and had its full effect.[1]

Just before the reception of the information regarding the stoppage of mails, Anderson had posted his acknowledgment of the war department's letter of the 4th and a report by Foster to the chief-engineer of the army; both letters were opened by the Confederate authorities, and gave full confirmation of the accuracy of the telegram from "A Friend." Anderson said that "the resumption of work yesterday (Sunday) at various points on Morris Island, and the vigorous prosecution of it this morning, . . . shows that they have either received some news from Washington which has put them on the *qui vive*, or that they have received orders from Montgomery to commence operations here. I fear" that Fox's attempt "cannot fail to be disastrous to all concerned. . . . We have not oil enough to keep a light in lanterns for one night. The boats will have

[1] Nicolay and Hay, *Abraham Lincoln*, IV., 31, 32.

therefore to rely at night entirely upon other marks. I ought to have been informed that this expedition was to come. Colonel Lamon's remark convinced me that the idea merely hinted at to me by Captain Fox would not be carried out. We shall strive to do our duty, though I frankly say that my heart is not in the war which I see is to be thus commenced." [1]

As shown by despatches which Anderson had no means of sending, and carried north, eight guard-boats and signal-vessels were on duty out far beyond the bar; a fourth gun had been added to the new battery on Sullivan's Island, which had until the 8th been masked by a house now torn down, and which bore directly upon any boat attempting to land stores on the left bank. There was bread enough to last, using half-rations, until dinner-time Friday (12th). Anderson reported the command in fine spirits. It was evident that a hostile force was expected. The iron-clad floating battery appeared the morning of the 11th at the west end of Sullivan's Island. Anderson, in ignorance that his own intercepted letter and Harvey's telegram had given them all they needed to know, said: "Had they been in possession of the information contained in your letter of the 4th instant they could not have made better arrangements than these they have made and are making to thwart the contemplated scheme." [2]

[1] *War Records*, Serial No. 1, p. 294.   [2] *Ibid.*, pp. 249–251.

Chew, who, as mentioned, had been selected as
the messenger to carry to Charleston the notice of
the president's intention to attempt to provision
Sumter, left Washington Saturday, April 6, at 6
P.M., in company with Captain Talbot, and reached
Charleston forty-eight hours later; finding no action taken against Sumter, he delivered a copy of
his memorandum to the governor, who called General Beauregard into the consultation. Captain
Talbot's request to join the garrison at Sumter was
referred to Beauregard, and peremptorily refused,
Beauregard remarking the instructions from Montgomery required that no communication whatever
should be permitted with Anderson except to convey an order for the evacuation of the fort.[1] The
return of the envoys to Washington was much delayed by disarrangement of trains by order of
Beauregard, who also held all telegrams from Chew
to Lincoln.[2]

Sumter now mounted fifty-nine guns, twenty-
seven of the heaviest of which were in barbette (the
upper and open tier). In the lowest tier there were
also twenty-seven, four of which were 42-pounders
and the remainder 32's. The ports of the second
(or middle tier), eight feet square, were closed by
a three-foot brick wall, laid in cement and backed
in twenty-seven of the more exposed by two feet of
sand kept in place by planks or barrels. On the

[1] Talbot's report, in *War Records*, Serial No. 1, p. 251.
[2] Roman, *Beauregard*, I., 33.

parade were one 10-inch and four 8-inch guns, mounted as howitzers, the former to throw shells into Charleston, the latter into the batteries on Cummings Point. The guns bearing upon the three batteries on the west end of Sullivan's Island were ten 32-pounders; on Fort Moultrie, two 43-pounders. Five guns bore upon the mortar battery at Fort Johnson. Seven hundred cartridges had been made up, material of every kind, even the woollen shirts of the men, being used.[1]

Bearing upon Fort Sumter there were on Sullivan's Island three 8-inch, two 32-pounders, and six 24-pounders in Fort Moultrie; two 32-pounders and two 24-pounders in the new enfilade battery; one 9-inch, two 42-pounders, and two 32-pounders at the Point and aboard the floating battery, and six 10-inch mortars; on Morris Island, two 42-pounders, one 12-pounder Blakely rifle, three 8-inch guns, and seven 10-inch mortars; at Fort Johnson, one 24-pounder and four 10-inch mortars; at Mount Pleasant, one 10-inch mortar: a total of twenty-seven guns and eighteen mortars.[2] The latter were particularly to be feared, as mortar fire under the conditions of a fixed target and perfectly established distances is extremely accurate. The interior of the fort was thus as vulnerable as the exterior.

Governor Pickens at once sent to Montgomery a

[1] *War Records*, Serial No. 1, pp. 12–25, 213–216.
[2] *Ibid.*, pp. 25–58.

telegram reporting the visit of the president's messenger. A lengthy discussion ensued in the Confederate cabinet. Toombs, the secretary of state, said: "The firing upon that fort will inaugurate a civil war greater than any the world has yet seen; and I do not feel competent to advise you."[1] In the state of southern feeling, however, the only thing possible was for Secretary Walker to order Beauregard, April 10, "If you have no doubt of the authorized character of the agent who communicated to you the intention of the Washington Government to supply Sumter by force, you will at once demand its evacuation, and if this is refused proceed, in such manner as you may determine, to reduce it."[2] Beauregard answered the same day, "The demand will be made to-morrow at 12 o'clock." To this came reply from Montgomery, "Unless there are special reasons connected with your own condition, it is considered proper that you should make the demand at an earlier date." Beauregard replied (all these of the same date, the 10th), "The reasons are special for 12 o'clock."[3] These imperative "reasons" proved to be shortness of powder, then on its way, and which arrived from Augusta, Georgia, that evening,[4] and the placing of a new rifled 12-pounder.

---

[1] Statement of Ex-Confederate secretary of war to writer; Crawford, *Fort Sumter*, 421.

[2] *War Records*, Serial No. 1, p. 297.　　　　　[3] *Ibid*.

[4] Crawford, *Fort Sumter*, 422.

Shortly after noon, April 11, a boat bearing a white flag and three officers, the senior being Colonel James Chesnut, recently a United States senator, pushed off from a Charleston wharf and arrived at Sumter at half-past three. The officers being conducted to Anderson, a demand for the evacuation of the work was delivered. The officers of the fort were summoned, and after an hour's discussion it was determined, without dissent, to refuse the demand, and a written refusal was sent, in which Anderson regretted that his sense of honor and his obligations to his government prevented his compliance.[1] Anderson accompanied the messengers as far as the main gate, where he asked, "Will General Beauregard open his batteries without further notice to me?" Colonel Chesnut replied, "I think not," adding, "No, I can say to you that he will not, without giving you further notice." On this Anderson unwisely remarked that he would be starved out anyway in a few days if Beauregard did not batter him to pieces with his guns. Chesnut asked if he might report this to Beauregard. Anderson declined to give it such character, but said it was the fact.[2]

This information telegraphed to Montgomery elicited the reply: "Do not desire needlessly to bombard Fort Sumter. If Major Anderson will state the time at which, as indicated by him, he

[1] *War Records*, Serial No. 1, p. 13.
[2] *Ibid.*, p. 59; Crawford, *Fort Sumter*, 424.

will evacuate, and agree that in the mean time he
will not use his guns against us unless ours should
be employed against Sumter, you are authorized
thus to avoid the effusion of blood. If this or its
equivalent be refused, reduce the fort as your judgment decides to be most practicable." [1]

A second note from Beauregard was presented
that night, and after a conference with his officers
of three hours, in which the question of food was
the main consideration, Anderson replied, "I will,
if provided with proper and necessary means of
transportation, evacuate Fort Sumter by noon on
the 15th instant . . . should I not receive prior to
that time controlling instructions from my Government or additional supplies." The terms of the reply were considered by the messengers "manifestly
futile," and at 3.20 A.M. of the 12th the following
note was handed by Beauregard's aides, Chesnut
and Lee, to Anderson: "By authority of Brigadier-
General Beauregard, commanding the provisional
forces of the Confederate States, we have the honor
to notify you that he will open the fire of his batteries on Fort Sumter in one hour from this time." [2]

Meantime Fox, intrusted with the general charge
of the relief expedition, was sent by the president,
March 30, to New York, with verbal instructions
to prepare for the voyage but to make no binding
engagements. Not having received the written au-

---

[1] *War Records*, Serial No. 1, p. 301.
[2] Crawford, *Fort Sumter*, 425, 426.

thority expected, he returned to Washington April 2, and on the 4th the final decision was reached, and Fox was informed that a messenger would be sent to the authorities at Charleston to notify them of the president's action. Fox mentioned to the president that he would have but nine days to charter vessels and reach Charleston, six hundred and thirty-two miles distant. He arrived at New York April 5, bearing an order from General Scott to Lieutenant-Colonel H. L. Scott (son-in-law and aide-de-camp to the general-in-chief), embracing all his wants and directing Colonel Scott to give in his name all necessary instructions. Colonel Scott ridiculed the idea of relief, and his indifference caused the loss of half a day of precious time, besides furnishing recruits who, Fox complained, were "totally unfit" for the service they were sent on.[1]

Fox at once engaged the large steamer *Baltic* for troops and stores, and, after great difficulty, obtained three tugs, the *Uncle Ben*, *Freeborn*, and *Yankee*, the last fitted to throw hot water. The *Pocahontas*, *Pawnee*, and the revenue-cutter *Harriet Lane*, as already mentioned, were to be a part of the force, which thus, with the *Powhatan*, included four armed vessels, the last being of very considerable power. The *Pawnee*, Commander Rowan, sailed from Washington the 9th; the *Pocahontas*, Captain Gillis, from Norfolk the 10th; the *Harriet Lane*, Captain Faunce, from New York the 8th; the

[1] *Naval War Records*, IV., 248.

Baltic, Captain Fletcher, the 9th. The *Powhatan* was already far on her way to Pensacola.

The *Baltic* arrived at the rendezvous, ten miles east of Charleston bar, at 3 A.M. of the 12th, and found there the *Harriet Lane;* at six the *Pawnee* arrived; the *Powhatan* was not visible. The *Baltic*, followed by the *Harriet Lane*, stood in towards the land, when heavy guns were heard and the smoke and shells from the batteries which had opened that morning on Sumter were distinctly visible. Fox stood out to inform Rowan, of the *Pawnee*. Rowan asked for a pilot, declaring his intention of going in and sharing the fate of his brethren of the army. Fox went aboard the *Pawnee* and informed him that he would answer for it that the government did not expect such a sacrifice, having settled maturely upon the policy in instructions to Captain Mercer and himself. The *Nashville*, from New York, and a number of merchant vessels off the bar, gave the appearance of the presence of a large naval fleet.

The weather continued very bad, with a heavy sea. No tugboats had arrived; the tug *Freeborn* did not leave New York; the *Uncle Ben* was driven into Wilmington by the gale; the *Yankee* did not arrive off Charleston bar until April 15; all too late for any service; neither the *Pawnee* nor the *Harriet Lane* had boats or men to carry supplies; the *Baltic* stood out to the rendezvous and signalled all night for the expected *Powhatan*. The next morning, the 13th, was thick and foggy, with a heavy ground swell, and the *Baltic*, feeling her way in, touched on Rattlesnake shoal, but without damage; a great volume of black smoke was seen from Sumter. No tugboats had yet arrived, and a schooner near by, loaded with ice, was seized and preparations made to load her for entering the following night. Going aboard the *Pawnee*, Fox now learned that a note from Captain Mercer of the *Powhatan* mentioned that he had been detached by superior authority and that the ship had gone elsewhere; though Fox had left New York two days later than the *Powhatan*, he had had no intimation of the change. At 2 P.M., April 13, the *Pocahontas* arrived, and the squadron, powerless for relief, through the absence of the *Powhatan* and the tugs, was obliged to witness the progress of the bombardment.[1]

"About four A.M. on the twelfth," says Doubleday, "I was awakened by some one groping about my room in the dark and calling out my name." This was Anderson, who had come to inform his second in command of the information just received of the intention of the Confederates to open fire an hour later.[2] At 4.30, the Confederates being able to make out the outline of the fort, a gun at Fort Johnson was fired as the signal to open; the first shotted gun was then fired from Morris Island by Edmund Ruffin, an aged secessionist from Virginia, who had long, in pamphlet and speech, advocated

[1] Fox's report, in *Naval War Records*, IV., 245–251.
[2] Doubleday, *Sumter and Moultrie*, 142.

separation from the Union. The fire from the batteries at once became general.

The fort began its return at seven o'clock. All the officers and men, including the engineers, had been divided into three reliefs of two hours each, and the forty-three workmen yet remaining all volunteered for duty. It was, however, an absurdly meagre force to work such a number of guns and to be pitted against the surrounding batteries, manned by more than six thousand men. The number of cartridges was so reduced by the middle of the day, though the six needles available were kept steadily at work in making cartridge bags, that the firing had to slacken and be confined to the six guns bearing towards Moultrie and the batteries on the west end of Sullivan's Island. The mortar fire had become very accurate, so that when the 13-inch shells "came down in a vertical direction, and buried themselves in the parade-ground, their explosion shook the fort like an earthquake." [1] The horizontal fire also grew in accuracy, and Anderson, to save his men, withdrew them from the barbette guns and used those of the lower tiers only. Unfortunately, these were of too light a caliber to be effective against the Morris Island batteries, the shot rebounding without effect from the face of the iron-clad battery there, as well as from the floating iron-clad battery moored behind the sea-wall at Sullivan's Island. The withdrawal of the men from the

[1] Doubleday, *Sumter and Moultrie*, 147.

heavier battery could only be justified by the already foregone result, and no doubt this was in Anderson's mind. The garrison was reduced to pork and water, and, however willing, it could not with such meagre food withstand the strain of the heavy labor of working the guns; to add to the difficulties, the guns, strange to say, were not provided with breech-sights, and these had to be improvised with notched sticks.[1]

The shells from the batteries set fire to the barracks three times during the day, and the precision of the vertical fire was such that the four 8-inch and one 10-inch columbiad, planted in the parade, could not be used. Half the shells fired from the seventeen mortars engaged came within, or exploded above, the parapet of the fort, and only about ten buried themselves in the soft earth of the parade without exploding. Two of the barbette guns were struck by the fire from Moultrie, which also damaged greatly the roof of the barracks and the stair towers. None of the shot came through. The day closed stormy and with a high tide, without any material damage to the strength of the fort. Throughout the night the Confederate batteries threw shell every ten or fifteen minutes. The garrison was occupied until midnight in making cartridge bags, for which all the extra clothing was cut up, and all the coarse paper and extra hospital sheets used.[2]

[1] Doubleday, *Sumter and Moultrie*, 147.
[2] Foster's report, in *War Records*, Serial No. 1, pp. 20, 21.

At daylight, April 13, all the batteries again opened, and the new 12-pounder Blakely rifle, which had arrived but four days before from abroad,[1] caused the wounding of a sergeant and three men by the fragments thrown off from the interior of the wall by its deep penetration. An engineer employed was severely wounded by a fragment of shell. Hot shot now became frequent, and at nine o'clock the officers' quarters were set afire. As it was evident the fire would soon surround the magazine, every one not at the guns was employed to get out powder; but only fifty barrels could be removed to the casemates, when it became necessary from the spread of the flames to close the magazine. The whole range of the officers' quarters was soon in flames, and the clouds of smoke and cinders sent into the casemates set on fire many of the men's beds and boxes, making the retention of the powder so dangerous that all but five barrels were thrown into the sea.[2]

By eleven o'clock the fire and smoke were driven by the wind in such masses into the point where the men had taken refuge that suffocation appeared imminent. "The roaring and crackling of the flames, the dense masses of whirling smoke, the bursting of the enemy's shells, and our own which were exploding in the burning rooms, the crashing of the shot and the sound of masonry falling in every direction, made the fort a pande-

[1] *War Records*, Serial No. 1, p. 293.   [2] *Ibid.*, p. 22.

monium. . . . There was a tower at each angle of
the fort. One of these containing great quantities
of shells . . . was almost completely shattered by
successive explosions. The massive wooden gates,
studded with iron nails, were burned, and the wall
built behind them was now a heap of debris, so
that the main entrance was wide open for an as-
saulting party." [1]

But however great the apparent damage and the
discomfort and danger while the fire lasted, the firing could have been resumed "as soon as the walls
cooled sufficiently to open the magazines, and then,
having blown down the wall projecting above the
parapet, so as to get rid of the flying bricks, and
built up the main gates with stones and rubbish,
the fort would actually have been in a more defen-
sible condition than when the action commenced." [2]

But want of men, want of food, and want of powder together made a *force majeure* against which
further strife was useless; and when, about 1 P.M.,
the flag-staff was shot away, though the flag was at
once flown from an improvised staff, a boat was
sent from the commanding officer at Morris Island,
bringing Colonel (Ex-Senator) Wigfall and a com-
panion bearing a white flag, to inquire if the fort
had surrendered.

Being allowed entrance, Major Anderson was
sought for, and Wigfall, using Beauregard's name,

[1] Doubleday, *Sumter and Moultrie*, 158.
[2] Foster's report, in *War Records*, Serial No. 1, p. 24.

offered Anderson his own terms.   Wigfall exhibited
a white handkerchief from the parapet, and this
being noticed brought from Beauregard himself
Colonel Chesnut, Colonel Roger A. Pryor, Colonel
William Porcher Miles, and Captain Lee, followed
soon by Beauregard's adjutant-general, Jones, Ex-
Governor Manning, and Colonel Alston.   It tran-
spired that Wigfall had not seen Beauregard for
two days, and that his visit was wholly unauthor-
ized.   The proper authorities, however, being now
at hand, arrangements were concluded at 7 P.M.,
Anderson surrendering (after some correspondence),
with permission to salute the flag as it was hauled
down, to march out with colors flying and drums
beating and with arms and private baggage.[1]

Noticing the disappearance of the colors, a flag of
truce was sent in from the squadron outside, and
arrangements made for carrying the garrison north.
Next morning, Sunday, April 14, with a salute of
fifty guns the flag was finally hauled down.   It had
been Anderson's intention to fire a hundred guns,
but a lamentable accident occurred in the prema-
ture discharge of one, by which one man was killed,
another mortally wounded, and four others seriously injured.   This accident delayed the departure
until 4 P.M., when the little company of some eighty
men, accompanied by the forty laborers,[2] marched

[1] Foster's report, in *War Records*, Serial No. 1, pp. 23, 24.
[2] Doubleday, *Sumter and Moultrie*, App., where the names
appear.

out of the gate with their flags flying and drums beating. The steamer *Isabel* carried Anderson and his men to the *Baltic*, and at nightfall they were on their way north.

April 15, the day after the surrender, the president issued his proclamation calling "forth the militia of the several states of the Union" to the number of seventy-five thousand men, in order to suppress "combinations too powerful to be suppressed by the ordinary course of judicial proceedings, or by the powers vested in the marshals by law," and "to cause the laws to be duly executed." Congress was called to convene July 4. An immediate effect of the proclamation was the secession of Virginia, April 17, the conservative elements of the state convention, although in the majority, being overwhelmed by the enthusiasm and impetus of the secession attack. Another prompt result was the formation of the northwestern counties into what is now West Virginia.

Fox's expedition, however abortive in a physical sense, did much more than attempt to succor Sumter; it was the instrument through which the fort was held to the accomplishment of the fateful mistake of the Confederacy in striking the first blow. It prevented the voluntary yielding of the fort, and was an exhibition of the intention of the government to hold its own. It was thus elemental in its effects. Had Anderson withdrawn and hauled down his flag without a shot from the South, it

would have been for the Federal government to
strike the first blow of war; and its call for men
would have met with a different response to that
which came from the electric impulse which the
firing upon the flag caused to vibrate through the
North. This expectation was the basis of Lincoln's determination. Almost alone, unmovable by
cabinet or war department, he saw with the certainty of the seer what holding Sumter meant, and
continued on the unchangeable way which from
the first he had taken. In his letter of sympathy
to Fox, May 1, he said: "You and I both anticipated
that the cause of the country would be advanced
by making the attempt to provision Fort Sumter
even if it should fail, and it is no small consolation
now to feel that our anticipation is justified by the
result."[1]

The enthusiastic response of the North to the
proclamation was witness to the truth of Lincoln's
view, as well as to the North's determination that
the offended dignity of the Union should be avenged,
its strongholds regained, its boundaries made intact, and that the United States be proved to be a
nation. It was for this the Union fought; the freeing of the blacks was but a natural and necessary
incident. The assault upon Sumter was the knife
driven by the hand of the South itself into the
vitals of slavery.

While the struggle thus begun was to desolate

[1] *Naval War Records*, IV., 251.

the South and wring the hearts of millions, it was to revivify the Union as a whole and arouse the South into a life far exceeding, in its moral and economic sides alike, any which could have been possible under its ancient régime. However great the loss of life and property, however distressing the destruction of so much of the flower of northern and southern manhood, and of a social organization which had been the growth of two centuries, the outcome, besides the vital one of nationality, has been one of greatest good for both sections; for the North, through the ideals which come through such self-sacrifice; for the South, immeasurable in freeing both whites and blacks from conditions which made development impossible to both. The negro is now given the greatest and most favorable opportunity in his race history, in having the uplift of association on fair terms with a numerous and highly civilized race, an association necessary for his success. The whites are freed from the enforced segregation of the great mass on lonely farms, with no outlook beyond, which was their sole portion; they have been drawn into the highways of progress, and can take, and are taking, a fair and equal share in the expansion of the country such as never could have come under slavery. The South's salvation demanded that it should, through freedom, take up the march of the world. Even the shade of Calhoun cannot be altogether dissatisfied.

CHAPTER XX

CRITICAL ESSAY ON AUTHORITIES

BIBLIOGRAPHICAL AIDS

THE materials bearing upon the initial subject of this book, the earlier causes leading to the war, are largely cited in the critical essays in other volumes of this series; notably in Albert Bushnell Hart, *Slavery and Abolition* (XVI.); George P. Garrison, *Westward Extension* (XVII.); Theodore C. Smith, *Parties and Slavery* (XVIII.); and James K. Hosmer, *Appeal to Arms* (XX.). An excellent general list is John Russell Bartlett, *Catalogue of Books and Pamphlets Relating to the Civil War in the United States* (1866); also, J. T. Ritchie, *Lincolniana, a List of Lincolniana in the Library of Congress* (1906); C. H. Van Tyne and W. G. Leland, *Guide to the Archives of the Government of the United States in Washington* (Carnegie Institution, *Publications*, No. 14).

GENERAL SECONDARY WORKS

Hermann E. von Holst, *Constitutional History of the United States* (7 vols., 1885–1892), is the completest study of the constitutional aspects of events up to 1860, but is wanting in any true comprehension of the South and its conditions. James Schouler, *History of the United States under the Constitution* (6 vols., 1880–1897), is an excellent record of events, told with entertaining vigor, with accuracy, and with good references. James Ford Rhodes, *History of the United States from the Compromise of 1850* (7 vols., 1893–1906), gives in the introductory chapters an excellent review of the political aspects of slavery; the first three volumes cover the period of the present work; it is eminently fair and judicial in treatment; its notes and references are of great value to the student, and it must long remain the most complete study of the events of this period. *The American Statesmen* series, edited by John T. Morse, Jr., is of value for a general view of the first half of the last century, but its deficiency in references is a great defect. Horace Greeley, *The American Conflict* (2 vols., 1864), is strongly partisan, but the first volume contains much valuable material in extracts from documents and references. Henry Wilson, *Rise and Fall of the Slave Power* (3 vols., 1875–1877), is suggestive, but it must be remembered that it is the work of a strong partisan. William Henry Smith, *A Political History of Slavery* (2 vols., 1903), has some value as the work of a journalist conversant with the newspaper world of the period immediately preceding the Civil War. John Codman Ropes, *The Story of the Civil War* (2 vols., 1899, unfinished), devotes the first seven chapters to an excellent analysis of the beginning of the war. E. W. R. Ewing, *Northern Rebellion and Southern Secession* (1904), though ill-arranged and discursive, is of value in giving a southern view of northern action and legislation in the period of the incubation of secession. John C. Reed, *Brothers' War* (1905), is a book of value dealing with the causes of divergence, with appreciations of Calhoun, Webster, Davis, and Toombs, and with a study of the negro. George Lunt, *Origin of the Late War* (1866), gives the views of a Massachusetts moderate Whig in sympathy with the South; the book is a good, conservative presentation of the subject. J. W. Draper, *History of the Civil War* (3 vols., 1871), highly philosophical but suggestive; John W. Burgess, *Civil War and the Constitution* (2 vols., 1903), I.; and Samuel H. Harding, *Missouri Party Struggles in the Civil War Period* (Am. Hist. Assoc., *Report*, 1890), are of interest in connection with the beginnings of the strife.

Of particular value in the story of Fort Sumter, on which hinged the great question of the time, is Samuel W. Crawford (surgeon at Sumter, later brevet major - general),

Genesis of the Civil War (1887); the book contains much concerning events at the end of 1860 and the beginning of 1861 found in no other single work. Two works supplementing Crawford's account are Alfred Roman, *Military Operations of General Beauregard* (2 vols., 1884); and Abner Doubleday (captain, later major-general), *Reminiscences of Forts Sumter and Moultrie in 1860–1861* (1876).

COLLECTIONS OF DOCUMENTS

James D. Richardson, *Messages and Papers of the Presidents* (10 vols., 1896–1897); Albert Bushnell Hart, *American History Told by Contemporaries* (4 vols., 1897–1901), a valuable collection of papers and extracts; Thomas H. Benton, *Thirty Years' View* (2 vols., 1854–1856); Edward Stanwood, *History of the Presidency* (1898); Thomas Hudson McKee, *National Conventions and Platforms of all Parties from 1789 to 1901* (4th ed., 1901). Frank Moore, *Rebellion Record* (1865), is divided into a "Diary of Events," made up from newspaper clippings, "Documents and Narratives," "Rumors," "Poetry," and "Incidents"; it is a "scrap book" of considerable value. Under this heading of documents may be placed also Appleton's *Annual American Cyclopedia* for 1861, a very valuable and accurate work; *Battles and Leaders of the Civil War*, R. U. Johnson and C. C. Buel, editors (4 vols., 1884–1887); *Tribune Almanac* (1859–1861), with much political information. Attention is called to the collection of Confederate MSS., generally known as the *Pickett Papers*, in the treasury department, Washington (tabulated in C. H. Van Tyne and W. G. Leland, *Guide to the Archives of the Government of the United States in Washington*), which include the correspondence of the Confederate government with its commissioners in Washington, March and April, 1861, and other important papers of the period.

PUBLIC DOCUMENTS

The views of the leaders of public opinion, and particularly of those of the South, are more fully expressed in the speeches in Congress than in any other documents. *The Congressional Globe*, expresses voluminously the sentiment of men in public life, and it was these who directed southern sentiment. It was different in the North, where the public men, in the main, followed in the rear of an anti-slavery sentiment nourished by societies, by a voluminous literature, and by the then potent lecture system. *The House and Senate Journals, Executive Documents, Miscellaneous Documents,* and *Reports of Committees* for 1859–1861, need to be referred to; these are best reached through *Tables and Annotated Index to the Congressional Series of United States Public Documents* (1902), prepared in the office of the superintendent of documents; and Ben Perley Poore, *Descriptive Catalogue of the Government Publications of the United States, September 5, 1774–March 4, 1881* (1885).

Of the official publications covering the months November, 1860–April, 1861, the most valuable are the extensive publications of the war department, entitled *War of the Rebellion, Official Records of the Union and Confederate Armies* (130 vols., 1880–1902), and of the navy department, *Official Records of the Union and Confederate Navies in the War of the Rebellion* (20 vols., 1894–1905); *Journal of the Congress of the Confederate States of America, 1861–1865* (*Senate Documents*, 58 Cong., 2 Sess., No. 234).

PERIODICALS

Second only to the official publications are *Niles' Register* (1811–1849), a weekly of high order, published in Baltimore, without which the student of the history of the period would be distinctly poorer; and the *National Intelligencer*, a Washington daily. Both of these papers took more pains to print contemporary documents than the ordinary newspapers. *De Bow's Review* (New Orleans and Washington, a monthly established in 1846) gives the fullest expression of southern views in a literary form, notably in the crisis of 1859–1860; besides important political contributions, particularly upon the proposed reopening of the African slave-trade, it contains valuable data of southern agriculture, commerce, and conditions. *Harper's Weekly*, 1859–1861, contains a valuable summary of events; *The North American Review*, *The Atlantic Monthly* (then under the editorship of Lowell), and *Harper's Magazine* contain important articles on the subject of secession, scattered throughout the period from 1859 to the present, as does also *The Century*, established in 1881. The newspaper files of most libraries are very defective in those of the period treated; those in the Library of Congress are the most valuable and complete. The more powerful journals of 1859–1861 were the *National Intelligencer; New York Tribune; New York Times; New York Evening Post; Boston Advertiser; Albany Evening Journal*, of which Thurlow Weed was editor, and which was largely Seward's organ; *Chicago Tribune; Philadelphia North American; Baltimore American* (unionist); *Richmond Enquirer* (secessionist); *Charleston Mercury* (rabidly secessionist); *Washington Union* (Mr. Buchanan's organ, until it became so violently secessionist that he parted from it). A large number of the weekly papers of the South published in the country towns are of much value as giving truer views of popular opinion than the papers in the cities; the *Edgefield* (South Carolina) *Advertiser* may be mentioned as typical of the class.

WRITINGS OF PUBLIC MEN

Daniel Webster, *Works* (6 vols., 1851); Abraham Lincoln, *Complete Works* (edited by John G. Nicolay and John Hay, 2 vols., 1904); *Lincoln-Douglas Debates* (reissued 1899); and William H. Seward, *Works* (edited by G. E. Baker, 5 vols., 1853–1884), cover more fully than anything else, or than all else, the northern view of the constitutional questions involved in the great divergence of the sections. The three notable contributions of southerners to the constitutional aspect of the question are John C. Calhoun, *Works* (edited by Richard K. Crallé, 6 vols., 1851–1855); Alexander H. Stephens, *War between the States*

(2 vols., 1867); and Jefferson Davis, *Rise and Fall of the Confederate Government* (2 vols., 1881). The work of Stephens is the ablest exposition of the southern view yet made, and is fair and temperate in tone. The small book of J. L. M. Curry, *The Southern States considered in their Relations to the Constitution of the United States and to the Resulting Union* (1894), is the work of one who took a prominent part in the secession movement and was later in the diplomatic service of the United States; it deals with the subject with fairness and ability. James H. Hammond, *Letters and Speeches* (1866), and Thomas L. Clingman, *Writings and Speeches* (1877), are important from the southern side.

AUTOBIOGRAPHIES AND REMINISCENCES

James Buchanan, *Mr. Buchanan's Administration on the Eve of the Rebellion* (1866) and *Autobiography of William H. Seward* (edited by Frederick W. Seward, 1877), both of value; Gideon Welles (secretary of the navy), *Lincoln and Seward, Remarks upon Memorial Address of Charles Francis Adams upon William H. Seward*, of historical importance, as are Welles's articles, "The Election and Administration of Abraham Lincoln," in the *Galaxy* magazine (XXII., XXIII., 1877); Winfield Scott, *Autobiography of Lieutenant-General Scott* (2 vols., 1864), a work of little value through omissions and inaccuracies; John Sherman, *Recollections of Forty Years* (2 vols., 1895); Thurlow Weed, *Autobiography* (edited by his daughter, Harriet A. Weed, 1884); George W. Julian, *Political Recollections* (1884); James G. Blaine, *Twenty Years in Congress* (2 vols., 1884), the first half of the first volume of which gives a fair and readable review of events leading to secession; A. K. McClure, *Lincoln and Men of War Times* (2d ed., 1892), a book of personal recollections of considerable value; A. G. Riddle, *Recollections of War Times* (1895), by a member of Congress; Donn Piatt, *Memories of Men who Saved the Union* (1887), by a journalist; John W. Forney, *Anecdotes of Public Men* (1873), by a journalist.

From the side of the southerners there are Reuben
Davis, *Recollections of Mississippi and Mississippians*
(1900), a straightforward, honest book; (Bishop) Richard
W. Wilmer, *The Recent Past from a Southern Standpoint*
(1900); (Mrs.) Victoria V. Clayton, *White and Black under
the Old Régime* (1899), an excellent little book, describing
the life and events of the period with great fairness and
frankness; (Mrs.) Roger A. Pryor, *Reminiscences of Peace
and War* (1904); Moncure D. Conway, *Autobiography* (2
vols., 1904), interesting as giving the views of the one
prominent Virginian allied with the New England tran-
scendentalists.

BIOGRAPHIES

John G. Nicolay and John Hay, *Abraham Lincoln, a History* (10 vols., 1890), a work of highest value in connection with the Civil War, through the intimate knowledge
which came to the authors as Lincoln's private secretaries;
John G. Nicolay, *Abraham Lincoln* (1902), a condensation
of the preceding work and an inspiring volume; Ward H.
Lamon, *Life of Abraham Lincoln* (1872), of value as being
by a former law partner. For the many other lives of Lincoln, see G. T. Ritchie, *Lincolniana*, cited above. George
Ticknor Curtis, *James Buchanan* (2 vols., 1883); this and *Buchanan's Administration*, admirable in many ways as they
are, are the works of lawyers and have the defect of dealing
with the great events of the eve of secession and with secession itself from the strictly legal stand-point, recognizing in
too slight a degree the overpowering psychical causes; they
are really *apologiae* for a great failure to measure the men
and movements of the time. Frederick Bancroft, *Life of
William H. Seward* (2 vols., 1900); Frederick W. Seward,
Seward at Washington (2 vols., 1891); (Mrs.) Chapman
Coleman, *Life of John J. Crittenden* (2 vols., 1871), a valuable book, but far from being as complete as it should be;
Thurlow Weed Barnes, *Life of Thurlow Weed* (1884), being
the second volume of a work of which the first is the
Autobiography already quoted; Albert Bushnell Hart,

Salmon Portland Chase (1899); George C. Gorham, *Life of Edwin M. Stanton* (2 vols., 1899); Robert C. Winthrop, Jr., *Memoir of Robert C. Winthrop* (1897); Morgan Dix, *Memoirs of John Adams Dix* (2 vols., 1883); William Salter, *Life of James W. Grimes* (1876); James Russell Soley, *Admiral Porter* (1903); Thomas Sergeant Perry, *Life and Letters of Francis Lieber* (1882); Chauncey F. Black, *Essays and Speeches of Jeremiah S. Black, with a Biographical Sketch* (1885).

Of southerners, Frank H. Alfriend, *Life of Jefferson Davis,* (1868); Richard Malcolm Johnston and William Hand Browne, *Life of Alexander H. Stephens,* (1878), a very valuable book, inasmuch as it gives the views of the sanest and wisest of the southern men in political life regarding the events of these years; John Witherspoon Du Bose, *Life and Times of William Lowndes Yancey* (1896); Barton H. Wise, *Life of Henry A. Wise* (1899); Henry A. Wise, *Seven Decades of the Union, a Memoir of John Tyler* (1881), a work of moderate value; Lyon G. Tyler, *Letters and Times of the Tylers* (2 vols., 1885).

JOHN BROWN

The John Brown episode has occasioned a voluminous literature, most of which is of northern origin and of extreme partisan character. The chief authorities are the report of the Mason Senate Committee (*Senate Reports*, 36 Cong., 1 Sess., No. 278); Frank B. Sanborn, *Life and Letters of John Brown* (1891); Richard J. Hinton, *John Brown and his Men* (1894); James Redpath, *Public Life of Captain John Brown* (1860); Hermann E. von Holst, *John Brown* (1888). These last four are excessively laudatory and treat the subject as one of martyrdom. F. B. Sanborn published in the *Atlantic Monthly* (XXXV., 1875) a series of articles which are practically embodied in his work just mentioned. Others bearing on the subject are: Octavius Brooks Frothingham, *Gerrit Smith* (1878); Octavius Brooks Frothingham, *Theodore Parker* (1864). Two offsets to the extreme laudation of Brown are Eli Thayer, *The Kansas Crusade* (1889), and Charles Robinson, *The Kansas Conflict* (1892). Other less important works bearing upon the character of Brown are named in connection with the subject of Kansas in Theodore C. Smith, *Parties and Slavery* (*Am. Nation*, XVIII.), chap. xxi. Two small books, Osborne P. Anderson (one of Brown's party at Harper's Ferry), *A Voice from Harper's Ferry* (1861), and Theodore Parker, *Letter of Francis Jackson reviewing John Brown's Expedition* (1860), have some slight value as side-lights upon the episode.

ECONOMIC CONDITIONS

The basic information is, of course, contained in the Census Reports of the United States. The general economic conditions of the South before the war are most excellently depicted in the very valuable works of Frederick Law Olmsted, *Seaboard Slave States* (1856, new ed. 1904), *A Journey through Texas* (1857), *A Journey in the Back Country* (1860, a new ed. 1907), and a condensation of these three published as *The Cotton Kingdom* (2 vols., 1861). These and James D. B. De Bow, *The Industrial Resources of the Southern and Western States* (3 vols., 1852–1853), and *De Bow's Review*, passim, contain information of great value upon southern life and conditions. J. C. Ballagh, *Southern Economic History; Tariff and Public Lands* (Am. Hist. Assoc., *Report*, 1898); and Samuel Davis, *Some of the Consequences of the Louisiana Purchase* (*Ibid.*, 1897), are of value. Attention is called to additional lists of works upon the South in Albert Bushnell Hart, *Slavery and Abolition* (*Am. Nation*, XVI.), chaps. iv., xxii., and Theodore C. Smith, *Parties and Slavery* (*Am. Nation*, XVIII.), chap. xxi.

OUTBREAK OF THE WAR

Besides the discussion in J. F. Rhodes, *United States*, James Schouler, *United States*, Nicolay and Hay, *Abraham Lincoln*, J. W. Draper, *Civil War*, and other good secondary books, there is a body of first-hand materials. Some of the most significant are: William H. Russell (correspondent of the *London Times*), *My Diary North and South* (1863); Adam Gurowski (an on-looker in Washington), *Diary from March 4, 1861, to November 12, 1862* (1862); J. S. Pike, *First Blows of the Civil War* (1879); Abner Doubleday, *Reminiscences of Forts Sumter and Moultrie* (1876), and Samuel W. Crawford, *Genesis of the Civil War* (1887), two books by participants; Thomas S. Goodwin, *Natural History of Slavery* (1864), strongly anti-slavery; Richard Grant White, *New Gospel of Peace* (1862 and later eds.), a clever satire.

Southern views in William C. Fowler, *Sectional Controversy* (1865), strongly pro-slavery; and the controversial books of James Buchanan, Jefferson Davis, and Alexander H. Stephens.

DIPLOMACY

The diplomacy of 1859–1860 affecting the questions involved in the on-coming war relates almost entirely to Mexico, Cuba, and Central America, which were regarded as fields for slavery extension. The desire and the attempt for a more intimate political relation with these regions, or for actual annexation, were a marked feature of the situation. Reference should be made to the list under this heading in Smith, *Parties and Slavery* (*Am. Nation*, XVIII.), chap. xxi. Particular mention, however, should be made of John H. Latané, *The Diplomacy of the United States in regard to Cuba* (Am. Hist. Assoc., *Report*, 1897); John H. Latané, *Diplomatic Relations of the United States and Spanish America* (1900); William Walker, "General Walker's Policy in Central America," in *De Bow's Review*, XXVIII. (February, 1860); William C. Scroggs, "Walker and the Steamship Company," in *American Historical Review*, X. (July, 1905); Howard L. Wilson, "Buchanan's Proposed Intervention in Mexico," in *American Historical Review*, V. (July, 1900).

INDEX

END OF VOL. XIX